THE FORNES FRAME

ANNE GARCÍA-ROMERO

THE FORNES
FRAME

*Contemporary Latina Playwrights and
the Legacy of Maria Irene Fornes*

THE UNIVERSITY OF
ARIZONA PRESS

TUCSON

The University of Arizona Press
www.uapress.arizona.edu

Printed in the United States of America
21   20   19   18   17   16   6   5   4   3   2   1

ISBN-13: 978-0-8165-3144-8 (paper)

Cover designed by David Drummond

Publication of this book is made possible in part by support from the Institute for Scholarship in the Liberal Arts, College of Arts and Letters, University of Notre Dame.

Library of Congress Cataloging-in-Publication Data
Names: García-Romero, Anne, author.
Title: The Fornes frame : contemporary Latina playwrights and the legacy of Maria Irene Fornes / Anne García-Romero.
Description: Tucson : The University of Arizona Press, 2016. | Includes bibliographical references and index.
Identifiers: LCCN 2015032996 | ISBN 9780816531448 (pbk. : alk. paper)
Subjects: LCSH: Hispanic American women dramatists. | Fornes, Maria Irene—Influence. | Cram, Cusi—Criticism and interpretation. | Hudes, Quiara Alegría—Criticism and interpretation. | Romero, Elaine (Elaine D.)—Criticism and interpretation. | Svich, Caridad—Criticism and interpretation. | Zacarías, Karen—Criticism and interpretation.
Classification: LCC PS153.H56 G367 2016 | DDC 812/.609928708968—dc23 LC record available at http://lccn.loc.gov/2015032996

For my mother,
Barbara Clarke García–Romero

CONTENTS

ILLUSTRATIONS

ACKNOWLEDGMENTS

F IRST, I MUST thank Maria Irene Fornes, whose remarkable work and career have inspired this book. Next, I thank the Latina playwrights who have generously shared their plays with me, especially Caridad Svich, Karen Zacarías, Elaine Romero, Cusi Cram, and Quiara Alegría Hudes. This book would not exist without them.

The University of Notre Dame has significantly supported my work on this book. I thank Don Pope-Davis and Susan Ohmer for inviting me to Notre Dame through the Moreau Academic Diversity Postdoctoral Fellowship Program. Thanks to Dean John T. McGreevy and the College of Arts and Letters for generously supporting my research. Thanks to Agustín Fuentes, Thomas V. Merluzzi, Kenneth Garcia, and Patricia Base in the Institute for Scholarship in the Liberal Arts for supporting my research. Thanks also to Gilberto Cardenas, José E. Limón, Timothy Matovina, and Luis Ricardo Fraga at the Institute for Latino Studies for their ongoing support of my work. Thanks to my colleagues in the Department of Film, Television, and Theatre, especially James Collins, Don Crafton, Peter Holland, Anton Juan, Kevin Dreyer, Pamela Wojcik, and Mary Kearney, for their mentorship. Many thanks to my colleagues across campus, whose encouragement and work continue to inspire me, especially Christine Cervenak, Paulette Curtis, Elizabeth F. Evans, Jason Ruiz, Maria Tomasula, and Azareen Van Der Vliet Oloomi.

In the Department of Theatre and Dance at the University of California, Santa Barbara, I received generous mentorship during my PhD program. I offer huge thanks to Leo Cabranes-Grant, whose invaluable guidance and wonderful artist/scholar model inspired this book. I give many thanks to Naomi Iizuka for her continual support throughout my academic career. Thanks to Suk-Young Kim, Catherine Cole, and Kum-Kum Bhavnani for inspiration in the classroom and guidance on my committee. I thank Mark Bly, director of my MFA in Playwriting program at the Yale School of Drama, for his dramaturgical generosity and for inviting Fornes to teach our class. Thanks to Murray Mednick and the Padua Hills Playwrights Festival for creating a stunning theatrical environment where he, Fornes, Julie Hébert, Marlane Meyer, and the other playwrights taught their students to seek truth in the theatre. At Occidental College's Department of Theater, I thank Alan Freeman for his theatrical mentorship and Susan Gratch for teaching me to love theatre history.

Thanks to the staff at the University of Arizona Press, especially my editor, Kristen Buckles, for her generous and continued guidance, and my copy editor, John Mulvihill, for his detailed attention to each page of my book. Thanks to the anonymous readers whose careful consideration of my manuscript hugely influenced the shape of this book.

My colleagues greatly inspired my work on this book. First, I thank Yael Prizant for her outstanding friendship, endless encouragement, and rigorous review of my manuscript. Next, I thank Elena Glasberg for her expert guidance throughout my entire writing process. And thanks to Chantal Rodriguez, my dissertation buddy, who read early drafts of my work. Many thanks to Jorge Huerta for consistently encouraging me throughout my career; to Tiffany Ana López for inspiring my scholarship; to Juliette Carrillo for enduring friendship and inviting me to dramaturg at the Hispanic Playwrights Project; to Henry Godinez for generously sharing his expertise as a Latin@ theatre pioneer in Chicago; to Linda Saborío for carefully considering my play in her scholarship; to Tlaloc Rivas for sharing this Latin@ theatre journey; to Melissa Huerta for inviting me into her Latina theatre studies scholarship process; to Dorinne Kondo for her ongoing guidance and exemplary artist/scholar model; to Sarah Wells for her support and guidance; to Colleen Baker for her insight and expertise; to Michelle Memran for graciously helping me connect with Fornes; to Polly Carl for her enthusiasm and ongoing support of my work; to Todd London for his exemplary leadership at New Dramatists and his impeccable writing about new plays; and to

Susan Gurman for her ongoing advocacy of my work as a playwright and translator.

My University of Notre Dame students' enthusiasm, intelligence, and insights were immensely helpful to my process with this book. Special thanks to Lucas Garcia, my talented and tireless research assistant. Thanks also to Charles O'Leary and Dylan Parent for their valuable engagement with my research.

On a personal note, I thank my family in the United States, Barbara and Alethea García-Romero, Toño and Alicia García-Romero, Paul Fariello, Libby and Dan Anderson, and Ellen Clarke, for their constant love and support. I especially want to thank my mother, Barbara, whose vibrant career as a professor of Spanish literature truly inspires my life's work. I also want to thank my family in Spain, especially Mercedes García-Romero, for their love and encouragement. I need to acknowledge my late father, José Antonio García-Romero, and my late grandmothers, Ana Romero Campos and Margaret Hauck Clarke, who paved the way for me to pursue a life in the arts and academia. I thank my dear friends whose wisdom and love have sustained me, especially Gina Gold, Leah C. Gardiner, Irene Meisel, Heather Brodhead, Heather Ehlers, Marcia Newman, and Susan E. Bowen. Lastly, I thank Rodolfo Montecinos MacAdoo, who arrived toward the end of this journey, but whose enthusiasm, love, and encouragement helped me to complete this book. Mil gracias.

THE FORNES FRAME

INTRODUCTION

Defining the Fornes Frame

A REVERENTIAL HUSH DESCENDS as the teacher enters a room full of writers. Soon, she starts a writing exercise, instructing, "Close your eyes. Picture a character . . ." So begins my training with Maria Irene Fornes, the prolific, Cuban American, Obie-award-winning playwright who taught hundreds of playwrights over her fifty-year career in the American theatre. Fornes was one of my first professional playwriting teachers when I was a recent college graduate. I studied with her for two summers at the Padua Hills Playwrights Festival, located at that time on the campus of California State University at Northridge. Murray Mednick, Fornes, and Sam Shepard founded the Padua Hills Playwrights Festival in 1978 as a haven for professional playwrights to create and direct site-specific work while also training a new generation of theatre artists. Next, I studied with Fornes during my MFA in Playwriting program at the Yale School of Drama. Fornes generously provided me with a profound access to creativity, innovative methods for generating new play material, and an exemplary theatre artist path, which helped me to build my career as a playwright and later as a scholar and university theatre professor.

After graduation from Yale, I briefly worked for Fornes as a typist. One afternoon, we met for tea at an elegant café in New York City's Greenwich Village and ran into playwright Nilo Cruz, her former student. I witnessed how Fornes's presence elicited joyful reverence from this acclaimed writer, who several years later would become the first Latino to win the Pulitzer Prize for Drama. While I watched her graciously and warmly reconnect with Cruz, I was reminded of Fornes's stature and influence. Afterward, we discussed my discouragement over a workshop production of my latest play. Fornes asked me, "Did you learn one new thing?" "Yes," I replied, "I learned how my main character needs to express a deeper level of honesty toward the end of her journey in act 2." She affirmed, "Good. Then you did your job." As we left the café, she could see that my spirits had lifted. She then pronounced, "We should have a parade celebrating playwrights. Playwrights unite!" and we marched down Seventh Avenue, arm in arm.

My professional playwriting career began a decade before I returned to academia in the mid-2000s to pursue my doctorate in theatre studies. During those ten years I presented my plays with a vibrant community of Latin@ theatre artists. (I'll discuss the orthography of the term Latin@ later in this chapter.) My playwriting colleagues introduced me to many diverse views of Latin@ culture. I started to see more fully the variety of possibilities that can exist when dramatizing the intricacies of Latin@ society. In academia, however, the Latin@ theatre studies scholarship I encountered did not include many contemporary Latina playwrights whose work had been recently produced in the American theatre to national and international acclaim. I had witnessed newer theatrical voices that I thought merited inclusion in the archive. Also, Latin@ theatre studies tended to focus more on male rather than female playwrights. Therefore, in 2005, I approached my Latina playwriting colleagues and requested their plays so I could write about their work. This book is the result of five Latina playwrights generously sharing their writing with me over the past decade.

The Fornes Frame: Contemporary Latina Playwrights and the Legacy of María Irene Fornes examines the work of Caridad Svich, Karen Zacarías, Elaine Romero, Cusi Cram, and Quiara Alegría Hudes through the frame of Fornes's legacy as a playwright and teacher. As a theatre studies scholar, a playwright, and a student of Fornes, I bring a unique perspective in placing the work of these early twenty-first-century Latina playwrights into the archive. In this study, I emphasize that the key to understanding Latina theatre today is through the model Fornes established. The Latin@ community encompasses a vast array of cultural differences. Fornes embraces the notion that a Latina playwright can explore cultural complexity in her plays or create theatrical worlds that might have no connection to her heritage, but are inspired by her unique artistic point of view. Plays by these five Latina playwrights expand past a consideration of a single culture toward broader, simultaneous connections to diverse cultures. This cultural expansion often reflects how these Latina playwrights dramatize the supernatural. These Latina playwrights also experiment with the theatrical form as they redefine what a Latina play can be. Following Fornes's legacy, these playwrights continue to contest and complicate Latina identity, thus redefining Latina theatre in the early twenty-first century.

THE FORNES FRAME

Fornes, author of *Fefu and Her Friends* and *Sarita* and a nine-time Obie award winner, serves as the entry point to this study, as she represents the genesis of Latina playwriting. In addition to her work as a playwright and director, Fornes founded and ran the seminal INTAR Hispanic Playwrights-in-Residence Laboratory in New York City from 1981 to 1992, where she trained numerous award-winning and widely produced Latin@ playwrights. Her students have won Obie Awards, National Endowment for the Arts Fellowships, a MacArthur Fellowship, and a Pulitzer Prize. She went on to teach at some of America's most prestigious universities, including Yale, Princeton, Brown, Wesleyan, and Iowa, and led workshops at leading theatres, such as the Mark Taper Forum in Los Angeles and the Traverse Theatre in Edinburgh, Scotland. Her teaching methods arose from her training as a visual artist and provide innovative ways to create and develop a new play. Fornes's work laid the foundation for the careers of the playwrights in this study. Her singular vision, her embrace of both Latin@ and non-Latin@ cultures in her work, and her excellence as a teacher of playwriting continue to influence contemporary Latina playwrights.

I will utilize what I am calling the "Fornes frame" to consider the work in this study. I chose the word "frame" because it describes the many ways in which Fornes influences Latina playwrights. A frame can be a grouping of ideas, a border, a pair of glasses, a human or animal body, a foundational structure, a proscenium arch of a theatre, or a doorway. The word "frame" comes from the Middle English *framian*, which means "be useful."[1] Fornes's work provides innovative and useful models of what a Latina play can be. She offers groundbreaking theatrical ideas to theatre artists and audiences. Fornes's plays traverse cultural, spiritual, and aesthetic borders. Her work experiments with the use of stage space. Her plays and pedagogy highlight the importance of human and animal bodies in generating new play material. Fornes emphasizes the possibilities of the visual in new play creation. Her teaching and mentorship have opened many creative and professional doors for theatre artists. Her plays and career have established a foundational structure for future generations of Latina playwrights.

While Fornes's overall work addresses multiple subjects, I will focus on four concepts using the Fornes frame: cultural multiplicity, supernatural intervention, Latina identity, and theatrical experimentation. As a playwright and teacher, Fornes engages cultural multiplicity in her plays. She employs supernatural interventions to illuminate her characters' paths. She delves into identity, whether Latina or non-Latina. She also conducts theatrical experiments to create new forms and structures that facilitate her characters' journeys. I have chosen these four concepts for several additional reasons. First, Latin@ culture continues to grow in complexity. Therefore, considering how playwrights incorporate multiple cultures in their work is key to understanding this expansion. Next, staging the supernatural can be fraught with the danger of audiences misunderstanding these moments and labeling them as "magical." Considering the nuances of spirit world negotiation in Latina theatre contributes to a broader understanding of the role of spirituality in these plays. As Latina culture diversifies, Latina playwrights craft characters whose journeys are shaped by this multiplicity. Examining how these playwrights dramatize this identity is a significant means of understanding the transformations in twenty-first-century Latin@ society. How Latina playwrights experiment with form and language has been undertheorized in Latin@ theatre studies scholarship. The formal choices that these playwrights make instruct audiences as to how cultural multiplicity can be reflected in a play's aesthetic landscape. I will begin this study by considering how Fornes addresses these concepts in her work. However, I first need to define each concept.

CULTURAL MULTIPLICITY

Cultural multiplicity in these plays reflects the diverse twenty-first-century Latin@ community in the United States, which encompasses a wide array of cultures from Latin America, to the Caribbean, to Spain and onward. These playwrights' works establish an ever-shifting Latin@ cultural landscape. It is not that previous generations of Latin@ playwrights did not provide important views of the Latin@ community. However, early twenty-first-century Latina playwrights generate a wider and more ample theatrical presentation of contemporary Latin@ culture.

Late twentieth-century Latina plays frequently delve into the lives of characters who exist only in one of the three predominant Latin@ populations: Mexican American, Puerto Rican, or Cuban. Plays by authors such as Migdalia Cruz and Cherríe Moraga, both Fornes's students, explore characters that are often negotiating their Latina lives within a single cultural world. In *Miriam's Flowers*, Cruz examines Miriam, a young Puerto Rican woman, and her violent surroundings. In *Heroes and Saints*, Moraga considers the struggles of a Mexican American family as they navigate farmworker life. Fornes's plays often contain multilayered cultural considerations. She also invites Latina playwrights to negotiate and examine a variety of cultural worlds.

The plays in this study expand the definition of what a Latina play can be. These Latina playwrights dramatize the interactions between Mexicans, Puerto Ricans, Cubans, Dominicans, Bolivians, Chileans, Argentineans, Spaniards, Latin@s, and Anglo-Americans, among many other cultures. While knowledge of this diversity may be most prevalent within the Latin@ theatre community, there are those who fail to acknowledge or value this multiplicity. The Latina playwright who expands the notion of Latin@ theatre can thus be marginalized by those who privilege a limited view of Latina identity. As Latin@ theatre studies scholars Alberto Sandoval-Sánchez and Nancy Saporta Sternbach reflect, "Once a playwright . . . de-essentializes her work by setting it outside of . . . expected . . . locations, she may find herself at odds with the very community her writing serves" (i.e., the larger Latin@ community).[2] However, the playwrights discussed in this study de-essentialize their work by upending cultural expectations within and outside of Latin@ communities. Just as Fornes complicates cultural presumptions with her plays, these play-wrights display the rich cultural diversity that continues to redefine early twenty-first-century Latina theatre.

SUPERNATURAL INTERVENTIONS

Latina playwrights dramatize supernatural interventions in which the spirit world intersects with the natural world on stage. However, the staging of the supernatural in Latin@ theatre is often exoticized as magic realism. When American theatre audiences perceive it as such, they fail to engage with the complex realities of supernatural interventions in Latin@ plays. Magic realism is perhaps best known as a description of the novels written by the Latin American "boom" generation; however, the term is problematic. When told that readers were often aware of the "magic" in his novels, but did not see the "reality" behind it, the Colombian novelist and Nobel laureate Gabriel García Márquez responded, "This is surely because their rationalism prevents them from seeing that reality isn't limited to the price of tomatoes and eggs. Everyday life in Latin America proves that reality is full of the most extraordinary things."[3] The term "magic" may reduce a supernatural intervention to an idealized fantasy that has little or no connection to reality. If some audiences find staged Latin@ worlds to be foreign, they ought to seek new levels of understanding of these cultural differences, rather than define the experience as merely fantastical.

In her plays, Fornes often includes moments where her characters seamlessly traverse borders between the physical and spiritual realms. Fornes and the Latina playwrights discussed in this study theatricalize engagement with the spirit world as their characters create sacred space, explore ritual, and gain *facultad* (i.e., supernatural sight). Their plays provide audiences with access to a deeper understanding of supernatural worlds. These playwrights construct theatrical illuminations of the supernatural that are expansive and allow audiences to witness the heterogeneity of spirit-world interactions.

These spirit-world negotiations begin through the creation of sacred space. Historian of religion Mircea Eliade defines the sacred "as a reality of wholly different order from 'natural' realities."[4] On one level, sacred space is different from space in the natural world, but in these plays the sacred is not necessarily "wholly different." It is still considered part of the "natural reality." Focusing on this sacred space as an alternate reality can lead to respectful observation, rather than dismissive assignation of it as a "magical" realm with no connection to everyday existence.

Once sacred space is established, ritual can occur. Eliade sees ritual as an "enactment of a creation event or story recounted in myth,"[5] thus focusing on ritual as secondary to the sacred. In contrast, ethnographer Arnold Van Gennep argues that "ritual can actually define what is sacred, not simply react to something already and for always fixed."[6] Phenomenologists such as Eliade emphasize the primacy of sacred mythology over ritual, while functionalist-structuralists such as Van Gennep focus on the "practicality of ritual and how it facilitates social life."[7] However, rituals here function on multiple levels. They create both sacred space and social change. By creating rituals in a performed space, these playwrights also highlight worlds in which characters' actions can forge direct links to the sacred.

Ultimately, the use of rituals to create sacred space in these plays leads to *facultad*, which in Spanish means "faculty," "ability," or "power." Cultural theorist Gloria Anzaldúa defines *facultad* as "the capacity to see in the surface phenomena the meaning of deeper realities, to see the deep structure beneath the surface."[8] She links this ability to extraordinary vision or a supernatural sight. Anzaldúa argues that *facultad* is apt to be most strongly developed in those who are "pounced on . . . the females, the homosexuals of all races, the dark skinned, the outcasts, the persecuted, the marginalized, the foreign."[9] Anzaldúa posits that this shift in perception then allows the individual to access sacred space:

> It deepens the way we see concrete objects and people, the senses become so acute that we can see through things, view events in depth, a piercing that reaches the underworld (the realm of the soul). As we plunge vertically, the break, with its accompanying new seeing, makes us pay attention to the soul, and we are thus carried into awareness—an experiencing of soul (self).[10]

Facultad thus traverses the borders between the natural and supernatural realms and emphasizes connection to an individual's soul or spirit.

Anzaldúa links *facultad* to indigenous spirituality yet juxtaposes this against "the Catholic and Protestant religion, [which] encourages fear and distrust of life and of the body."[11] Anzaldúa maintains that "the spirit world, whose existence the whites are so adamant in denying, does in fact exist."[12] Anzaldúa's position, first published in 1987, reflects an oppositional stance to Anglo culture. However, the Latin@ community has significantly diversified in the past three decades. *Facultad* now incorporates racial and cultural difference, so that belief in the spirit world cannot be categorized solely as non-white. The development of *facultad* mirrors a diverse Latin@ reality that is constantly negotiating multiple dualities: Latin@/Anglo, Latin@/indigenous, natural/supernatural. The playwrights here present characters that access extraordinary visions of the spirit world.

LATINA IDENTITY

Latina identity can refer to the ways that contemporary Latinas define and inhabit their cultural worlds. Fornes visualizes and writes plays that continually complicate what it means to be a Latina playwright. As a teacher, she encourages her students to explore multifaceted characters. Her work provides a frame in which to coalesce diverse elements influencing Latina identity. These Latina playwrights create characters that reflect a rich cultural multiplicity, which informs their journeys through the plays. Their plays question rather than reinforce homogeneous cultural identity.

Anzaldúa's consideration of the term *mestiza* is fundamental to an examination of Latina identity. Anzaldúa defines the mestiza dynamic as a "racial, ideological, cultural, and biological cross-pollinization."[13] Anzaldúa delves into the multiplicities that arise from female identity forged by two or more cultures. This consciousness must "break down the subject-object duality . . . and to show how this duality is transcended."[14] Reflecting on the term *mestiza*, performance studies scholar Diana Taylor states: "Its root, from *mixtus*, means both the child of racially mixed parents and also the cross breeding of plants and animals. But it stresses the biological over the botanical."[15] The term *mestiza* therefore reflects the physical realm created by disparate cultures. By linking the notion of consciousness to the term *mestiza*, Anzaldúa highlights the significance of remaining ever mindful of complex identity. Her stance values engagement with each cultural influence so that the mestiza can then negotiate her identity in light of this diversity.

Anzaldúa emphasizes cultural multiplicity and the frictions caused by these intersecting, diverse worlds. She contends that the mestiza navigates her terrain by "developing a tolerance for contradictions, a tolerance for ambiguity."[16] Here Anzaldúa jettisons a single Latina identity and embraces a complicated and multifaceted Latin@ culture. She encourages an awareness of the cultural complexities in the Latin@ community that empowers the Latina to remain actively engaged in her own identity formation. Anzaldúa suggests the mestiza inhabits the liminal space between differing cultures, while she acknowledges the challenges that arise from redefining one's cultural identity.

Anzaldúa points to the chasm between cultural worlds and suggests a variety of options for mestiza consciousness that she feels must be proactive and not reactive. Anzaldúa uses the metaphor of a river separating cultures living on opposite shores. She offers that this new mindfulness must depart from the rancorous divisive stance of the past. The mestiza must either exist on both shores simultaneously, "disengage from the dominant culture, write it off as a lost cause, and cross the border into a wholly new and separate territory,"[17] or choose to "go another route."[18] Her first option reflects an approach whereby the mestiza will engage with both of her cultures equally. However, the ground has shifted. The newest mestiza crosses various tributaries and simultaneously navigates on multiple lands between disparate shores.

Corporeality becomes an important hallmark of mestiza consciousness. Anzaldúa asserts that the mestiza must remain active and tolerant while engaging with multiple cultures in a variety of ways. She champions the mestiza's ability to "transform herself into a tree, a coyote, into another person."[19] Here Anzaldúa emphasizes that the mestiza's body can metaphorically shape-shift and change into diverse physical forms. The Latina body is a sign of the inner shifting awareness that must acknowledge and interact with numerous cultural impulses.

Latina playwrights have previously explored the centrality of the Latina body as a site of representation, but the emphasis has been on a single national identity. Latina playwrights such as Cruz, Moraga, and Milcha Sanchez-Scott (also a Fornes student) examine issues of corporeality that focus primarily on Puerto Rican and Mexican American cultures. In Cruz's play *Miriam's Flowers*, Miriam resorts to self-mutilation as a means of dealing with the tragic death of her brother. Latin@ theatre studies scholar Tiffany Ana López writes: "Cruz has said that the only thing any of her female characters fully owns is her own body. The physical body is the site for understanding the issues of identity that charge Cruz's plays."[20] In Moraga's play *Heroes and Saints*, Cerezita is a woman born without a body as a result of pesticides being used in the farmlands, highlighting the plight of the Chicana/o farmworker's fractured body. At the climax of Sanchez-Scott's play *Roosters*, in a moment of supernatural intervention, Angela's body levitates. The five Latina playwrights in this study continue this conversation by engaging in a wider cross-cultural embrace of the diverse Latin@ community. Their female protagonists' bodies become sites of representation as they negotiate and define the impact of cultural complexity.

Plays by Latina playwrights in the late twentieth century often contain characters whose survival depends on the reinforcement of a national identity. Latina culture has gained agency in the American theatre in the past twenty years due to work by award-winning playwrights such as Cruz, Moraga, and Sanchez-Scott. As audiences encountered such compelling Puerto Rican and Mexican American female characters as Miriam, Cerezita, and Angela, a new level of cultural visibility entered the American theatrical dialogue. However, in the early twenty-first century, with a greater heterogeneity in Latin@ culture, plays that champion a single national perspective do not reflect the ever-growing diversity within the Latin@ community.

THEATRICAL EXPERIMENTATION

Latina playwrights conduct theatrical experimentation by challenging prevailing dramaturgical norms such as linear narrative, naturalistic characters, and monolingualism. A spectacular tension can exist between theatrical experimentation and commercial viability. If a playwright writes a play that challenges traditional notions of structure, character, and language, will her play get produced? If her play adheres to prevailing dramaturgical norms, is it more likely to get produced? Influenced by her background in visual arts, Fornes's plays closely consider aesthetics. Fornes experiments with nontraditional structures, spare poetic language, and unconventional characters. Fornes and these Latina playwrights are writing plays with fractured narratives, linguistic hybridities, and multicultural characters. Theatrical experimentation, created by employing and subverting diverse artistic models, is carried out in these plays, which are not only commercially viable but vital to twenty-first-century American theatre.

Theatrical experimentation in Latin@ theatre has been underexplored in Latin@ theatre studies. Perhaps this is due to the primary work of field formation in studies such as *Chicano Drama: Performance, Society, and Myth* by Jorge Huerta and *Latina Performance: Traversing the Stage* by Alicia Arrizón, for example, which focus largely on the thematics and politics of Latin@ theatre and not as much on the formal innovations of the playwrights. Sandoval-Sánchez and Saporta Sternbach, in *Stages of Life: Transcultural Performance and Identity in U.S. Latina Theatre*, provide a critical lens on this issue when they remark: "A primary characteristic of this new genre [of Latina theatre] is its non-linear structure: it tends to be fragmented and non-chronological, allowing for the staging of short scenes and vignettes that are frequently autobiographical."[21] Sandoval-Sánchez and Saporta Sternbach offer the bildungsroman, the coming-of-age novel that "chronicles the phases of a woman's life in the course of her education and conscientización," as a model for Latina plays that often use "vignettes, each signaling a moment in the path of life."[22] However, Sandoval-Sánchez and Saporta Sternbach's bildungsroman model correlates more with how structure might illuminate identity, as opposed to how specific structural choices themselves can elucidate multiple themes and issues. This general lack of attention to theatrical experimentation in Latin@ theatre studies can also be attributed to the fact that plays that challenge traditional dramaturgical elements often exist on the margins of American mainstream theatre. Yet, as Latin@ theatre studies scholars continue to analyze the works of contemporary Latina playwrights, consideration of nontraditional dramaturgical choices is vitally important to illustrate the growing complexities of Latina theatre.

WHO IS LATIN@?

Throughout this study, I will be using the term "Latin@," which utilizes the "@" symbol to replace the previous "a/o" ending. The symbol is used to translate and include the masculine and feminine ending. As Latin@

theatre studies scholar Jean Graham-Jones notes, this new use of the "@" symbol "attempts to counter the masculinism implicit in the Spanish adjective *latino* by including both gender endings."[23] The "@" symbol extends a concern for gender into a term that also includes new considerations about location, time, and technology. The "@" symbol can replace the word "at," which connotes a locality or temporality. This echoes the role that geography and history can play in shaping Latin@ identity. The "@" symbol is now most frequently used to link monikers and internet domain names so one can send e-mail, today's global communication medium. This relates to the fact that the Latin@ community is increasingly globalized in the early twenty-first century. With respect to the pronunciation of Latin@, both Latina/o and Latin@ are pronounced as "Latina/Latino." Thus, this new orthography has relevance only in a print context.

The "@" symbol translates to the word *arroba* in Spanish, which means a quantity of solid or liquid measure and is part of a colloquial term, *por arrobas*, which means a large quantity. This Spanish definition speaks to the need to remeasure preconceived notions of what it means to be Latin@. Also, the Spanish meaning relates to the fact that past definitions of Latin@ do not always add up; some aspects are left out and meaning needs to be recalibrated.

The "@" symbol appears above the number 2 on the English keyboard and to the right of the number 2 on the Spanish keyboard. This placement speaks to a layering of meaning in the term, which must now contend with not one but numerous cultural worlds. In order to type the "@" symbol, one must "Shift" or "right-Alt," then hit the key, suggesting that current comprehension of the term necessitates shifting or altering one's perception. The plays by the Latina playwrights in this study investigate globalization, shift views on migration, question cultural multiplicity, and alter the understanding of contemporary Latin@s.

Definitions of Latin@ have varied over the past decade. In their study of Latin@ culture, *Latinos: Remaking America*, based on papers presented at the Harvard University conference "Latinos in the 21st Century: Mapping Research Agenda," anthropologist Marcelo Suárez-Orozco and education scholar Mariela Páez define Latin@ as "that segment of U.S. population that traces its descent to the Spanish-speaking, Caribbean, and Latin American worlds."[24] This delineation favors genealogy but does not address individual identification. Sandoval-Sánchez and Saporta

Sternbach privilege the individual's choice when they define Latin@ as "all persons who ethnically . . . and culturally identify with Latin American origins or roots and who reside permanently in geographically dispersed locations within the U.S."[25] However, the definition needs to go beyond a focus on Latin America. Graham-Jones widens the scope of the designation, which she feels ought to be invoked "as shorthand reference for the many cultures—indigenous and immigrant, Western and non-Western—that make up what the dominant U.S. culture insists on generalizing as '*la vida latina*.'"[26]

To be Latin@ is no longer limited to being part of one of the three majority Spanish-speaking cultures in the United States: Mexican, Puerto Rican, or Cuban. Today, Latin@ is a heterogeneous term that includes the diversity of all Spanish-speaking and indigenous cultures existing in the United States from Mexico, to the Caribbean, to Central and South America and Spain, in addition to the multiplicities that arise from the intersections of these cultures with other world cultures. This definition highlights the globalization of the Latin@ community, yet may necessitate a shift in perception or alteration of position, for the Latin@ plays produced in the American theatre rarely reflect this view. Historically, U.S. theatre producers and audiences have considered the term "Latino/a" solely through the lens of Mexican, Puerto Rican, or Cuban cultures. One might understand this perception since, according to the 2010 U.S. Census, Mexican Americans, Puerto Ricans, and Cuban Americans make up 76 percent of the U.S. Latin@ population, which constitutes 16 percent of the U.S. population. Central American, South American, Caribbean, and "all other Hispanic" groups[27] represent the remaining 24 percent, which continues to grow and diversify the community. In this study, "Latin@" refers to both genders and the term "Latina" means a female.

My definition of Latin@ has been largely informed by my work as a playwright and theatre studies scholar. During my drama school years, which I mentioned earlier, my identity as a Latina playwright developed more fully when I started to explore the intersection of languages and cultures in my work. A decade later, as a theatre studies scholar, I continue to hone a more nuanced definition of my Latina identity while researching the field of Latin@ theatre. My Spanish artist father immigrated to the United States a year after he married my American professor mother (who is of English-Irish-German descent). Growing up in an artistic, academic, bicultural, and bilingual household in New England, and then California, deeply influenced my writing. Living in and around Boston, San Francisco, Los Angeles, New York City, Minneapolis, and now Chicago, I have experienced and found my place among the many cultural collisions within the Latin@ community. Some may refute my definition of Latin@ and ask, "How can a Spanish American woman be a Latina?" This definition, however, is reflective of my artistic and personal experience.

I write plays about diverse cultural connections that echo my heritage. I often explore how Latin@, Anglo, and other worlds collide to create a complex cultural reality on stage. I will not be discussing my plays in this study, but here I will offer two examples to contextualize my position as a professional playwright analyzing works written by my colleagues and to underscore my in-depth knowledge of, and ongoing commitment to, the field.

My play *Paloma* considers an interfaith relationship between a Moroccan American devout Muslim man and a Puerto Rican–Spanish American nominally Catholic woman as they navigate the challenges of their religious differences in 2004 New York City and Spain. *Paloma* was the runner-up for the 2011 National Latino Playwriting Award, and received its world premiere at the National Hispanic Cultural Center in Albuquerque, New Mexico, produced by Camino Real Productions, and its West Coast premiere at the Los Angeles Theatre Center. *Paloma* was also included in the anthology *New Playwrights: Best Plays of 2013*, published by Smith and Kraus.

In addition, my play *Earthquake Chica* examines the life of a bicultural Mexican American legal secretary in present-day Los Angeles, who learns to embrace her heritage through her relationship with a shy Mexican American accountant who loves Latin American literature. *Earthquake Chica* was a finalist for the 2002 National Latino Playwriting Award, produced by Borderlands Theater in Tucson, Arizona, and published by Broadway Play Publishing and NoPassport Press.[28] Existing in the liminal spaces between cultures inspires me to explore the intricacies of early twenty-first-century Latin@ society, which has broadened to include a larger array of world cultures, a linguistic terrain that encompasses varieties of Spanish and indigenous languages, and a wider sense of inclusiveness amid its growing diversity.

EARLY TWENTY-FIRST-CENTURY
LATINA PLAYWRIGHTS

Latina playwrights emerged as a significant influence in U.S. theatre beginning with the work of Fornes in the 1960s. Fornes first established her career in the burgeoning Off-Off-Broadway movement with plays such as *Tango Palace* and *The Successful Life of 3*, which both won Obie Awards.[29] In the 1970s, Fornes's plays, such as *Fefu and Her Friends*, continued to garner Obie awards as well as numerous U.S. and international productions.[30] Latina playwrights such as Moraga and Sanchez-Scott gained prominence in the 1980s with plays produced regionally and Off-Broadway. The next generation of Latina playwrights in the 1990s includes Migdalia Cruz and Carmelita Tropicana (also a Fornes student.) Unlike Fornes, whose plays only occasionally deal with Latin@ culture, Moraga, Sanchez-Scott, Cruz, and Tropicana each have explored the specificity of their cultural, political, and social environs.

From 2000 through the present, the current generation of early twenty-first-century Latina playwrights has emerged to national and international recognition. Their work is not defined by adherence to a single cultural identity, but by an exploration of a variety of cultural collisions, which fosters theatrical experimentation and innovation. This study examines the work of this most recent generation of Latina playwrights, including Caridad Svich, Karen Zacarías, Elaine Romero, Cusi Cram, and Quiara Alegría Hudes. Each playwright, raised in the United States, hails from a diverse cultural background, and these formative cultural multiplicities often inspire their plays as they mine the expanse of the Latin@ experience.

This study focuses solely on early twenty-first-century Latina playwrights for several reasons. First, the majority of Latin@ plays that have been produced in the United States are written by men. Each of the Latina playwrights included here has an equally remarkable body of work that merits greater exposure, acknowledgment, and production. These specific playwrights are also included because their work has not been substantially documented in the archive. Work by prominent Latina playwrights such as Cruz, Moraga,[31] and others, whose plays first premiered in the 1980s and 1990s, have been documented in books by Alicia Arrizón, Jorge Huerta, Jon Rossini, Alberto Sandoval-Sánchez and Nancy Saporta

Sternbach, Linda Saborío, Elizabeth Ramirez, and Catherine Casiano. The five playwrights in this study have received national and international acclaim, yet many scholars have not previously considered their plays.

Next, while past works of Latin@ theatre studies scholarship have focused on contemporary Latin@ playwrights, none has emphasized the vast cultural diversity within the Latin@ experience. These scholars primarily focus on plays that reflect the influences of the three major cultural groups in U.S. Latin@ culture: Mexican Americans, Puerto Ricans, and Cuban Americans. Their works have covered late-twentieth-century Latina playwrights in depth. Latina plays produced within the first two decades of the twenty-first century encompass a greater cultural multiplicity. A close examination of these plays by Latina playwrights is now necessary.

Lastly, these Latina playwrights offer a unique and important window into contemporary Latin@ society. Their protagonists contend with a wide range of cultural questions: What does it mean to be Latina in early twenty-first-century America? How do Latinas negotiate cross-cultural intersections in their identities? How do Latinas engage with cultural difference in their communities? This engagement in turn provides a rich, complex view into early twenty-first-century Latin@ culture for audiences and offers inspiration for the next generation of Latina playwrights.

LATINA PLAYWRIGHTS: FIVE VOICES

These diverse theatrical voices include some of the most celebrated Latina playwrights working in the American theatre today. The word "voice" comes from the Latin *vocare*, meaning to call or summon. Each of the playwrights explored in this study calls forth and summons a new way of viewing Latin@ theatre. Some of these playwrights studied with Fornes, while others are indirect beneficiaries of Fornes's writing and pedagogy. These playwrights compose a network of emerging early-to-midcareer playwrights and represent a new generation of theatre artists that is significantly contributing to our national discourse on Latin@ theatre. In addition, these early twenty-first-century playwrights hail from multicultural backgrounds and engage with a variety of cultural complexities in their work, which continually expands the definition of Latin@. Many of their plays also experiment with structure and language in ways that mirror complex cultural interactions.

These five playwrights are professionally trained and enjoy award-winning playwriting careers. Each received a graduate degree in playwriting from a significant U.S. theatre program, and their work has been developed in nationally recognized theatres and arts organizations, which is unprecedented in previous generations of Latina playwrights. Since I began this project in 2005, these playwrights have continued to rise to greater prominence. They have won many prestigious awards, including the 2010 Steinberg Citation–Best New Play, 2010 Edgerton New American Play Award, 2012 Obie Award for Lifetime Achievement, 2012 Pulitzer Prize for Drama, among many others.

Caridad Svich, author of *Prodigal Kiss* and *Tropic of X*, is a playwright of Cuban-Spanish, Argentinean-Croatian descent. Her mother's family emigrated from Galicia, Spain, to Cuba, and her father's family emigrated from Croatia to Argentina. She describes her background thus: "I self-identify as Latina hybrid. . . . I was raised with memories (and photos and music) of my parents' homelands and brought up in seven U.S. states by the time I was twelve."[32] She completed her undergraduate work at the University of North Carolina, Charlotte, and her MFA in playwriting at the University of California, San Diego. Her plays have been presented across the United States and abroad at diverse venues, including Denver Center Theatre, Mixed Blood Theatre, Cincinnati Playhouse in the Park, Women's Project Theater, Repertorio Español, INTAR, Victory Gardens, Salvage Vanguard Theatre, Teatro Mori (Chile), ARTheater (Germany), and Ilkhom Theater (Uzbekistan). She has been an NEA/TCG playwright-in-residence at the Mark Taper Forum and is an alumna playwright of New Dramatists. Her many awards include a 2003 National Latino Playwriting Award for *Magnificent Waste*, a 2013 National Latino Playwriting Award for *Spark*, and the 2012 Obie Award for Lifetime Achievement. Svich is also the founder of NoPassport, "an unincorporated, artist-driven, grass-roots theatre alliance and press devoted to cross-cultural, Pan-American performance, theory, action, advocacy, and publication."[33] As NoPassport's founder, Svich organizes national gatherings of artists and scholars to discuss the state of the field and serves as the editor of NoPassport Press, which publishes new plays, translations, and criticism.

Karen Zacarías, author of *Mariela in the Desert* and *The Sins of Sor Juana*, is a playwright of Mexican-Lebanese-Danish descent, who immigrated to the United States at a young age. She reflects: "I am Mexican/Lebanese on my father's side, Danish on my mother's side. I am an immigrant, coming to this country from Mexico when I was ten. I think of myself as a Latina, sometimes specifically Mexican. More and more, I have also started thinking of myself as an American playwright."[34] She received her undergraduate degree from Stanford University and her MA in creative writing from Boston University. Her plays have been produced at theatres such as Arena Stage, the Kennedy Center for the Performing Arts, Goodman Theatre, Denver Center Theatre, Round House Theatre, Cleveland Play House, La Jolla Playhouse, GALA Hispanic Theatre, and Alliance Theatre. She is the founding artistic director of Young Playwrights' Theater, "an award-winning non-profit dedicated to enhancing literacy, arts empowerment, and conflict resolution through playwriting in Washington, DC area schools."[35] She has been a resident playwright at Arena Stage. She won the 2006 Francesca Primus Prize, the 2005 TCG/ATT First Stages Award, and the 2004 National Latino Playwriting Award, all for *Mariela in the Desert*. She won the 2010 Steinberg Citation–Best New Play for *Legacy of Light*.

Elaine Romero, author of *Secret Things* and *¡Curanderas! Serpents of the Clouds*, a Mexican American playwright, outlines her heritage in this way: "My mother's family has a four-hundred-year history in New Mexico. The family predates the takeover of Northern Mexico by the U.S. My great-grandparents on my father's side were from Spain. I was raised closer to my mother's family, so my identity is much more of a Mexican American one. I've also lived in the Southwest for much of my life, so I'm constantly re-infused with that culture."[36] She received her undergraduate degree from Linfield College and earned her MFA in playwriting at the University of California, Davis. Her plays have been developed and produced by Actors Theatre of Louisville, Alley Theatre, Goodman Theatre, Magic Theatre, Arizona Theatre Company, Kitchen Dog Theater, INTAR, Women's Project and Productions, the Lark Theatre, Borderlands Theater, and Miracle Theatre. Romero won the 2010 Edgerton New American Play Award for *Ponzi*. She has been the TCG/Pew National Theatre artist-in-residence at Arizona Theatre Company, where she cofounded their National Latino Playwriting Award, which was established "to create a greater awareness of the work being done by Latino and Latina playwrights across the nation."[37] She has been a member of the Goodman Theatre Playwrights Unit, and is a resident playwright at Chicago Dramatists.

Cusi Cram, author of *Lucy and the Conquest* and *Fuente*, is a playwright of Bolivian-Scottish descent, with parents originally from those two countries. She recounts her childhood as "growing up in New York in a mostly Anglo world. My parents separated when I was very young and I would visit my Dad in Latin America. . . . That world was very specific, it was a very Bohemian and artistic world filled with tons of interesting characters."[38] Cram went on to do her undergraduate work at Brown University and is a graduate of the Lila Acheson American Playwright's Program at the Juilliard School. Her plays have been developed and produced at theatres such as Denver Center Theatre, Williamstown Theatre Festival, LAByrinth Theater Company, Barrington Stage, South Coast Repertory's Hispanic Playwrights Project, Primary Stages, The New Group, New York Theatre Workshop, the NYSF/Public Theater, PS122, and the Dag Hammarskjold Theater at the United Nations. She is the recipient of the 2004 Herrick Theater Foundation New Play Prize for *Fuente*, and is a three-time Daytime Emmy nominee for her work in children's television. She is a company member of the LAByrinth Theater Company. Cram, also a professional actor, originated the role of Cassie Callison on the soap opera *One Life to Live*.

Quiara Alegría Hudes, author of *Yemaya's Belly* and *Elliot, A Soldier's Fugue*, is a playwright with Puerto Rican and Jewish heritage. She describes her formative years in Philadelphia: "I was raised by two Puerto Rican parents—my mom (Arecibo) and my stepfather (Barranquitas)—but I look white. I identify myself in two ways. I feel culturally very Puerto Rican, it's my identity. I also feel very biracial. It's part of my identity, too."[39] She received her undergraduate degree at Yale University and her MFA in playwriting from Brown University. Her plays have been developed and produced at theatres such as Second Stage Theatre, Hartford Stage Company, Goodman Theatre, Cleveland Playhouse, the Kennedy Center for the Performing Arts, Alliance Theatre, Teatro Vista, and Portland Stage Company. She has developed her work at the Sundance Institute Theatre Lab, the Eugene O'Neill National Playwrights Conference, and through her seven-year residency at New Dramatists.

She was a 2007 Pulitzer Prize finalist for her play *Elliot, A Soldier's Fugue* and a Tony Award nominee for Best Book of a Musical for her work on *In the Heights*, which won the 2008 Tony Award for Best Musical.[40] She won the 2012 Pulitzer Prize for Drama for *Water by the Spoonful*, the first Latina playwright to receive this prestigious award.

I am fortunate to have professional connections with each writer included in this study. While a Jerome fellow at the Playwrights' Center in Minneapolis, I served as dramaturg on a workshop of Svich's *Prodigal Kiss* at the Midwest PlayLabs in 2000. I also served as dramaturg on a reading of Zacarías's *Mariela in the Desert* at the Hispanic Playwrights Project (HPP) at South Coast Repertory in 2003.[41] Svich, Hudes, and I shared membership in New Dramatists, the oldest U.S. nonprofit center for the development of playwrights, founded in 1949 and based in New York City.[42] Romero and I participated in a writing workshop at the Mark Taper Forum's Latino Theatre Initiative writers' retreat in 2000 and are both currently resident playwrights at Chicago Dramatists, an organization dedicated to the development and advancement of playwrights in the greater Chicago area since 1979.[43] Cram and I met through HPP, where we both developed our plays. My depth of connection to such a diverse range of playwrights provides me with a unique and substantial level of inquiry and access.

FRAMING THE BOOK

Fornes's career as a playwright and teacher frames this book. After the initial chapter on the generative work of Fornes, each chapter focuses on a different Latina playwright. The order of these chapters is related to several elements: the playwright's connection to Fornes as teacher, the playwright's career longevity in the field of Latina theatre, and the concepts in this study, which include considerations of culture, spirituality, identity, and aesthetics in Latina theatre.

In chapter 1, "Maria Irene Fornes: The Fornes Frame," I examine the teaching and writing of Fornes, which has influenced a generation of Latin@ playwrights. In *Fefu and Her Friends*, Fornes presents a group of Anglo women as they gather for an educational fund-raiser in 1935 New England. In *Sarita*, Fornes chronicles the struggles of a Cuban American woman in the South Bronx of 1939 to 1947. I consider how Fornes questions the essentialist view of the hyphenated writer and shows that the Latin@ playwright can explore different ideas that don't have to be ethnically connected to one's heritage but only connected to one's artistic experience.

In chapter 2, "Caridad Svich: Imprinting the Fornes Frame," I argue that Svich is a direct theatrical descendant of Fornes. Svich has addressed cultural multiplicities, supernatural interventions, Latina identity, and theatrical experimentation throughout her playwriting career, which began in the early 1990s. In *Prodigal Kiss*, Svich follows the migration of a Cuban woman to the United States. Svich's *Tropic of X* reimagines a hip-hop sensibility while considering the lives of two Latin American lovers as they contend with dictatorship and censorship. I examine how Svich's plays exemplify Fornes's wide-ranging influence on Latina playwriting.

In chapter 3, "Karen Zacarías: Navigating Multiple Borders," I analyze how Zacarías addresses cultural multiplicities and the ensuing complexities in her work. Zacarías started her playwriting career in the early 1990s and did not study with Fornes. However, I trace how her works bear the imprint of Fornes's legacy. In *Mariela in the Desert*, Zacarías connects the lives of a family of Mexican painters and a Jewish American art historian in 1951 Mexico. Zacarías's *The Sins of Sor Juana* examines the seventeenth-century Mexican nun as she deals with her past in the Spanish Viceroyalty while confronting censorship in her present. How both plays forge connections to a variety of cultures is a key component of this chapter.

In chapter 4, "Elaine Romero: Viewing Latin@ Realism," I address staging of the spirit world and how Romero dramatizes sacred space, ritual, and *facultad* (i.e., supernatural sight) in her work. Romero, who also studied with Fornes, commenced her playwriting career in the early 1990s. In *Secret Things*, Romero presents a Latina reporter researching crypto-Jews in New Mexico. Romero's *¡Curanderas! Serpents of the Clouds* follows two Latinas, a healer and a physician, on a trip to Mexico. I consider how these plays engage the supernatural, moving past a restricted gaze toward a multifaceted way of seeing.

In chapter 5, "Cusi Cram: Performing Latina Identity," I focus on how Cram delves into the representation of Latina identity by investigating cultural complexities. Cram, who acted in Fornes's plays, started her playwriting career in the late 1990s. In *Lucy and the Conquest*, Cram explores a Latina actor's journey as she unearths her family history in Bolivia. Upending the soap opera genre, Cram's *Fuente* delves into the fractured lives of two couples in a small U.S. desert town. The questioning of cultural engagement in these characters' lives is a central aspect of this chapter.

In chapter 6, "Quiara Alegría Hudes: Conducting Theatrical Experimentation," I investigate how Hudes experiments with aesthetics in her work. Hudes commenced her playwriting career in the early 2000s and did not study with Fornes. However, I examine how her aesthetic choices echo those of Fornes. Hudes's *Yemaya's Belly* follows a boy who leaves his town, and later his island, to sail to the United States. In *Elliot, A Soldier's Fugue*, Hudes explores the life of a Puerto Rican Iraq war veteran from Philadelphia. I consider how Hudes reconfigures existing artistic and spiritual models in order to create innovative structures, characters, and language in her plays.

The Latin@ community in the United States continues to evolve in the new millennium. American theatre audiences may not be familiar with the breadth of this rapidly diversifying population. Each of these plays provides a unique view into the intricacies and nuances of early twenty-first-century Latin@ culture. These Latina playwrights engage a multiplicity of viewpoints, including Mexican, Puerto Rican, Cuban, Dominican, Bolivian, Argentinean, Chilean, Spanish, Yoruban, Incan, Aztec, urban, suburban, international, bicultural, multicultural, bilingual, polylingual, intellectual, political, musical, whimsical, and historical, among many others. Therefore, these Latina playwrights significantly contribute to the American theatre by creating a body of work that helps audiences experience Latin@ realities at the beginning of the twenty-first century.

1

MARIA IRENE FORNES

The Fornes Frame

I N 1945, CARMEN COLLADO DE FORNES, a former schoolteacher, emigrated from Cuba to the United States with her two youngest daughters, Margarita and Maria Irene. Maria Irene was fifteen. Earlier that year in Cuba, Carlos Fornes, her father, died of a heart attack at the age of fifty-three. So, Carmen Fornes, a widow, raised her two daughters in New York City in the South Bronx and then on the West Side near the future home of Lincoln Center. Maria Irene Fornes first trained as a painter in New York City before pursuing playwriting. During her award-winning career, Fornes created more than fifty works for the stage that have been produced throughout the United States and internationally, including in England, France, Spain, Denmark, Sweden, Russia, and India. She won an unprecedented nine Obie Awards, a distinction surpassed only by playwright Sam Shepard. Fornes is less well known than many of her playwriting peers, who include Edward Albee, Caryl Churchill, John Guare, Shepard, and Luis Valdez. However, her influence and legacy continue to significantly shape the field of American theatre.

Writers need models, esteemed and experienced professionals, who can help guide the journey of creation. Influential authors teach through the example of their successful artistic careers as well as through their excellence in the classroom. Latina playwrights especially need mentors to show them a path through the American theater, a world that often does not fully understand or showcase Latina plays. As a playwright and teacher, Maria Irene Fornes has had a substantial influence on the Latin@ theater community. Her significant body of work and her years of teaching have provided guidance and inspiration for a generation of Latin@ theatre artists.[1]

Fornes consistently complicates what it means to be a Latina playwright. In her Obie Award-winning play *Fefu and Her Friends*, Stephany (Fefu) Beckman addresses her colleagues Christina and Cindy in the living room of her New England country home and asks:

> Have you ever turned a stone over in damp soil? . . . And when you turn it there are worms crawling on it? . . . And it's damp and full of fungus? . . . Were you revolted? . . . Were you fascinated? . . . There you have it! You too are fascinated with revulsion. . . . You see, that which is exposed to the exterior . . . is smooth and dry and clean. That which is not . . . underneath is slimy and filled with fungus and crawling with worms. It is another life parallel to the one we manifest. It's there. The way worms are underneath the stone. If you don't recognize it . . . *(Whispering.)* it eats you. That is my opinion. Well, who is ready for lunch?[2]

Metaphorically, Fornes has constantly "turned a stone over" to examine "another life parallel" and has addressed the ensuing complexities in her playwriting. Fornes presents what theatre studies scholar Elinor Fuchs calls the "parable of the stone." Fuchs writes: "The stone, Fefu immediately makes clear, is not simply a metaphor for the difference between life and the grave. It is a metaphor for the crucial, characterological differences between men and women."[3] Fuchs asserts that the underside of the stone, the worm-infested side, correlates to the women in the play, as noted in the play's first line when Fefu cheerfully relays, "My husband married me to have a constant reminder of how loathsome women are."[4] Fuchs views the smooth side of the stone as corresponding to the world of men in Fornes's play, where men "are well together . . . out in the fresh and air and sun, while (women) sit . . . in the dark."[5] Fuchs claims this metaphor categorizes the types of women in the play, some of whom are "ecstatic," while others descend to "horrific depths." However, Fuchs's stone metaphor focuses solely on gender. The stone in damp soil also presents an ecology of dualities that involves sunlight/shadow, dry/damp, smooth/slimy, clean/fungus, and fascination/revulsion. A person must recognize this parallel life, as Fefu suggests, lest she be consumed by it. Fornes constantly rotates the metaphorical stone to consciously complicate many dualities in Latina playwriting: Latin@/Anglo, Spanish/English, female/male, homosexual/heterosexual, supernatural/natural, experimentation/realism, and artist/teacher.

Fornes creates an ecosystem of viewpoints in her work. Fefu asks her colleagues to consider her questions and opinions. Questioning as a mode of inquiry suggests a multiplicity of possibilities. Opinions allow for differing points of view. Fornes utilizes both these approaches as she contends that the Latina playwright is entitled to write about identities, spiritualities, and cultures that are not ethnically connected to her heritage but instead only to her artistic experience. She encourages the Latina playwright to question the playwriting art form and to generate an aesthetic approach organic to the world of her play.

FIGURE 1.   Maria Irene Fornes in New York City, 1990.
Photo by Robert Giard, © Estate of Robert Giard.

THE FORNES CONNECTIONS

I will utilize the "Fornes frame" to examine the plays of five twenty-first-century Latina playwrights: Caridad Svich, Karen Zacarías, Elaine Romero, Cusi Cram, and Quiara Alegría Hudes. This frame encompasses four concepts: cultural multiplicity, supernatural interventions, Latina identity, and theatrical experimentations, which I will delve into more deeply as I consider Fornes's plays later in this chapter. However, contextualizing the ways in which these writers connect to Fornes and her work will underscore the importance of considering their plays using the Fornes frame.

Caridad Svich is the only one of these Latina playwrights to have trained with Fornes for a substantial period of time. After receiving her MFA in playwriting from the University of California, San Diego, Svich studied with Fornes for four consecutive seasons from 1988 to 1992 at the INTAR Hispanic Playwrights-in-Residence Laboratory in New York City, while also serving as Fornes's assistant. Svich reflects:

> On my work the training impacted me in every way: the methodology forced me to never stop asking questions of the work and myself as an artist, to enjoy the practicality of theatre, and the ability for a theatre experience to be unique and absolutely human. As a playwright, my work was first seen in New York City whilst at the Lab so it was indeed a first step after the cocoon of grad school.[6]

Fornes also directed Svich's play *Any Place but Here* at Theatre for the New City in 1995. Fornes has not often directed her students' work. Thus this production was a significant artistic and pedagogical experience in which Fornes mentored Svich through her directorial expertise.[7] Svich feels Fornes taught her "rigor, playfulness, truthfulness, daring, formal enquiry, linguistic enquiry."[8] Svich here reflects Fornes's emphasis on questioning and experimentation. Svich has also continued Fornes's legacy by teaching playwriting at many universities, including the Yale School of Drama, Rutgers University, Barnard College, Bennington College, and the University of London.

Fornes has offered playwriting workshops in the United States and internationally. Elaine Romero studied with Fornes in the Latin

American Writers' Workshop in Taxco, Mexico. Romero later participated in a Fornes workshop at the Latino Theater Initiative writers'
retreat at the Mark Taper Forum in Los Angeles. Of her work with
Fornes, Romero affirms:

> I feel like Irene's great gift is teaching one access to oneself—to one's cre-
> ativity. I love her exercises. I feel like they are very liberating. I love the fact
> she does her own version of yoga. I now am a certified yoga teacher, and
> thankfully, Irene taught me it is good, if not necessary, to get up! . . . Study-
> ing with Irene made me more a part of the greater Latina/o playwriting
> community that she was so central to founding. My life in the playwriting
> world changed considerably after studying with her.[9]

Romero is an assistant professor of theatre at the University of Arizona.
Like Svich, she carries on the legacy of Fornes through her teaching.

Some Latina playwrights first engaged with Fornes's work through
acting in her plays. Cusi Cram acted in Fornes plays during her undergraduate years at Brown University. Though she never studied with
Fornes, Cram's immersion in Fornes's theatrical world influenced her
development as a young theatre artist. Cram reveals:

> I played Paula in *Fefu and her Friends* and it kind of rocked my world,
> opened up the idea of what a play could be. And I kissed a girl, which was
> pretty amazing and strange. I recall her being quite lovely and that I was
> thrilled. . . . It was my first all-girl play too—sort of started my interest in
> feminism and feminist literary theory. . . . It seems because Paula Vogel
> was such a big fan that everyone was doing Fornes plays. I saw *Sarita* and
> did a scene from *Mud* for acting class.[10]

Cram mentions Pulitzer Prize-winning playwright Vogel, who directed
Brown University's graduate playwriting program from 1984 to 2008.
Vogel, like Fornes, is an influential teacher who's trained a generation
of playwrights and theatre artists that have successful careers in American theater, including Cram and Quiara Alegría Hudes.[11] Cram teaches
playwriting in New York City at the Einhorn School of Performing Arts
at Primary Stages and the Fordham University/Primary Stages MFA in
Playwriting program.

Quiara Alegría Hudes and Karen Zacarías also never studied with Fornes. Hudes, the Shapiro Distinguished Professor of Writing and Theatre at Wesleyan University, struggled with Fornes's plays. But ultimately she connected to the visceral physicality of the work: "[Fornes's] work is extremely dark and I had trouble with it at first. . . . Some of [her] playworlds are so tasty and tactile you can smell them, and that is how I found my way in."[12] For her part, Zacarías, who has taught playwriting at Georgetown University, asserts, "I have the distinct feeling of loss of not having taken Fornes's class, of not knowing her when she was teaching. I am inspired by her role as a playwright and a teacher, as a cultivator of story and souls. She is a pioneer."[13]

While an influential teacher to many twenty-first-century Latin@ playwrights, Fornes's singular artistic vision is reflected in her own body of work. Her plays privilege artistic experience over ethnic exploration while never abandoning the influence of her Cuban heritage. In many ways, the work of the playwrights included here mirrors the cultural complexity of Fornes's work. Some of their plays directly explore Latina culture and others do not. In addressing the role of cultural influence in her Hispanic Playwrights-in-Residence Laboratory training, Svich emphasizes:

> This Lab was not only a place to train and develop your writing muscles under a master's guidance and supervision, but also a place where you could upset expectations of what a play could be and be part of a community of writers dedicated, in part, to the forging of an entirely different theatrical language, one that could borrow equally from Iberian and Latin American traditions, and European and American ones. Fornes would often say, "We are writing for the twenty-first century."[14]

Fornes is a playwright who defies classification, who complicates artistic and cultural norms, and yet whose Latina identity is never forgotten. *Fefu and Her Friends* delves into the lives of Anglo women in New England and does not address Latin@ culture. *Sarita* explores the life of a young Cuban American woman in New York City. However, both plays demonstrate how Fornes stages cultural multiplicities, devises supernatural interventions, shapes Latina and non-Latina identity, and conducts theatrical experimentations in her work.

FEFU AND HER FRIENDS: FORNES STAGES NEW ENGLAND WOMEN

In *Fefu and Her Friends*, her Obie-award-winning play that she directed and first produced in 1977, Fornes presents eight Anglo women in a New England country house in 1935 as they gather to rehearse for a fund-raiser to benefit the education of children. *Fefu and Her Friends* is one of her most produced works, with forty-five productions occurring between 1977 and 1999.[15] This play exemplifies the metaphor of the stone through the interiority/exteriority of space and character. At the beginning of part 1, Fefu mentions that Phillip, her husband, John, her younger brother, and Tom, the gardener, are all outside (off stage). In part 2, with the exception of Fefu and Emma, who are the two iconoclastic women in the group, the women remain inside. In part 3, all the women remain inside except for Fefu, who goes outdoors briefly at the end of the play. While movement occurs within the house, the women mainly remain separated from the world of men outside. Fornes emphasizes the visibility of the women, while the men never appear as characters in the play.

Fornes addresses female identity in this 1930s world by examining issues of gender, education, class, and sexuality, all of which contribute to the work's enduring influence. Fefu, ever the iconoclast, announces, "I like being like a man. Thinking like a man. Feeling like a man."[16] Christina, the epitome of feminine decorum, is scandalized by Fefu and interjects, "She's crazy."[17] Emma, the effusive world traveler, adores dramatic expression: "Life is theatre. Theatre is life. If we're showing what life is, can be, we must do theatre."[18] Paula, the only character from a working-class background, challenges the others' economic prosperity: "I think we should teach the poor and let the rich take care of themselves."[19] Julia, the mystical yet paralyzed woman who was injured in a hunting accident, enters in a wheelchair and explores the terrain of mental illness, stating, "My hallucinations are madness, of course, but I wish I could be with others who hallucinate also."[20] Cecilia and Paula, former lovers, address the complexities of homosexuality as they face the loss of their relationship. Paula confesses, "I'm not lusting after you."[21] Cecilia replies, "I know that . . . I'll call you."[22] After Paula's speech regarding the divide between the rich and poor, Fornes's stage directions state that "Cecilia opens her arms and puts them around Paula, engulfing her. She kisses Paula on the lips. Paula steps

back. She is fearful."[23] Fornes's characters either challenge or uphold varying aspects of the Anglo female status quo throughout the play.

While the play focuses primarily on Anglo culture, Fornes does engage
cultural multiplicities by referencing three iconic feminists, either from
or influenced by non-U.S. cultures. In part 1, Paula commends Fefu on
her talk about Voltairine de Cleyre. Named after the eighteenth-century
French philosopher Voltaire, Voltairine de Cleyre (1866–1912) was an
"American anarchist and feminist, attacked church, state, and the institution of marriage as colluding in the bondage of women."[24] De Cleyre
taught English to Jewish immigrants in Philadelphia, where she learned
to speak and write Yiddish. She later wrote an essay and raised funds to
support the Mexican Revolution.[25] Her lecture "Sex Slavery" denounced
married women as bonded slaves. Fuchs wonders whether this iconic
woman is included in *Fefu and Her Friends*

> as a kind of bulwark against the forms of feminine (un)consciousness rep-
> resented in the play, as if to say that somewhere, in the background of
> women's history, lay the possibility for a different path? Had Fefu not been
> in thrall to Phillip, had Julia not been vulnerable to the mysterious acci-
> dent, they might have been Voltairine de Cleyres?[26]

The inclusion of de Cleyre also provides an example of a feminist who
values immigrant cultures and global activism.

In part 2, Fornes incorporates Isadora Duncan (1877–1927), acclaimed
dancer and choreographer, "whose dancing was known in part for its new
emphasis on gravity, on connection of the lower body with the ground."[27]
Duncan, while born in the United States, spent a majority of her life in
Europe and was influenced by French and Russian cultures, bore two
children out of wedlock, and had both male and female lovers. "With
free-flowing costumes, bare feet and loose hair, Duncan restored dancing
to a new vitality using the solar plexus and the torso as the generating
force for all movements to follow."[28] Julia, in her hallucination, defends
Duncan as a woman who was not crazy and then girds herself against a
possible blow from imaginary malevolent judges who threaten to strike
and injure her.[29] Julia's sexual orientation is not directly addressed in the
play, but Fornes contrasts her lack of physical mobility with Duncan's
innovative physical performance style. Fornes therefore links Julia to

Duncan, an American bisexual female dancer who lived as an immigrant in Europe and performed internationally.

In part 3, Fornes highlights the writing of Emma Sheridan Fry (1864–1936), an actor and educator, whose 1917 book, *Educational Dramatics*, provides the text for Emma's speech to inspire attendees of the educational fund-raiser. Fry worked for the Educational Alliance in New York City from 1903 to 1909, teaching acting to children of Polish and Russian Jewish immigrant families on New York's Lower East Side. As theatre education scholar Beatrice L. Tukesbury describes, "Fry's work not only resulted in fine theatre for children, young people, and their parents, but reached into the lives of the players, raising their ethical, moral, and social standards, improving speech and appearance, stimulating imaginations, broadening horizons."[30] Fry utilized theater to educate and assimilate immigrant children. Fry's text serves as a centerpiece for the play, a testimony to the power of education written by a woman who was deeply influenced by children from non-U.S. cultures. By incorporating culturally complex iconic feminists into each part of the play, Fornes highlights the global influences on her Anglo characters and the importance of seeking inspiration from, and connection to, disparate world cultures.

Fornes has asserted that her Cuban heritage influences her writing whether she writes of Latin@ culture or other cultures. Fornes, while completely bilingual, speaks heavily accented English. Referring to her accent in relation to her Cuban heritage, Fornes reflects, "I have a strong accent, and I think it's because there's a part of me I don't want to eradicate."[31] Fornes similarly creates a theatrical language from which her Cuban heritage can never be eradicated. Fornes has posited that her Cuban identity influences her creative process. Her enduring connection to Cuba informs her subject matter and theatrical exploration on the level of form, language, and content. Fornes acknowledges:

> My writing has an off center quality that is not exactly deliberate, but that I have not tried to change because I know its origin lies in the temperament and language of my birth. Besides, my primary interest has never been to reproduce a realistic, everyday world. Outside of the language itself, I know there are character values and priorities that suggest a foreign source. I know that sometimes I am moved by something because of my Cuban upbringing and I know that sometimes I notice something because

of my Cuban upbringing. At the same time, in many ways, I think the way
Americans think, and I feel very much at home in the United States."[32]

Fornes engages culture here as well, for while her plays may not specifically address her Caribbean origin, she admits that her Cuban upbringing influences the very fabric of her dramaturgy.

Fornes shows that a Latina's writing can reflect not only her literal
ethnic heritage, but also her cultural imagination. In her 1985 preface to
Fornes's anthology, *Plays*, author Susan Sontag emphasizes that Fornes
"is unmistakably a writer of bicultural inspiration: one very American
way of being a writer. Her imagination seems to me to have, among other
sources, a profoundly Cuban one."[33] Both Sontag, and Fornes herself, put
forth the notion that one's culture can be an influence and inspiration,
regardless of the subject matter about which one writes. Fornes articulates that her Cuban and American cultures are equally intrinsic to her
theatrical language, and Sontag states that this bicultural orientation is
a very American approach to writing. The importance of two cultures
equally informing a Latina play also shifts the perception of what it
means to be a Latina playwright.

This artistic bicultural position can additionally be traced to one of
Fornes's earliest theatrical influences: the original production of Samuel Beckett's *Waiting for Godot*, directed by Roger Blin, which Fornes
attended while in Paris in 1953. At the time she did not speak French, but
was hugely inspired by the performance. Thus cultures collide as Fornes,
a Cuban American artist traveling from the United States to France to
study painting, sees the premiere of a play by an Irish playwright writing
in French. Education studies scholar Ann Beer posits: "Central to (Beckett's) bilingual art is . . . his constant ability to see artistic forms afresh.
. . . He renewed forms, often to vociferous protest, in ways that were
previously unthinkable and have since come to seem 'natural.' Godot is
a supreme example. Bilingualism and biculturalism are surely central to
this self-renewal."[34] In addition to being an artistic inspiration, Beckett
served as a model for Fornes, demonstrating that writing in one's second language can provide an opportune theatricality and a platform for
experimentation influenced by one's culture of origin.

The inspiration for *Fefu and Her Friends* also underscores a bicultural
reality. While she does not address Latin@ culture in the play, Fornes
reveals she was inspired by a Mexican joke:

The source of this play is a Mexican joke. There are two Mexicans in sombreros sitting at a bullfight and one says to the other, "Isn't she beautiful, the one in yellow?" and he points to a woman on the other side of the arena crowded with people. The other one says, "Which one?" and the first takes his gun and shoots her and says, "The one that falls." In the first draft of this play, Fefu explains that she started playing this game with her husband because of that joke. But in rewriting the play, I took out this explanation.[35]

In her play, Fornes does not address the Mexican machismo the joke skewers, but considers the effects of universal machismo on the lives of early twentieth-century Anglo women. The genesis of this play points to Fornes's link to Latin America. This cultural connection is less visible, just as the side of the stone in her parable is hidden from view. Yet this inspiration remains significant.[36]

Fornes devises supernatural interventions in her play through the character of Julia. When Julia enters the house in her wheelchair, her friends Cindy and Christina have a difficult time accepting Julia's paralysis. As Fefu brings Julia to her room, Cindy describes how a hunting incident caused Julia's condition. Cindy tells Christina that she was with Julia when a hunter shot a deer and "Julia and the deer fell. The deer was dead . . . dying and Julia was unconscious. She had convulsions . . . like the deer. He died and she didn't . . . apparently there was spinal nerve injury."[37] Thus, Julia is supernaturally paralyzed by the animal's death. In part 3, Fefu confronts Julia about her paralysis, telling her to fight and to try to walk. Their confrontation escalates in a ritualistic, almost liturgical exchange:

JULIA: May no harm come to your head.
FEFU: Fight!
JULIA: May no harm come to your will.
FEFU: Fight, Julia!
(Fefu starts shaking the wheelchair and pulling Julia off the wheelchair.)[38]

After her violent gesture, Fefu exits to clean her rifle. The women comfort Julia, whose fragility seems intensified by Fefu's actions. Then, a shot is heard. Fornes writes: "*(Julia puts her hand on her forehead. Her hand goes down slowly. There is blood on her forehead. Her head falls back. Fefu enters holding a dead white rabbit.)*" Then Fefu speaks: "I killed it . . . I just shot

FIGURE 2. *Fefu and Her Friends*, by Maria Irene Fornes, produced by the American Place Theatre, directed by Fornes, in 1978. Fefu (Rebecca Schull) threatens Julia (Margaret Harrington). Photo by Martha Holmes, reproduced courtesy of Billy Rose Theatre Collection, New York Public Library for the Performing Arts.

. . . and killed it . . . Julia. . . ."[39] Fefu's gunshot supernaturally causes the death of Julia. However, the death is handled realistically with no shift in lighting or scene design. Fornes merges the supernatural and natural worlds on stage as she closes her play.

Fornes conducts theatrical experimentation in *Fefu and Her Friends* through her innovative use of theatrical space in part 2. Parts 1 and 3 are located in the living room of Fefu's home, a New England country house. Part 2 takes place in four separate locations in and around the house: a study, the kitchen, a bedroom, and the lawn. In her description of part 2, Fornes writes, "The audience is divided into four groups. Each group is led to the spaces. These scenes are performed simultaneously."[40] Fornes therefore instructs that the audience must leave the proscenium setting of part 1 and physically move to different areas of the theatre or performance venue to witness the four scenes of part 2 and then reconvene in the proscenium setting for part 3.[41] This innovation was inspired by the layout of the New York City loft where the play was first performed. Fornes explains:

> When I was about to finish the first part, Barbara suggested we see a loft that was advertised as a performance place. We went to see it and I liked it. The person running it was used to renting it for parties or concerts. He took us to his office, which was simply a small partition in the loft. There he had a beautiful Persian carpet, a lovely antique desk, bookshelves on the walls filled with books, and several Victorian chairs. I said to Barbara, "This could be Fefu's study." I asked the man if we could use the whole space and he said, "Yes. Would you like to use the kitchen too?" How thrilling, I said to Barbara, "I think I'm going to do the play here." I did and it was thrilling. Besides the living room, the study, and the kitchen, there was a room in back that became the bedroom, and the lawn was part of the set to the side of the living room.[42]

Part 2 thus creates a spatial migration, as each audience member must travel from location to location throughout the entire theatrical space.[43] Fornes, a Cuban-born playwright living in New York City, wrote this play in which audiences too must migrate in order to gain access to her theatrical world. The audience must enter another "culture," the world of Fefu's house, travel to various locations within Fefu's world, and then return to their location of origin, the main auditorium or proscenium seating area.

As each audience member migrates from room to room, the close proximity to the performance creates a sense of intimacy, transformation, and potential assimilation into the imaginary of these characters. In the study, Christina confesses she is a conformist, and Cindy recounts a nightmare where a policeman tortured her: "[He] grabbed me and felt my throat from behind with his thumbs while he rubbed my nipples with his pinkies."[44] In the kitchen, Sue and Paula discuss the length of a love affair being "seven years and three months."[45] After Sue exits, Cecilia enters. Soon, she and Paula exchange views on their past relationship.[46] On the lawn, Emma reveals her obsession with genitals, and Fefu admits to being in constant pain due to a lack of a "spiritual lubricant."[47] In the bedroom, Julia hallucinates and battles invisible judges who mentally torture her, forcing her to repeat a prayer, which includes a recitation on gender: "The human being is of the masculine gender. . . . Women are evil. Woman is not a human being."[48] After experiencing their separate journeys, the entire audience reconvenes to witness part 3, which includes the rehearsal for their fund-raiser, a water fight, and, ultimately, Julia's mysterious death. Parts 1 and 3 are more exterior, while part 2 is a more interior exploration of character.

In a production, there are four different versions of her play, depending on the order each audience member experiences part 2. In the published script, the order of part 2 is the lawn (Fefu and Emma), the study (Cindy and Christina, then Fefu), the bedroom (Julia, then Sue), and the kitchen (Sue, Paula, and Cecilia, then Fefu). However, if an audience's migration is from the study to the kitchen to the lawn to the bedroom, then that group begins their journey with an intimate revelation of a nightmare. Next they listen to theories of relationships ending. Then they hear a discourse on genitalia and spirituality. Their travels end with witnessing a harrowing monologue that lingers as they reconvene to view the living room for the start of part 3, when the women sing "Who Is Sylvia," a nineteenth-century art song by Franz Schubert, with lyrics from act 4, scene 2 of Shakespeare's *Two Gentlemen of Verona*, when Proteus, a young nobleman, declares his love for Sylvia, daughter of the Duke of Milan. This particular journey from tragic hallucinations to a sprightly art song inspired by Shakespearean romance creates a jarring tonal shift, which may serve to emphasize the complexity of these women's struggles to survive in this 1930s society. Thus, Fornes has her audience simulate migration to show the importance of traveling to multiple, disparate worlds in order to create a compelling piece of theater that champions female education.

SARITA: FORNES CHRONICLES
A SOUTH BRONX LATINA

Fornes directly addresses Latin@ culture in *Sarita*, another Obie-award winner, which she wrote and directed in 1984. However, *Sarita* is also one of her least produced plays—only four times between 1984 and 1988.[49] Employing an innovative use of dance and song, Fornes considers the world of Sarita, a young Cuban American woman who lives in New York's South Bronx from 1939 to 1947. Eleven songs written by Leon Odenz punctuate the play with musical styles that range from tango and bolero to ballad and gospel. Through twenty short scenes with music, Fornes addresses the connection between Latin@ and Anglo worlds and highlights the cultural complexities in these characters' lives.

Sarita Fernandez, a young Cuban American, searches for personal and sexual empowerment. She oscillates between her lover Julio, an unemployed Cuban American from her neighborhood, and her husband Mark, an Anglo U.S. soldier. She begins her relationship with Julio when she is thirteen and suffers through his infidelities while remaining passionately involved with him. At eighteen, Sarita is suicidal over Julio's latest betrayal. In the final scene of act 1, Mark saves Sarita from jumping off the Empire State building out of distress over Julio's new lover. As Mark enters Sarita's world, Fornes begins to complicate the cultural intersections in her life.

Fornes first portrays Mark exoticizing Sarita when he sings the song "You are Tahiti": "You are the flower. I am the snow. You are Tahiti. I am Gauguin."[50] Through this song, Fornes addresses race and culture in the world of these characters. Sarita, a Latina, becomes a flower, an organism often displaying color, and Mark, an Anglo from Cleveland, represents the snow, white precipitation that descends on the earth. Mark does not identify Sarita as Cuba or Puerto Rico but surprisingly chooses a Polynesian island instead. This choice may relate to his time in the military service, although he never mentions being stationed in the South Pacific.

Mark identifies himself as Gauguin (1848–1903), the French painter who traveled to Tahiti in the late nineteenth century and chronicled his experience there through his paintings. Flora Tristan (1803–1844), Gauguin's grandmother and a French feminist author of Peruvian descent, wrote *The Peregrinations of a Pariah*, a chronicle of her 1836 round-trip journey between France and Peru, which became a groundbreaking feminist text. In addition, Gauguin spent the majority of his first seven years of life in Peru. Biographer David Sweetman says of Gauguin and Peru: "Lima was always with him. 'I am a Savage from Peru,' [Gauguin] repeated, mocking his disbelieving listeners, knowing that it was true."[51] Gauguin never met his grandmother; she died four years before his birth. Sweetman continues: "Flora had, in the years since her return to France, been trying to find ways to give practical expression to the radical political views which had been aroused by her experiences in Peru and it is here that her activities again prefigure those of her grandson."[52] So Gauguin and Tristan both remained connected to their Peruvian identities after immigrating to France.

By aligning Mark with Gauguin, a man with a multicultural heritage, Fornes provides a cultural lens through which Mark can view Sarita. Upon Gauguin's return to France from Tahiti in 1893, the artist carried on various affairs, including one with Annah the Javanese, a South Asian woman. Gauguin's nude portrait of Annah is one whose "final effect is of a placeless, timeless scene, neither East nor West, North nor South, not a bad metaphor for Gauguin's curiously suspended existence."[53] A "Gauguin" Mark would be a bicultural man who not only exoticizes a "Tahitian" Sarita, but has an abiding connection to Latin American culture and therefore could potentially have a unique understanding of Sarita's world.

Fornes continues to define Sarita's identity through her sexual relationships with Julio and Mark. At age fourteen, she was so distraught by Julio's infidelity that she had sex with many men and became pregnant, not knowing the identity of the father. She had her child, a boy named Melo, whom she asked her mother to care for when she and Julio ran away together at age sixteen. At age seventeen, Sarita returned home after Julio left her. Then in 1944, at age eighteen, she meets Mark. Two months later they are in a relationship, which lasts through the end of the play in 1947. However, during the three intervening years, Sarita also clandestinely has an affair with Julio. In a letter to Julio, Sarita writes, "It's like a sickness that lives in my heart and I have tried to tear it out but I can't. I am sick with it and I want to die. May God help me."[54] Sarita had fallen in love with and married Mark. Yet an unbridled passion for Julio continued to consume her in spite of their tumultuous history.

Sarita exists between two men with different cultural backgrounds. Her sense of self fluctuates as her actions raise questions: Does Julio love her? Does Mark love her? Can she live without Julio? She even seeks spiritual guidance when she prays, "God. I am serious. I cannot breathe. I'm burning. I'm turned inside myself. Do you know what I'm saying?—I feel my life's leaving me. I feel I'm dying God, I want to love Mark and no one else."[55] Julio's Latino world consists of unbridled passion, unemployment, and illegal behavior. Mark's Anglo world includes faithful love, gainful employment in the military, and conservative behavior. Fornes constructs questionable representations, with Julio as the Latino criminal, Mark as the Anglo savior, and Sarita as the sex-obsessed Latina. These character constructions do not appear to be in service of a larger context and therefore seem to be intentionally reinforcing cultural stereotypes.

Though these character constructions are unsettling, Fornes emphasizes the resulting tragedy when this young Latina defines herself through her sexual relationship to men, at the cost of her own freedom and sanity. As Mark and Sarita's relationship begins to unravel, Sarita's passion ultimately results in tragedy. When Julio threatens to tell Mark about their ongoing affair unless she gives him money, Sarita stabs and murders him. After Julio's death, Sarita is committed to a mental hospital. At the close of the play, Mark arrives to visit Sarita. Her crime of passion sends her to a space where she is devoid of a cultural context and remains disconnected not only from Mark but also from the world at large. In the final gesture of the play, Mark and Sarita's hands lock together in an attempt to forge a bridge toward a new existence.

Fornes devises supernatural interventions by establishing sacred space through performed ritual, which results in *facultad*, or supernatural sight. In the first scene of act 2, Sarita and Fela, her mother, throw a party during which they make flower and food offerings to Oshun, the Santería goddess of love, who is syncretically associated with the Virgin of Charity (La Virgen de la Caridad del Cobre), the patron saint of Cuba.[56] Fornes emphasizes the spiritual disjunctions within Sarita's home when Fernando, a boarder in Fela's apartment, states, "I'm a Catholic and I don't see why you have to give food to the Virgin."[57] Fela explains that "Oshun likes that I feed her." As Juan, a friend and drummer, joins the party, a Santería ritual song, "Ofe Isia," begins first as a prayer to help Fernando join the ritual. Soon all, including the doubtful Fernando, are dancing and singing in Spanish and Yoruba to worship Oshun.[58] Through this ritual of song, drumming, and dance, a sacred space is created where these characters can access the spirit world.

Fornes stages the spiritual and cultural multiplicities in this world through text, music, and movement as she presents a Caribbean religious ritual that next intersects with an American popular dance. After Mark enters, he and Sarita begin the foxtrot, a popular dance originally created by W. C. Handy, a young African American, in Memphis, Tennessee, in the early 1900s.[59] As they dance, Mark again exoticizes Sarita, "You are a tropical beauty," while Sarita asks Mark, "And in Cleveland, all the fellows look like you?" Here Fornes juxtaposes the tropics (i.e., Cuba) and midwestern America (i.e., Cleveland), which intersect amid a dance with origins in African American culture.

Fornes continues by examining spiritual differences when Sarita, a devotee of Santería, asks Mark, "And is it true that they are all preachers' sons . . . all evangelists?" to which Mark replies affirmatively.[60] However, Fornes's consideration here seems more schematic than complex, furthering received notions of cultural identity. Sarita remains the exotic Caribbean beauty, while Mark, the American soldier, hails from Cleveland where all the men are religious and look the same. Fornes does not problematize these representations but perhaps intentionally reinforces them.

Fornes escalates Sarita's conflict with both men when Julio enters the party. Sarita now literally stands between the two significant men in her life. On meeting Julio, Mark begins to question him, and the stark differences between these two appear. Julio admits he receives welfare, is a pickpocket, and commences to steal from Mark's pockets. As Mark becomes agitated and wants to fight, Sarita intervenes, and she and Mark prepare to leave. However, her connection to Julio is reestablished, which will lead to her downfall.

Fornes next highlights the cultural and spiritual disparities between Mark and Sarita. As the scene ends, Mark sings a religious, nondenominational Christian song, "His Wonderful Eye": "For the lord / speaks in the darkness, / shines in the shadow, / walks in the swamp . . . And I see his eye / and his eye says come to me."[61] The sacred space created by the Santería worship followed by Mark's entrance results in Mark gaining *facultad*. Fornes writes, "Mark's shadow appears in the up left window."[62] Even though he is in the shadows, he has an ability to witness Sarita and Julio's reunion. Julio and Sarita rekindle their connection and stare at each other during Mark's song. In literature scholar Diane Moroff's interpretation, "Mark is not only spatially removed from the drama, but also spiritually removed; he does not belong in this world. And yet, since his song provides a kind of voice-over narration to Julio and Sarita's reunion, he seems to exercise some control over this world."[63] However,

FIGURE 3. *Sarita*, by Maria Irene Fornes, produced by INTAR, directed by Fornes, in 1984. Mark (Tom Kirk) and Julio (Michael Carmine) fight over Sarita (Sheila Dabney) as Fela (Carmen Rosario), Fernando (Rodolfo Diaz), and Yeye (Blanca Camacho) witness. Photo by Carol Halebian.

Mark judges Sarita's existence by singing words such as "shadow" and "swamp," implying that his deity is shining down on the degradation of Sarita's environment. Presumably, Oshun is also watching the actions of Julio and Sarita, but Mark does not have access to Santería.

Fornes conducts theatrical experimentations through the use of song. *Sarita* includes eleven original songs, with lyrics by Fornes and music composed by Leon Odenz. The majority of the songs address issues surrounding Sarita's passion, express characters' private sentiments, and do not necessarily forward the narrative. The songs function as moments where music intersects with the action of the play to illuminate characters' desires and longing. In act 1, scene 1, Yeye, Sarita's friend, sings, "He Was Thinking of You," referring to Julio. Then Sarita sings a short song, "I'm Pudding," describing her excitable response to being in Julio's presence. Next they sing a prayer, "Holy Spirit, Good Morning," and ask God to answer Sarita's prayers to be with Julio.[64] The songs juxtapose spiritual traditions: Santería, Catholicism, and Protestantism. Additionally, the songs cover a diversity of musical genres, including Cuban (guaguancó, guaracha, nañigo), Latin American (tango and bolero), as well as American (1940s ballad, swing, and gospel), highlighting the cultural multiplicities in the play.

Finally, Fornes also experiments theatrically through constructing twenty short scenes. American theatre scholar Scott T. Cummings labels Fornes's short scenes as "emotigraphs" and reflects, "Whether as brief as a few seconds or as long as a few minutes, these vignettes are always rigorously composed, iconographic, marked by stillness and pulsing with emotion."[65] Many of these scenes have no dialogue and consist of stage action. In act 1, scene 6, Fornes emphasizes how Sarita and Julio reflect each other. Her stage directions state: "Sarita and Julio are seen on the upper level. They sit side by side with their arms around each other. They face front and smile tenderly as if they are looking at each other in a mirror."[66] In act 2, scene 18, Sarita finds Mark unconscious next to a bottle of liquor. In the previous scene Julio returned his key to Sarita and Mark's apartment, confirming Sarita's ongoing affair with Julio. Fornes describes: "She starts to go to Mark, notices the key and picks it up. She is dejected."[67] Through these gestures of holding hands or picking up a key, Fornes communicates the complexity of Sarita's relationship with Julio, and the fact that Mark is not a savior but also a character with flaws. These short scenes, or "emotigraphs," become one of the hallmarks of Fornes's dramaturgy. Perhaps these painterly scenes highlight Fornes's foundation as a visual artist. Perhaps these scenes exist in a linguistic vacuum because even the cacophony and collisions of language are not enough to communicate the characters' struggles. Fornes experiments with time, space, gesture, and music, and the accumulation of these short scenes and songs gives depth and ferocity to Sarita's doomed love affair as she tries to navigate between Julio and Mark.

Fornes complicates the disparities between Sarita and Mark to call attention to conflicts surrounding the Latin@ community and its historical struggles to forge connections with U.S. Anglo society. The inequality of the characters propels the play toward its detailed examination of Sarita's world. Fornes presents a separatist view, emphasizing that Sarita cannot ultimately negotiate the divide between Latin@ and Anglo worlds and must remain literally separated from society in a mental institution.

By implication, Fornes's play puts forth the notion that a Latina's inability to integrate multiple cultures can lead to insanity. Through Sarita's journey, Fornes therefore encourages audiences to embrace cultural multiplicity in order to survive.

ENVIRONMENTAL PEDAGOGY

Fornes constructed an artistic and educational space for theatre artists to receive valuable playwriting training. Shortly after Fornes emigrated from Havana, Cuba, to New York City at age fifteen, she enrolled in a Catholic academy, but dropped out after six weeks.[68] She never completed a traditional formal education, yet Fornes is a true autodidact. She began teaching playwriting in 1966 at the Judson Workshop in New York City and continued teaching for the next thirty-three years at universities, theaters, and playwriting organizations across the United States as well as internationally, including in Mexico, India, Scotland, and England.

Fornes champions the cause of education in her plays. The culminating third act of *Fefu and Her Friends* centers on the rehearsal for an educational fund-raiser. As Emma performs Sheridan Fry's speech, an emphasis on environment emerges:

EMMA: Environment knocks at the gateway of the senses. . . . It shouts, "Where are you? Where are you?" But we are deaf. The signals do not reach us. Society restricts us, school straight jackets us, civilization submerges us, privation wrings us, luxury feather-beds us. . . . Environment finding the gates closed tries to break in. Turned away, it comes another way. . . . Environment, seeking admission, claiming recognition, signaling to be seen, shouting to be heard. The gates give. . . . Environment shouting, "Where are you?" and Center battering at the inner side of the wall crying, "Here I am," and dragging down bars, wrenching gates, prying at portholes. Listening at cracks, reaching everywhere, and demanding that sense gates be flung open. The gates are open![69]

The speech highlights that access to female education is limited during the 1930s. The environment, by which Fornes seems to mean an elemental interior voice, provides the foundation for feminist activism to address this inequity. She also describes the pervasive power of the environment to reach those who are resistant to awareness and action.

Fornes opens the gates to many environments by offering her students access to alternative modes of playwriting. She resists more traditional teaching methods that might "straight jacket" the student. Straitjacketing implies that the student has had a mental breakdown and must be restrained from harming herself or others. While these are Sheridan Fry's words, Fornes chooses her character Emma to recite them, offering a strong indictment that "school" could lead to insanity. However, here "school" may mean a 1930s, male-driven, pedagogical environment, for education remains paramount for these women.

I use the term "environmental pedagogy" to describe the ways in which Fornes has taught a generation of playwrights. Fornes radically departs from schools of playwriting that focus on teaching Aristotelian principles such as developing a premise, deciding upon a point of attack, generating rising action, building toward the climax, and then resolving the action with a dénouement. Fornes's aim is not to impart any type of playwriting formula. As she explains, "I tried not to teach them how to write but to present to them ways where they could find their creativity, how to become in touch with their own imagery and their own aesthetic."[70] Her methods encourage creating new play material through inhabiting multiple environments such as an interior meditative terrain, exterior diverse geographies, visual arts techniques, and yoga practice. Fornes leads her students into these environments so that playwrights can develop their individual voices over and above any cultural, political, and artistic agenda or a prescribed formula for writing a play.

Character creation is the cornerstone of Fornes's environmental pedagogy. Fornes guides playwrights through a process that helps them intuitively connect to creating characters rather than teaching her students to build an airtight structure that focuses on conflict and resolution. The character creation leads to the generation of scenes. Eventually, the scenes form a first draft. Thus character is the foundation of the play's construction. Fornes seems more interested in advocating for an idiosyncratic, character-driven theatrical world than a predetermined, well-made play.

Fornes's training as a painter also influenced the emphasis on character in her environmental pedagogy. She studied with pioneer German American abstract expressionist Hans Hofmann (1880–1966) in his New York City studio and for one summer at his school in Provincetown, Massachusetts. Cummings writes: "Hofmann focused on how the two-dimensional form of painting could achieve a sense of depth without resort to perspective. Though Fornes gave up painting before she was thirty, Hofmann's push-pull principle had a lasting, subliminal effect on her."[71] In his essay "The Search for the Real in the Visual Arts," Hofmann describes his push-pull principle as a relationship between forces of visual, spatial planes: "*Push* answers with *pull* and *pull* with *push*. . . . When a force is created somewhere in the picture that is intended to be a stimulus in the sense of a *push* the picture plane answers automatically with a force in the sense of *pull* and vice versa."[72] (Italics appear in the original essay.) Hofmann's principle highlights a dialogue between opposing forces. His very description implies a conversation, with each element "answering" the other. This dynamic could correlate to the world of playwriting, where characters are energetic "forces" that "answer" each other in the theatrical "plane" of a stage.

Fornes's characters generate the energies in each scene that propel her plays forward. Fornes explains: "I compose my plays guided not by storyline but more by energies that take place within each scene, and also the energies that take place between one scene and the scene that follows. It's like Hofmann's push-and-pull in that the narrative doesn't control how the play proceeds, but the development of the energies within the play."[73] These terms "energy" and "force" imply the significant role that the physical laws of nature can have in the creation of visual and theatrical art. If energy is generated through character, then the building of character propels narrative forward in Fornes's plays.

Translation of the playwright's inner environment and spiritual contact with the playwright's creativity are significant aspects of Fornes's plays as well as of her teaching methods. Hofmann emphasized the importance of nature as a source of inspiration and the spiritual nature of art: "Creation is dominated by three absolutely different factors: First, nature, which works upon us by its laws; second, the artist, who creates a spiritual contact with nature and his materials; third, the medium of expression through which the artist translates his inner world."[74] Rather than focus on a single approach, Fornes invites her students into an ecosystem of ideas, forms, and cultural influences on the path toward writing a play.

Fornes utilized many visual art techniques in her teaching, including visualization, drawing, utilizing found materials, and constructing set models. Visualization is the cornerstone of her method: she instructed her students to close their eyes and visualize character, location, and action. She asked her students to access an interior landscape and delve into their personal creative subconscious, which can then lead to the generation of compelling play material. She created many variations of these visualizations to locate new possibilities for the formation and development of character.

After the visualization, she asked her students to draw pictures of their characters and locations. This aspect concretizes the inner vision into a tangible artistic form. The student's level of drawing ability is not important. The valuable element here is the student's effort to capture and sketch the visualized image, which then provides an immediate visible environment on the page and supplies more material for the writing process.

Fornes also provided found material to help her students generate character, location, and action. She introduced vintage photographs and postcards to her students as a means of jump-starting creativity. Fornes often bought these images at a flea market or thrift store. Elaine Romero recalls: "I remember one exercise where [Fornes] passed out old photographs. Mine was of three old women sitting on the porch during the 1930s. . . . I felt as if I had stepped into a lucid dream where I could be volitional and force the dream to show me things that it had not planned on revealing."[75] Fornes allowed her students to repurpose the environment of another person's life to create an entry point to a new theatrical world.

Once a draft of the play was written, Fornes guided her students through the revision process. In one exercise, she had her students construct small, three-dimensional set models out of cardboard and construction paper to fully envision the world of their plays. Then, utilizing cardboard human figures created to scale, she instructed her students to move the figures throughout the scenic environment while looking over each scene in their plays. This exercise allows students to consider how the script will function in a theatrical space, which can then inspire the revision of their scripts.

While she taught her methods at theatres, universities, and arts organizations across the country and internationally, Fornes specifically nurtured some of the most significant playwrights in contemporary Latin@

theatre through her Hispanic Playwrights-in-Residence Laboratory at INTAR in New York City between 1981 and 1992.[76] The Lab offered fellowships to Latin@ playwrights from all over the United States. The program consisted of an intensive three-month writing workshop for six to eight writers in the fall and a series of staged readings of works in progress at the end of the theatre season in the spring. Her INTAR students' plays have been produced across the United States, from small storefront theatres, to regional theatres, to Off Broadway and Broadway. Reflecting on her time in the Lab, Caridad Svich wrote:

> Fornes, leading by example, did not require that the playwrights in the Lab address any ethnically specific subject matter or theme. Through daily visualization exercises, the writers were asked to discover the work within them, to create the forms that suited their visions, and under Fornes's rigorous, watchful eye, to speak the truth about their worlds.[77]

Her students teach or have taught at institutions such as the University of Southern California, Stanford University, New York University, the University of California at Los Angeles, California Polytechnic Institute, Pomona, Yale University, and Brown University. The alumni of the Hispanic Playwrights-in-Residence Laboratory continue to shape the present and future of twenty-first-century Latin@ theatre.

ENVIRONMENTAL PEDAGOGY—
ONE PLAYWRIGHT'S EXPERIENCE

Fornes never wrote a book about her teaching. Her pedagogy continues on through her students, who teach her methods in universities, colleges, and arts organizations. No book has been published on Fornes's teaching methods either. Therefore, I will reconstruct my personal experience as her playwriting student to further explain the concept of her environmental pedagogy.

On a warm July Southern California morning at Cal State Northridge during the Padua Hills Playwrights Festival,[78] I sat at a long table in a crowded classroom for my first workshop with Fornes. Her heavily accented Cuban voice commanded, "Close your eyes. Picture a character.

This could be a character you are already working on or a totally new character. Once this character is in your mind's eye, picture all aspects of your character, starting with the hair, then the face, the body . . ."[79] Fornes's hypnotic cadence drew us into our interior landscapes, our private writer's universe, a subconscious dreamlike state where characters from inside of our beings could arise, surprise, and inform us of their presence. Fornes's exercise presupposed that each writer had access to this wealth of creative material and needed only a shamanic guide to call it forth. Fornes's meditative method bordered on the spiritual, with characters presenting themselves to each writer as if culled from the ether, with a life all their own. Her exercise called on writers to access information from another realm, and said access required only acute listening and observation.

We next committed this vision to paper, as one records a dream. Fornes continued: "When your character is clear to you, you can open your eyes and briefly describe your character. Also draw a picture of your character."[80] I tried to remember every detail, often baffled by the information but paying close attention to embrace the mystery, which would hopefully be revealed in the future. Fornes then led us through visualizing a specific location, asking questions such as, "Is it interior or exterior? Is it day or night? Are there objects in this location? Are they man-made or natural?"[81] After we drew our locations, she told us to visualize a second character interacting with the first character in this specific location. She then instructed us to write a scene between these two visualized characters.

This intuitive, creative, visual, and unconventional method has significantly influenced many of her students' careers as playwrights and teachers. The power of her presence and the access she provided to create a character as the launching point for a play have been transformative. Fornes eschewed any type of conversation of what a play is, or the elements of plot, character, or conflict. Her method catapulted us right into the center of our creativity as playwrights with the task of internally and subjectively discovering the play we needed to write.

One of Fornes's writing exercises exemplifies her environmental pedagogy. She began with her usual prompt of having us close our eyes, picture our character, then opening our eyes, describing our vision, and drawing a picture. Next, she instructed: "Close your eyes again. Picture an animal. Look how it moves through space. Look at its body . . . its skin. Does it have fur? Does it have scales? Does it have legs or arms? Once your animal is clear to you, open your eyes and draw a picture." The next prompt was the essential one. She directed: "Close your eyes. Now picture your human character standing in front of your animal. Now picture the human character merging with the animal. The character remains human but assumes all the qualities of the animal so that he or she is now a transformed human character. When this is clear to you, open your eyes and begin writing a scene between your transformed human character and another human character." This exercise leads writers to consider how their characters may behave unexpectedly or exhibit animalistic qualities and how that might inform character development. This is an innovative exercise because the transformed human character must equally maintain both environments: human and animal. This exercise often yields compelling results, as students are free to explore uninhibited behavior by their transformed characters.

Fornes's workshops generate an atmosphere of intense creativity and exploration. First, Fornes leads the writers in a yoga-like physical warm-up where each writer performs a series of stretching and breathing exercises. This physically engaged movement environment aims to focus the body and mind in preparation for the writing. Next, the writers return to their respective seats and Fornes begins the aforementioned visualization writing exercises. After this, she instructs her students to begin writing a scene based on the characters visualized. A quiet, almost sacred space materializes as virtual strangers simultaneously engage with their own artistic worlds.

Through these ritual-like writing exercises, her students gain new levels of insight or *facultad*. During this in-class writing time, Fornes herself writes. Although she never shares her writing, I later learned that she wrote many of her plays during her workshops. Utilizing her method as a teacher, I came to understand the power of in-class writing, for the heightened quality of attention, intense focus, and engaged writing fosters an environment of charged creativity that can inspire and motivate one's writing. After the in-class writing period comes to a close, Fornes asks for volunteers to read their work. Fornes explains that for in-class writing there is no feedback whatsoever, that the sole purpose of reading in-class writing aloud is to experience one's work among fellow writers as well as provide the other writers with an example of what is possible given the same exercise.

Fornes's environmental pedagogy also values and empowers the playwright regardless of backgrounds, experience, or knowledge. Like her plays, her teaching defies categories, encourages theatrical experimentation, and embraces all identities. The writing I began in her workshop at Padua deeply influenced my training as a young playwright. Two years later, when she was one of my first instructors at the Yale School of Drama, the students met her unconventional methods with a mixture of enthusiasm and suspicion. The energetic attentiveness in the room at Padua was replaced by a cautious reception at Yale. Perhaps her methods, which fostered an unpredictable, physically creative environment over a more traditional, deductive, and cerebral writing process led to this response. Regardless of the setting, Fornes has unequivocally offered her methods as a means to successful playwriting.

Fornes's environmental pedagogy emphasizes process versus product in the formulation of a playwright's voice and craft. Her expansive, egalitarian, and pluralistic approach, devoid of deductive, formulaic instruction, establishes an atmosphere among the students where all have access to the same methods for inspiration. During the Yale workshop, she reiterated the importance of exploration by saying:

> In writing, investigate a scene that compels you. See what the characters do. Write a lot of things . . . scenes . . . characters . . . that might not necessarily be in the play but the writing of which benefits the play. Explore. There needs to be an exploratory period when you are beginning a play . . . getting to know the characters . . . getting to know who they are. . . . what they want . . . what their path is.[82]

Fornes's environmental pedagogy encourages complexity and mystery, engaging with a juxtaposition of worlds and ideas that emerge organically from the characters' needs. Fornes's method allows character discovery to spontaneously guide the early shape of a play as opposed to predetermining a theatrical narrative. She provides her students with the knowledge that numerous possibilities are valid subjects of exploration in the craft of playwriting as long as the play serves the truths of its characters.

FORNES'S THEATRICAL DAUGHTERS

Many consider Fornes to be the "mother of U.S. Latin@ theater," and she has nourished her "theatrical offspring" through her remarkable career. All Latina playwrights are in some way Fornes's theatrical daughters. The alumnae from Fornes's workshops are among the most celebrated writers in the field of Latina theatre. The word "alumna" in English means a female student who is a graduate of a particular school or university, and in Spanish simply means female student. The root of both the English and Spanish words is the Latin *alumnus*, which literally means foster daughter. "Alumna" is also derived from the verb *alere*,[83] which means to nourish. While using the term "student," or "alumna," might seem more appropriate than "daughter," in an unconventional way Fornes created a theatrical family through her work as a playwright and teacher. Many playwrights who have known her and studied with her remain devoted to her work and legacy.

While she did have lesbian partners throughout her life, Fornes never had children of her own. She was, however, a loyal daughter to her mother, Carmen Fornes (1891–1994), for whom she was a caregiver in her later years until Carmen died at age 103. Though frail and eventually deaf, Carmen Fornes remained an active presence in Fornes's professional career. Carmen Fornes radiated a vibrant, bohemian spirit. When Fornes was my drama schoolteacher, her mother would sit in the back of our classroom, content and alert. One evening, during a dinner after our class, Carmen Fornes held a fellow student's infant daughter. As we witnessed the one hundred years between them, Maria Irene looked on in admiration. Fornes once told our class, "My mother cannot believe my students listen to me." We did listen to Fornes, learned from her and became part of her theatrical family.

Fornes has been a pioneer and mentor. Her playwriting and teaching create theatrical environments that engage a multiplicity of cultural worlds, juxtapose divergent spiritualties, mine diverse identities, and encourage experiments in form. Her plays theatricalize Latin@ and Anglo worlds, consider the intersections of Santería, Catholic, and Protestant spiritualities, mine a range of feminist, immigrant, and Latina identities, and revel in spare, poetic language, site-specific work, innovative use of song and dance, and the collisions of English, Spanish, and Yoruba texts. Her teaching creates a foundation for her playwriting and a mechanism to transmit her artistic legacy to future generations of playwrights. Elaine Romero reflects:

> [Fornes's] work showed me that I could be a Latina writer without feeling I had to hit a Latina/o mark. There is, perhaps, a purposeful nonspecificity about one's own Latina/o experience. It can be in the play or not at all. It might exist there only on a subterranean level if it exists at all.[84]

Fornes's work, her legacy, and the key issues she raises compose the lens through which to examine plays by the Latina playwrights included in this study. Following in her footsteps, how do these five Latina playwrights stage cultural multiplicities in their plays? How do they devise supernatural interventions? In what ways do their protagonists engage with Latina identity? How do their plays involve theatrical experimentation? Fornes provokes these questions through her plays and her teaching and challenges this new generation of Latina playwrights to respond.

2

CARIDAD SVICH

Imprinting the Fornes Frame

L ATINA PLAYWRIGHTS TRAINED by Maria Irene Fornes have had award-winning careers in the American theatre. Fornes's environmental pedagogy and fervent commitment to her students' artistic growth have created a theatrical family. Caridad Svich is a prolific, Obie-award-winning playwright/translator/adapter of Cuban-Spanish and Argentinean-Croatian descent and a direct theatrical descendant of Fornes, whom she studied with at the INTAR Hispanic Playwrights-in-Residence Laboratory in New York City. Svich's innovative work exemplifies how Fornes's playwriting and teaching have influenced Latina playwrights.

The Fornes frame can be a grouping of ideas that delve into cultural multiplicity, supernatural intervention, Latina identity, and theatrical experimentations. A close examination of Svich's plays will reveal numerous ways in which the work of Latina playwrights bears the imprint of the Fornes frame. Svich's work demonstrates how Latina playwrights stage multiple cultures in their plays. *Prodigal Kiss* chronicles a Cuban American woman and her immigration to the United States. *Tropic of X* mines the struggles of a young couple in an unnamed Latin American city. Both plays engage Latin America, the Caribbean, Spain, and the United States. Svich considers the complicated formation of Latina identity through her protagonists, Marcela and Maura, as they both address violence, gender, and nationality. Svich also devises supernatural

FIGURE 4. Caridad Svich reading her work at the
Great Plains Theatre Conference, Omaha, Nebraska,
in 2011. Photo by Metropolitan Community College.

interventions, involving sudden apparitions, metaphysical objects, and
spiritual communications that transform Marcela and Maura's dramatic
trajectories. Finally, Svich states, "The playfulness and double-play with
words which is intrinsically Latin@ is present in my writing."[1] Svich conducts this linguistic experimentation in each play by employing a variety
of musical genres, which dramatize her protagonists' multilayered realities. Svich constructs complex theatrical worlds that reflect and contest
what a Latina play can be.

PRODIGAL KISS: A CUBAN *BALSERA*'S FRAGMENTED ASSIMILATION

In *Prodigal Kiss*, Svich illuminates a Cuban woman's immigrant journey to the United States. In this play, which is set in various cities, Marcela, a newly arrived Cuban *balsera* (i.e., raft person), interacts with immigrants from Spain, Chile, the Dominican Republic, and Argentina, as well as an Italian American. At first Marcela resists the problematic models of assimilation provided by these Latin@ immigrants. Yet, ultimately Marcela negates her Cuban culture by choosing a new American name. Svich does not include Mexican American or Puerto Rican immigrants in this play, pushing past the major Latin@ groups to problematize the definition of Latin@. Representation of the Latina immigrant in Latin@ theater has often emphasized a single cultural identity in which the Latina maintains the culture of her homeland. Svich complicates this representation as Marcela immediately engages with the variety of Latin@ cultures in the United States, whether derived from Latin America, the Caribbean, or Spain. Svich sends Marcela on a journey of fragmented assimilation as she attempts to forge a new Latina identity.

Throughout the play's multiple spaces, Svich stages supernatural moments that arise out of an experimental musical liminality. Marcela sings of her loss and longing as she tries to maintain her Cuban identity. Svich first presents Marcela standing on a small raft in the middle of the ocean. She begins as a Cuban woman leaving her country in hopes of surviving the treacherous waters and finding a new life in the United States. Her Cuban body seems to supernaturally float in this perilous location between Cuba and the United States as she sings, in Spanish and English, "*Me voy pa Santiago. / Pa Santiago me voy. /* I'm going to Santiago. / To Santiago I go."[2] Svich starts her play with a binguality that reflects Marcela's longing for her home in Santiago de Cuba. The Spanish that Marcela sings is distinctly Cuban, with the word "*pa*" standing in for "*para*" (i.e., "for"), an example of how Cubans often discard a word's final syllable. This ruptured word could also connote Marcela's own fracture, as she exists in a liminal space between Cuba and the United States. While she firmly clings to her memories, she is uprooted and drifting toward another existence. Svich's song ends with Marcela accepting that she will most likely never return to her homeland: "I dream of Santiago / As it fades into the void. / On a boat of black water, / Let my heart be destroyed."[3] The black water here could refer to the grave-yard filled with Cubans who did not survive their journeys across the ninety miles of ocean between Cuba and Florida. Marcela singing this section in English linguistically represents that Santiago is indeed van-ishing. Svich's poetic lyrics end with a rhymed verse that stands in direct opposition to Marcela's life, which is now untethered with no foreseeable structure or harmony.

Svich next introduces the friction between Marcela's Cuban identity and that of a Latino immigrant who resorts to prostitution and violence to survive in American culture. After her arrival in Florida, Marcela stands "on a road by a field of saw grass,"[4] suitcase in hand, where she encounters Ignacio, a Spanish American from Santiago de Compostela, Spain, who ambles toward her, "poorly clothed . . . sunburnt" and carrying a paper bag of cheap wine. Marcela reveals she has come to America to "set my eyes beyond the equator. . . . Past everything. Start new."[5] Marcela next relays that she survived her treacherous journey on a raft with four other Cubans, two of whom died at sea. She reveals that she has come to the United States to see her Aunt Lise in New Jersey. Ignacio advises her that there are many ways to make a living in this country but that "This is a whole new land you've come to. We're all the same—rich, poor, and in-between. Whores. That's all we are."[6] Ignacio prostitutes himself with men and implies that Marcela will also need to prostitute herself, at which she bristles. Ignacio accuses Marcela of being a *jinetera* (i.e., prostitute) in Cuba and states he wants to have violent sex with her: "I wouldn't mind ramming you from behind with the taste of sweet wine in your mouth."[7] However, Marcela, ever on the defensive, hits him with her suitcase, which opens to reveal a mound of dirt. Marcela rubs Ignacio's face in this transported Cuban soil and castigates him: "You are noth-ing. And I am nothing more than what I aim to be, which is as far from you as I can get in this world."[8] Marcela leaves her suitcase and Ignacio lying in the dirt as she journeys onward. Svich stages a complex cultural gesture as Marcela throws Cuban earth on the body of a Spaniard who is trying to "conquer" her while they stand on American land. She depicts Marcela as one who is still strongly connected to her Cuban identity, as she literally has been carrying her country. However, by dumping the dirt upon her first encounter (i.e., dropping the elements of her culture),

Svich exposes the challenges Marcela faces in maintaining her Cuban identity on this new shore.

Svich includes Spain in the Latin@ experience by using the trope of the pilgrimage to Santiago. Svich employs this pilgrim tradition to shed light on the many immigrants (i.e., pilgrims) who arrive in the United States with the faith that life in America will bring abundance, healing, and possibly supernatural transformation. Svich creates disparate points of connection between pilgrims from cities with the name Santiago across the Spanish-speaking world as they all navigate their life in the United States. The Camino de Santiago (the way of St. James), a pilgrimage that starts near Biarritz, France, and ends in Santiago de Compostela, Spain, draws international pilgrims from across the globe to walk the approximately five-hundred-mile journey, or parts thereof. St. James, and his brother John, disciples of Jesus, were nicknamed "sons of thunder" because of their bad temper.[9] Hispanic studies scholars David Gitlitz and Linda Davidson write: "Legend holds that just before His Crucifixion, Jesus divvied up the world among His Apostles, encouraging them to get the Word out as widely as possible. James was assigned the Iberian Peninsula. He traveled as far as Galicia, but seems not to have been very convincing, for he attracted only seven disciples. He decided to return to the Holy Land,"[10] where he was beheaded by Herod Agrippa in 44 CE and became the first of the apostles to be martyred.[11] Again according to legend, his friends snuck his body out on a boat that found its way back to Galicia, where St. James was buried. In the early ninth century, his relics were reported to have caused supernatural manifestations that resulted in a shrine being built at his tomb, which became a chapel and later a cathedral.

In Latin@ theatre, there has often existed a firm stance against Spain and its history of conquest. Svich emphasizes the spiritual and cultural influences from Spain that can serve to inspire Latin@s, while also referencing the problematics of conquest. Svich links her characters to the pilgrimages to Santiago that began in the early tenth century and continue to this day. Early pilgrimages were undertaken to seek physical healing. Many pilgrims arrived gravely ill in Santiago or died shortly thereafter. Some now take the journey as a Catholic religious pilgrimage, yet many walk the Camino for spiritual or personal reasons that have little to do with organized religion.

Additionally, Svich connects to the poetry of Spain, as her play was inspired by Spanish poet and playwright Federico García Lorca's *Poet in New York*, a collection of experimental poetry that Lorca wrote in 1929 during his yearlong residency in New York City to study English at Columbia University. Svich reflects:

> I had just translated thirteen of the poems from *Poet in New York* (for the publication *Impossible Theater*) and was immersed in the imagistic and emotional world of the whole poem cycle but those thirteen poems in particular. I wanted to deal with the issues of dislocation that those poems have, that feeling of being a person landing in a new country and finding their way, of the deeply conflicted sensual images in the poems in a play that focused on a balsera and the many immigrants of the Americas and Iberia that she meets on US soil as she makes her peregrination/pilgrimage in a new land and through the shifting mirrors of an unstable American Dream. Some of the images from the poems inspired whole scenes in the play, others simply moments. But for me the spirit of *Poet in New York* courses through *Prodigal Kiss*.[12]

In his brief thirty-eight-year life, Lorca traveled from his native Spain to pursue his writing in the United States, Cuba, and Latin America. Lorca's death by Fascist forces at the start of the Spanish Civil War in July 1936 deprived Spain and the world of one of its brightest literary and theatrical talents. Svich has translated a significant body of Lorca's work into English. That Svich's play is inspired by García Lorca's poetry reinforces the importance of this Spanish playwright's work to the world of Latin@ theater.

In addition to Spanish influences, Svich draws upon the American musical tradition of the blues, as her play is also infused with the music of Bessie Smith, the Empress of the Blues. Marcela gets on a train heading toward St. Louis, Missouri, explaining, "I took the first train that came by. Saw 'St. Louie.' I thought it might be close to New Jersey."[13] Marcela's ignorance of U.S. geography takes her on a train toward another city dedicated to a saint, Louis IX, the thirteenth-century devout Catholic and only canonized king of France, who was notable for his humility and his personal examples of Christian service.[14] As this Cuban immigrant travels toward this American city named after a French saint, she is confronted by Coral, a Chilean immigrant in her seventies from Santiago de Chile, who came to the United States on August 29, 1929. She arrived with her father (who would work on Wall Street) only two months before the stock market crash and the start of the Great Depression. Coral tells Marcela that as a girl of five she met Smith, who lived on their block in New York City. Coral idolized Smith: "That's the kind of woman I want to be: someone who belongs to everyone and no one, a self-made, self-possessed bird with a taste of poison on her lips."[15] Coral then sings parts of Smith's song "St. Louis Blues," "St. Louis woman, where's your diamond ring." Marcela reveals that she too loves Smith's music and continues singing: "I got the St. Louie blues, and that's as blue as I can be."[16] This musical interjection briefly unites the two women with Smith, one of the highest paid African American entertainers of her day, who succeeded in a highly racially polarized country. Smith offers the kinship spirit of a woman who physically and spiritually defended herself from the societal forces that aimed to subjugate her, but who triumphed through her music.

The women's unifying moment through the blues echoes the 1929 *St. Louis Blues*, a seventeen-minute film with a scenario that dramatizes the song. In the narrative, Bessie is driven to drink over her philandering boyfriend, Jimmy. In her room in a boarding house, Bessie finds Jimmy in bed with another woman. Bessie violently beats the young woman until she leaves. Then Jimmy hits Bessie and she crumples to the floor. Later, in a bar, she drowns her sorrows in a mug of beer as she sings her signature song, "St. Louis Blues," while the bar patrons become a harmonizing and dancing chorus. Jimmy then returns to the bar, tap dancing and joyous. Bessie is thrilled to be reunited with him. As they embrace, he steals money from her pocket and escapes. The film ends with Bessie drowning her sorrows at the bar. Jazz historian Chris Albertson writes, "*St. Louis Blues* was but a drop in a celluloid ocean of prejudice." Albertson, however, emphasizes that the film "represents the only footage of one the greatest performers America has produced."[17] Coral and Marcela too have faced and experienced prejudice and violence as immigrants. Yet they are united by an African American singer, not a Latin@ performer, which speaks to the global reach of Smith's career. As women, they all have had to contend with gender discrimination and economic hardship. As with Smith, Coral and Marcela's strength and their song carry them onward.

Svich expands the cultural complexity in her play through the musical tradition of the blues, which began in the African American communities in Mississippi in the early twentieth century. However, the blues' origins can be found in West African musical traditions. Blues historian Elijah Wald explains that "many blues melodies are based on a pentatonic or five-note 'blues scale' that is frequently used by West African performers."[18] Svich's use of this musical genre with roots in Africa echoes the cross-cultural experiences of Marcela and Coral. This U.S. musical form also recalls the brutal legacy of slavery. Blues historian Francis Davis writes: "Despite its origins in field hollers and work songs the blues has from the very beginning been an activity reserved for stolen moments . . . [and] many of its first performers were men exempted from picking cotton by virtue of blindness or some other physical handicap, or wastrels for whom music was a way of avoiding back-breaking labor."[19] Marcela and Coral are not enslaved but are unemployed Latin American immigrants trying to survive. Yet, these women's mutual attachment to the blues speaks to their struggle to live in America despite the challenges of their immigration status, their minority position, and their lack of economic power. Presenting a Chilean American woman and a Cuban American woman who both adore a famous African American blues singer emphasizes the cultural intersections within the Latin@ experience.

This choice of Smith additionally echoes the life of Lorca. During his stay in New York City in 1929 (the year Coral moved to the city), Lorca loved the music and culture of Harlem. Theatre historian Leslie Stainton writes that Lorca "often went with friends to Harlem's jazz clubs . . . would sit motionless, his head bowed, eyes lost in reverie," and the first poem he wrote in New York was titled "King of Harlem."[20] Like Lorca, Smith died young, at the age of forty-three, in a car accident on a highway between Mississippi and Tennessee. Thus in this interaction on the train, Svich expands the Latin@ experience to include Cuban, Chilean, Spanish, African, and African American cultures.

Both Marcela and Coral have experienced radical shifts in their Latina identity through rupture from family and children. Coral relays how she traveled to St. Louis as a poor, orphaned thirteen-year-old to see the city memorialized in Smith's song. In St. Louis, Coral ended up working in a brewery where people couldn't understand that she was from Chile and called her "the Spanish bit." Coral has since lived a life of poverty and despair, and now exists by riding the trains because, as she laments, "I don't see much point in setting myself down anywhere."[21] Coral once married and had a daughter, but now her daughter does not speak to her. Marcela reveals that she had a lover, Chucho, and bore a son, Ambrosio, whom she left behind in Cuba because she could not care for him any longer. Coral claims that Marcela does not have what it takes to survive in the United States. Marcela counters by revealing details of her challenging life in Cuba, including bathing out of a bucket, foraging for food by collecting mangoes from the road, and spending a year in prison for disturbing the peace. Marcela asserts her indomitable spirit: "And I didn't lie down then. I kept going. Cause I knew there was something else."[22] As both women struggle to survive alone in their new country, Svich suggests that the Latina immigrant experience can destroy the roles of mother and daughter.

When Coral injures Marcela, Svich further complicates Latina identity. After Marcela relays her plans to visit her Aunt Lise in New Jersey, the women's relationship turns violent when Coral robs Marcela at gunpoint. Marcela, confused and frightened, hands Coral her money and warns she will get caught. Coral replies, "How'm I gonna get caught because there's no one here? Cause that's what you are, no one. Got no one to claim you, come right off the boat, you'll be lucky if you get a proper grave."[23] Coral then shoots Marcela and escapes. While Marcela could flee from Ignacio, she cannot evade Coral. Svich does not indicate what kind of gunshot Marcela sustains, yet she does recover. Svich underscores the violence within the Latin@ immigrant community when a Latina chooses to attack another Latina in order to survive. This destructive altercation between Latinas further fragments their attempts to assimilate.

As Marcela sings again of Cuba, Svich creates a supernatural intervention in a liminal space on a nameless dirt road. Earlier she sang on a raft, but now she sings on land while injured and lost: "Where is my Cuba? / Where is my son? / My lips turn silver / Looking for your tomb."[24] These English lyrics reflect Marcela's increasing immersion in America. While she longs for her homeland and her child, she attempts to move forward in her new country. Marcela then turns to see a woman "wearing a dress of silver rose petals on the edge of the road."[25] This mysterious woman hands Marcela a red sash, which she puts on; she then follows the woman's trail of silver petals as the first part of the play comes to a close. Having just been injured by a Latina, Marcela is now somehow empowered by a supernatural woman who leads her onward. This woman's ethnicity is not clear; however, Svich's stage directions state that her appearance is accompanied by the Carlos Núñez recording of the song "Black Shadow," by Rosalía de Castro and Juan Montes. This song is an adaptation of the nineteenth-century poem by de Castro, a Spanish Galician poet. Galicia is also the region in Spain where Santiago de Compostela is located. De Castro's poem ends with the lines, "You will never abandon me, / Shadow that always shadows me,"[26] which echoes the mysterious woman aiding Marcela. Most of the musicians in this recording are from Galicia: composer Montes, musician Núñez, and singer Luz Casals. However, U.S. music legend Ry Cooder plays guitar on this song. In an interview, Cooder states of recording Núñez's music, "There are a lot of people in the United States who will be hearing this music for the first time and they will be very grateful and happy about it. . . . This is like opening up another door."[27] Thus, this emergence of a supernatural woman accompanied by Spanish-American lyrics of longing and darkness amid an echo of pilgrimage opens a spiritual door through which Marcela continues her journey.

Marcela encounters another commodified Latino immigrant body when she next appears by a harbor in San Diego, California. The city is named after the fifteenth-century Spanish Saint Didacus of Alcalá, who was known for caring for the sick and administering miraculous healing.[28] San Diego was once part of Mexico and is therefore deeply influenced by Mexican, Spanish, and Latin@ cultures. Marcela arrives injured, faint from hunger, and in need of healing. She comes upon Rafael, an immigrant from Santiago de los Caballeros in the Dominican Republic, who has been in the United States for ten years. He began earning a living through working-class jobs, but then began prostituting a young Anglo man, Rider, to businessmen and sailors. Svich juxtaposes Dominican, Anglo, and Cuban cultures in a U.S. city with a complicated history of Spanish and Mexican influence. Yet a Latino brutalizes the Latina body and Anglo body here. At first, Rafael attempts to help Marcela by giving Rider twenty dollars to buy her food. Rider returns with only French fries. Rafael grills him about the lack of change, growing agitated and violent when he feels Rider is lying to him about the cost of the food. Marcela eats the fries as the two men argue. When Marcela tries to intervene, Rafael hits Marcela twice, knocking the food out of her hands. Marcela continues to eat off of the ground as Rafael confronts Rider, accusing him of turning a trick with a man and using that money, plus the change from the food, to buy cocaine. At one point, Rafael says Marcela could pay for Rider's services, but she declines. Marcela then watches Rafael abuse Rider and cut him with a switchblade. When the aggression subsides, Rafael comforts a bleeding Rider as the men leave. This is the second Latino immigrant Marcela encounters who earns his living through prostitution. Marcela ends this encounter in a weakened state, yet still trying to hold onto her Cuban identity and journey toward her Aunt Lise in New Jersey.

Svich continues to expand the notion that the female immigrant body must fight against a patriarchal system in order to survive. By the harbor, Marcela implores assistance from Miriam Mocha, a wheelchair-bound Argentinean immigrant in her thirties who hails from the city of San-tiago de Estera. Miriam enters singing a Bessie Smith song, "Reckless Blues," "And I wasn't nothing but a child . . . All you men tried to drive me wild,"[29] which echoes Coral's and Marcela's obsession with Smith. Smith's lyrics speak to a reality where a woman views her worth through her desire for male attention and love, underscoring Marcela's interactions with male immigrants who define and dominate women. These lyrics from a blues song with a mournful tone communicate the pain and suffering that can result from this oppressive perspective.

Marcela's Latina identity soon begins to transform when Miriam offers to comb her hair and give her a hair ribbon. Miriam wants to make Marcela presentable for her trip to New Jersey to see her aunt. Marcela proclaims that her former self has perished: "Marcela has died, drowned in the ocean's well, covered in seaweed and stagnant black water."[30] She defines herself as a spirit who must now take on a new identity: "Oh, the ghost of Marcela cries like a fresh sea-wind. . . . Oh to be christened now with another name, a name that will fit this sun-patched, stone-bruised I."[31] She then demands that Miriam grant her a new name, or she will take Miriam's name.

Marcela receives a new American identity when Miriam renames her Sharon. Marcela repeats the name and decides to accept it. The name Sharon derives from the Hebrew verb *yashar*, meaning to be level or straight, but can have various connotations such as a road being straight, leading a virtuous life, obtaining someone's approval, or a soul being at peace.[32] Sharon was also a popular name in the United States in the mid-twentieth century. The name Marcela derives from Mars, the Roman god of war. Thus, Marcela discards her "warrior-like" Cuban name for a "peaceful, virtuous, plain" American name with Hebrew origins. By accepting a new name, which is culturally complex in its etymology but on the surface is American, Marcela jettisons her Cuban culture, aiming to transform into an Anglicized woman.[33]

However, this transformation results in Marcela descending into criminality. During her journey to New Jersey, Marcela turns to prostitution and robbery. While waiting on a train platform, she sings in Spanish of her longing for Santiago: "*Santiago. / Te busco en los escombros, / En los altos y los bajos, / En la sangre del anhelo, / De tu grito redentor.*" Then, on the train, with a half-dressed man on top of her, she sings the same song in English: "Santiago, / I look for you in the arms, / In the far-off and the strange, / In the rupture and the hollows of your / seductive soul."[34] After she has sex with this man, he throws dollars at her feet. She leaves her name Marcela and her Spanish language on the platform, as she is now English-speaking Sharon who prostitutes herself. The musical reminder of her lost city of Santiago causes her to fully disconnect from her homeland and continue to experience degradation and violence.

As in Fornes's *Sarita*, Svich suggests that this rupture of Marcela's Latina identity drives her to engage in physical violence in order to survive. On a road by a kiosk, which echoes her encounter with Ignacio, she seduces Paco, a newly arrived Cuban immigrant who asks if she is from Cuba. She denies her Cuban heritage by repeating that her name is Sharon and then robs him at knifepoint of what little money he has. By fully negating her Cuban culture, Marcela continues to try to deny her Latina identity while perpetuating the cycle of violence she encountered with Ignacio, Coral, and Rafael.

After Paco walks away, Svich supernaturally rewards Marcela with greater wealth, which she must purge from her commodified body. When Marcela tucks the stolen money into her bra, she doubles over as if to vomit and "*silver coins begin to tumble out of her mouth as music comes up: Bessie Smith's 'Do Your Duty.'*"[35] Marcela sweeps up the coins, pockets them, and moves on. The final stanza of Smith's song is heard, asserting female agency: "I'm not tryin' to make you feel blue / I'm not satisfied with the way you do / I've got to help you find somebody to / Do your duty / Do your duty."[36] Marcela, now Sharon, fully embraces a survival stance, which includes violence and prostitution. Svich delineates the fragmentation in Marcela's assimilation; she is financially rewarded at the cost of her Cuban identity.

In the penultimate scene of the play, Marcela finally arrives in Union City, New Jersey, to search for her Aunt Lise. Union City has been called Havana on the Hudson due to its large Cuban immigrant population. Journalist Mary Jo Patterson writes: "Only 49 blocks long and fewer than 10 blocks wide, Union City acquired an outsized reputation within the Cuban diaspora. This densely populated town came to be regarded as Cuba's northernmost province, second only to Miami in Cuban flavor and influence."[37] Union City's industry of embroidery and lace textile factories initially drew immigrants from across the globe. Thus, Marcela's journey ends in a city with a rich history of not only Cuban immigration but a union of diverse cultures.

Marcela meets Carlo, an Italian American man from the neighborhood, who knew her Aunt Lise. The fact that Marcela meets an Italian American and not a Cuban American underscores how Union City has diversified culturally since Lise's immigration there years before. In an abandoned lot covered with snow, Marcela bristles when Carlo tries to offer her his coat. After she accepts his help, he questions her name being Sharon: "Funny kind of name for someone from Cuba." Marcela responds: "It's my given name. Lise knew me by another . . . but it suits me. It suits me better than my own. I don't know Marcela anymore. But I know Sharon. I pass by a window; I can spot her in a second with or without a hat."[38] Marcela's Cuban body now literally reflects her new American identity. Marcela confronts Carlo's cultural assumptions as she fights to hold onto her new life as Sharon, the American resident:

MARCELA: You must think I'm some kind of Cuban trash. . . . That I'm only good for dirt jobs and fucking, that I'm not good enough to be called Sharon or any other name except whore, and worm, and wetback, even though I got about as much right as anybody to seek out what I came for. You've done nothing but look me up and down like I just came out of water and ash, like some kind of prodigal who's come here to steal snow from your lots.[39]

Svich portrays Marcela's pessimistic view of the immigrant position that she now aims to escape. However, in order to gain power, Marcela attempts to renounce her Cuban background entirely and align herself more fully with American culture.

Marcela's journey to see her aunt ends in loss. Carlo tells Marcela that Lise would sometimes buy Spanish wine at the corner store where he worked and that she would attend church wearing a red sash. Then, Svich reveals that Lise connected her sash to the spirit-world. Carlo recounts: "[Lise] said she had to keep the spirits of the earth in line, keep protected, and red was the only color strong enough to do it. Any other color would put the earth off balance."[40] However, finally, Carlo reveals to Marcela that Lise has died. In her grief, Marcela tears up Lise's letter. After Carlo leaves, Marcela performs a ritual to honor her deceased aunt: *"Marcela slowly unties the red sash around her waist. As she does so, the faint sound of the sea. Marcela lays out the sash carefully on the snow."*[41] Marcela's public commemoration of Lise juxtaposes sea and snow, earth and spirit, as she relinquishes the last vestige of her connection to her aunt and to her Cuban heritage.

Marcela's struggle to assimilate ultimately leads to cultural disempowerment. The play closes with Marcela reciting Lise's letter from memory. In the letter, Lise describes her experience of life in Union City and its physical and spiritual parameters. She also refers to the Camino de Santiago: "Sometimes I swear I can see the lights of Santiago shining in this mad sky, And hear the voice of Saint James himself whisper to me in the clear of night."[42] Svich highlights how Marcela has been spiritually guided on her pilgrimage to Union City. She then sings a variation of the opening song, completely in English, "A pale arm of Santiagos / All around me. / A rain of silver light / That longs to guide me."[43] She acknowledges the "arm" of the community of immigrants she has encountered that has shaped her new U.S. existence.

Yet, as Marcela's pilgrimage comes to an end, her American identity denies the complexities of mestiza life in the United States, a life of old world and new, Spanish and English, loss and compromise, and ultimately melancholy and freedom. Anzaldúa states that the mestiza identity is a "conscious rupture with all oppressive traditions of all cultures and religions," and that the mestiza "communicates that rupture, documents the struggle . . . strengthens her tolerance (and intolerance) for ambiguity."[44] Marcela is not able to fully embrace her mestiza self.

Svich illuminates that while there is cultural multiplicity within the U.S. Latin@ community, this diversity is in danger of disappearing when the immigrant renounces her Latina identity and loses her connection to the culture of her homeland. Svich dramatizes the fragmented assimilation these immigrants face and signals how their struggles can end with cultural erasure in exchange for survival.

TROPIC OF X: HIP-HOP DECONSTRUCTION IN THE AMERICAS

Svich's *Tropic of X* examines the lives of a young couple struggling to survive in an unnamed Latin American country. Svich experiments with musical forms that reflect heterogeneous Latin@ culture and bills the play as a "poetic, Latin, Hip-hop-infused drama." Written in twenty-three scenes, Svich's linear narrative considers the lives of Maura, an "arcade junkie and petite wannabe-assassin," Mori, her male lover and accomplice, and Kiki, a "part-time hustler of fluid gender,"[45] living in a city with a history of coups and disappearances. In part 1, Fabian, a European tourist, hires Mori for a sexual encounter. However, in part 2, Fabian, "now in another guise,"[46] becomes a torturer who arrests Mori for loitering. As Maura fights to find her lost love, Fabian is erasing Mori's identity. When the two lovers are finally reunited, their connection is irrevocably lost, ultimately expressed in their subsequent deaths. Svich presents a fractured, multilayered, Latin American reality via a hip-hop aesthetic that she ultimately deconstructs, mirroring the oppression of a dictatorial regime.

Svich orchestrates a collision of musical forms that highlights heterogeneity and globalization in the Americas. While she employed the blues in *Prodigal Kiss*, Svich states that *Tropic of X* "rhythmically, sonically places the Latin American world in a more globalized sphere where the sounds of hip-hop, bolero, and British punk are reflected in a story of dictatorship, loss of freedoms, and censorship."[47] Therefore, the intersection of hip-hop, bolero, and punk, three musical genres that share notions of generative multiplicity, is symbolic of the play's world, which first allows for a variety of cultural intersections.

Hip-hop encourages collisions of poetry, rhythm, and protest. Hip-hop has been defined as "a U.S.-based musical style marked by rhythmic, spoken-sung declamation [i.e., rap] over prerecorded backing tracks or beats."[48] Africana studies scholar William Jelani Cobb states that hip-hop "began as a multicultural movement. It represented the artistic communion between young Latinos, West Indians, and post-migration African Americans."[49] Cobb asserts that the musical genre is "literally a product of the African Diaspora . . . that body of Africa-derived cultures specifically those of North America and the Caribbean."[50] Influential early hip-hop artists include Public Enemy, Run–D.M.C., and N.W.A. In the United States, hip-hop began in the African American and diasporic urban communities of New York City and expanded across the country and internationally. The form is associated with challenging injustice and giving voice to urban youth culture.

Boleros evoke romance through ballads of longing. Cuban music historian Ned Sublette explains that the bolero, a Cuban-originated romantic song style, was by the mid-twentieth century "a thoroughly pan-Latin music, popular everywhere Spanish was spoken,"[51] with growing influence from Mexican, Puerto Rican, and Dominican Republic musicians. Sublette describes that bolero singers would "declaim in a full-voiced dramatic style that hearkened back to the aria and the unamplified Spanish music theater."[52] The bolero genre has been popularized by artists such as Beny Moré (Cuba), Los Panchos (Mexico and Puerto Rico), and Luis Miguel (Mexico). Boleros, with their soaring vocals, often reflect a desire for love and confront unrequited sentiments.

British punk grew out of class discontent as expressed through driving guitar and drums, accompanying aggressive lead vocals that are sung, yelled, or growled. Media theorist Dick Hebdige describes British punk as originating from "a whole range of heterogeneous youth styles": glitter rock, American proto-punk, London pub-rock, Southend R&B bands, northern soul, and reggae.[53] Like hip-hop, punk incorporates and synthesizes these divergent forms, which Hebdige describes as an "unlikely alliance of diverse and superficially incompatible musical traditions."[54] Iconic British punk groups include the Sex Pistols and the Clash. The British punk genre embraces anarchy and antiestablishment stances.

While hip-hop, boleros, and British punk inspire the play, hip-hop, in particular, implies that worlds coexist and collide through an urban and diasporic identity. Amid spoken word, rhythmic beats, and preexisting recordings, hip-hop allows for a greater flexibility of cultural worlds. Hip-hop theatre scholar and director Daniel Banks[55] explains: "Hip Hop also recognizes the ability—as well as the frequent necessity for its members—to hold seeming contradictions in the same space. Hip Hop heads know that multiple truths can coexist harmoniously and do not need to be resolved."[56] By using this hip-hop model, Svich utilizes the manipulation of sound and the collision of rap as a reflection of the oppressed peoples who live under Latin American dictatorships and struggle to make their voices heard.

Svich's hip-hop model elaborates on the global exchange within the Latin@ community. She locates her play in the "polyglot Americas leaning south: a market of video arcades, old and new drugs, Nescafe internet cafes, swift-changing political regimes, fluctuating currency, cheap sex for the tourist trade, ex-bullrings turned into discos and hotels, white cars and bright blue houses with peeling paint, fresh murals on ruined walls, and a view of the limitless, dirty sea."[57] Through her Latin American setting with its hip-hop ethos, Svich extends the definition of the Latin@ experience to include intersections of mediated spaces, governmental instability, repurposed locations, transformative decay, racial and cultural difference, sexual tourism, illicit substances, and expansive nature.

In part 1 of *Tropic of X*, Svich strongly employs this hip-hop model as Maura, Mori, Kiki, and Fabian collide. The linear structure includes scenes that function as episodic fragments illuminating the characters' lives. Each scene title summarizes an aspect of its action. For example, scene 2, entitled "The arcade junkies, Maura and Mori, look at the tourist,"[58] represents these two Latin Americans as they scrutinize a male European tourist. Maura describes Fabian: "He thinks he's in some foreign movie, some tropical exotica fascist propaganda flick."[59] However, the title does not express the violence brimming underneath their gaze as Maura plots to attack the tourist: "Screwy Euro. We should jump him now. We should annihilate him like an effing Ninja matrix warrior."[60] The scene titles serve as duplicitous framing devices that announce a surface perception, but often do not reveal the violent nature of each character's actions. Through Maura, Mori, Kiki, and Fabian, cultures and realities begin to ricochet off of one another: Latin America and Europe, local and foreign, anarchy and fascism, peace and violence, as Svich complicates the dualities of her characters' lives.

Svich's hip-hop model can also be seen through linguistic collisions in the Americas. Banks explains: "The wordsmiths of Hip Hop reveal a

FIGURE 5. *Tropic of X*, by Caridad Svich, produced by Single Carrot Theatre, directed by Nathan A. Cooper, in 2013. Maura (Genevieve de Mahy) connects with her lover, Mori (Nathan Fulton). Photo by Britt Olsen-Ecker/Single Carrot Theatre.

history where the Word is crucial to the self-definition and perpetuation of the culture."[61] Svich revels in the generative energy of the Word to define character and multilingual realities. Her characters communicate in poetic riffs infused by an anachronistic ferocity. Their speeches brim with pop culture references that collide with English, which intersects with Spanish, then includes Biblical terminology. These characters generate as well as perpetuate a multifaceted linguistic landscape. Anzaldúa writes: "There is no one Chicano language just as there is no one Chicano culture."[62] She refers to the reality that Chicano culture is diverse and, as such, Chicanos speak a variety of languages, including "1. Standard English 2. Working class and slang English 3. Standard Spanish 4. Standard Mexican Spanish 5. North Mexican dialect 6. Chicano Spanish . . . 7. Tex-Mex 8. *Pachuco* (*caló*)."[63] Anzaldúa highlights the iterations and hybridities of language in Chicano culture. Likewise, Svich proposes that there is no single Latin@ language as there is no single Latin@ culture.

In scene 1, Svich declares the linguistic complexities of her play through Hilton, "the DJ cowboy of the island airwaves." By starting her play with a disc jockey, Svich emphasizes the historical importance of radio communication in Latin America to raise public consciousness and broadcast musical forms. Hilton begins with a hip-hop rant:

HILTON: *Oye oye oye oye oye oye oye*
This is the voice
The voice
The voice . . .
This is the voice of radio *Dos Equis*
In the A, B, D and number four,
you hear me?[64]

Hilton's monologue with a spoken-word tonality includes Spanish and English as well as multilayered meanings. For example, *Dos Equis*, which means "double X" in Spanish, is the name of a Mexican beer, echoes the title of the play, can refer to a doubly nondescript location (i.e., X marks the spot . . . twice), a nondescript signature for someone unable to sign his or her proper name, female chromosomes, and signals the end of the life (i.e., the end of the alphabet . . . or the end of things). Thus in one term, Svich evokes an alcoholic beverage, geography, handwriting, gender, and termination. This multilayered linguistic approach initiates the plurality of the Latin@ landscape she constructs.

Svich additionally employs the hip-hop model as she depicts gender identity through the character of Kiki. When Kiki first appears, Maura proclaims, "You're such a sorry-ass girly girl"; to which Kiki replies, "I'm hundred percent male, honey. No eggs in my basket."[65] Kiki later kisses Maura and tries to seduce Mori with drugs. When Maura and Mori take Kiki's cocaine, Kiki delivers a monologue on the origins of the drug:

KIKI: From Colombia through Poland to Italy,
from the UK to Holland to Kansas City,
from Moscow to Peru to Argentina,
from Oklahoma to Miami to new Arcadia.
Oh, Spain, oh Portugal, coca breathes.
Hosanna of the most heavenly currency.
Protect me, oh Morpheus, god of dreams.[66]

Kiki's fluid gender mirrors the influence of cultural hybridity on drug trafficking, which includes Western Europe, Eastern Europe, Latin America, and the United States. While Kiki does call out to the Greek god of dreams, Morpheus, for protection, it's unsettling that Svich assigns her to the drug trade, for it suggests the possibility that gender and cultural hybridity are states that need to be chemically altered or annihilated. In part 2, Kiki attempts to prostitute herself to a passerby: "Honey, come closer. Be rough. Come on. I can take it. My body can take anything."[67] Here Svich also links Kiki to violent aggression within prostitution. Therefore, while the hip-hop model mirrors the complexities of Kiki's gender fluidity, the paradigm breaks down when the transgendered identity exists in service to drugs and violence, which threaten to extinguish the very existence of this transgender voice.

Toward the middle of part 1, Svich's hip-hop model begins to collapse. The rise of another fascist regime, which obliterates multiplicity, causes this breakdown. This deconstruction can be seen most starkly in the characters of Fabian and Mori. When they first meet, Fabian expresses a range of linguistic options and identities, whereas Mori remains rooted in his culture.

FABIAN: In what language do you want me to speak?

[*French*] *Combien voulez-vous?*

[*German*] *Wievel wunschen Sie?*

[*Italian*] *Quanto desiderate?*

[*Chinese*] . . .

[*Spanish*] *Cuanto deseas?*

How much do you want, my friend?

MORI: However much you'll give me.

FABIAN: You are innocent.

MORI: Screw you.

FABIAN: . . . What's your name?

MORI: What do you care? I rim you and we're done with. This ain't no relationship we're going to set up house and have kids and watch TV.

FABIAN: I'm Fabian.

MORI: You're Spanish?

FABIAN: It doesn't matter where I'm from.

MORI: You say your name like a Spaniard, like an Iberian . . . whatsit: "Fabian."
FABIAN: I say it how I was taught.[68]

Fabian and Mori begin a transactional relationship, with Fabian asking Mori how much money he wants for this sexual encounter. Fabian offers to speak in a variety of European languages and Chinese, implying that Mori, as a prostitute, may have had international customers and that this is a world where many languages interact. Mori at first does not reveal his name to Fabian, preferring to remain anonymous. The possibility that Fabian is Spanish suggests that he is colonizing, exploiting, or conquering Mori, yet at the beginning of their meeting Mori still has agency to challenge Fabian. Mori eventually reveals his name as they engage in linguistic foreplay. Mori implies he will dominate Fabian when he rims him (i.e., oral stimulation of the anus). However, this power struggle soon devolves into violence. Fabian ends their sexual encounter by gagging Mori and cutting him with a knife. The hip-hop multivocal plurality dissipates as violence begins to silence voices and strip away freedom of expression.

By the end of part 1, only one voice dominates the linguistic discourse and shapes identity through a dictatorial methodology, which outlaws diversity. The country's political landscape becomes a violent, militarized state as Hilton announces that the "capture and torture of dissidents is now allowed."[69] At the beginning of part 2, Fabian begins to strip away Mori's language and his identity. He finds Mori sleeping outside and harasses him. The altercation escalates as Fabian launches into a barrage of questions:

FABIAN: Where are you from?
What's your language?
Papers?
Name?
. . .
Repeat after me. A.
MORI: A.
FABIAN: Ass.
MORI: Ass.
    Fabian strikes Mori

FABIAN: No language. Rules.

B. Repeat.

MORI: B.

FABIAN: Bull-crap.

MORI: What?

FABIAN: Repeat.

MORI: Bull-crap.[70]

Fabian tries to teach a language of oppression, but Mori resists. This linguistic system is not based in nuance but in strict rules where letters signify derogatory terms. After Mori continues to refuse to learn these terms, Fabian announces he is completely removing Mori's identity by reassigning his gender and renaming him with numbers.

FABIAN: . . . You are number 015125.

You will answer to this number and this number only.

You are now a female, understand? A girl. No trace.

MORI: What?

FABIAN: You have no memory.

Fabian blindfolds Mori and drags him away.[71]

Fabian eviscerates Mori through violence, torture, gender reassignment, and kidnapping. There is no multiplicity of hip-hop voices any longer. Fabian echoes the Spanish conquistadors who fought to eliminate indigenous language and culture in the Americas to solidify their power and dominance. In a modern context, Fabian represents the Latin American dictatorships that disappeared and tortured citizens, stripping them of language, identity, and/or their lives.

In scene 21, titled "Mori and Maura share a dream," Svich deploys a supernatural intervention. Maura cross-dresses as a man and travels through the countryside to find Mori. She encounters various obstacles in her quest to locate her disappeared lover. As in *Prodigal Kiss*, Svich constructs a liminal, flexible space. In this dreamscape, Maura and Mori communicate spiritually or perhaps psychically. The location is nebulous, and it's at times unclear who is speaking as Svich does not assign character names to the lines of dialogue, which also mirrors the characters' transgender liminality. However, the two lovers connect in word and spirit:

Where are you now?
On the path.
In the dark.
Yes.
Your voice is funny.
So is yours. Why don't you curse at me?
I don't want to. I'm a boy now.[72]

Their spiritual communication leads them to a new language. This new language is one of disembodied voices, disempowered citizens, and irreversible ruptures. The construction contains only European, non-Spanish phrases, emphasizing the eradication of the colonizer's Spanish and the indigenous languages as well.

There's graffiti.
What does it say?
I can't make it out.
Try.
Salt words in a salt sea.
Read them.
[French] Une nouvelle langue,
[Portuguese] uma lingua nova,
[German] eine neue Sprache
A new language
Your voice is clear.
My accent's crap. I learned the wrong alphabet.[73]

Its alphabet seems insurmountable for Maura and Mori, yet the language exists in a double liminality: in a dreamscape, written on water. However, this unfamiliar, fascistic language, generated in this sacred dream space, ultimately reunites these two lovers in the waking world.

As in *Prodigal Kiss*, Svich implies that the loss of language is directly linked to the loss of personal and cultural identity. When Maura arrives to save Mori, she finds he is completely brainwashed and does not recognize her. Maura tries to tell him his name, but he replies, "I am 015125. I was born in another country. I am a girl, age twenty. I am dead. Stop looking at me."[74] When Maura tries to connect with him, Mori spits out the language of his torturers: "Lesson number one thousand and two: do not leave, do not try to leave, never leave, or much drowning, head in bucket, pulling of limbs."[75] Finally, as Maura tries to say Mori's name, he is seemingly irretrievably damaged and replies, "Erase memory."[76] Here Svich also connects linguistic erasure to destruction of gender.

At the close of the play, Svich effectively demonstrates how dictatorship and torture silence multiplicity. Hilton's final monologue reveals the death of Mori and Maura, the victims of the violence and oppression in this fascist state. While it is unclear how the couple dies, Hilton says that, "Two pure ones have been found hard as mules on the sand against the rough sea, they are seen we are told through a night of lucid silver."[77] At first the hip-hop aesthetic permeates the characters' cultural landscapes, underscoring the varied lives of Maura, Mori, Kiki, and Fabian. However, this very model gives rise to the oppressive and dominant Fabian, who eradicates any hint of nonconformity. By constructing and deconstructing the hip-hop paradigm, Svich problematizes Latin@ culture as well as the multiplicity of voices in the Americas that struggle to be heard.

IMPRINTING THE FORNES FRAME

Svich received sustained mentorship from Fornes, and her resulting work reflects many aspects of Fornes's playwriting legacy. Svich states that Fornes taught her "rigor, playfulness, truthfulness, daring, formal enquiry, linguistic enquiry."[78] Svich's plays underscore rigorous mobility in their pursuit of truths about diverse cultures, immigration, and injustice in Latin America. She creates works driven by characters who seek truth about cultural identity and dare to engage with the spirit world. She conducts linguistic and structural experimentation in her work. Her creation of music-filled worlds at times suggests a playful whimsy while presenting unflinching views of oppression and violence.

The female characters in plays by Fornes and Svich confront violence and engage the supernatural as they attempt to redefine their identities. Fefu and her friends exist in a patriarchal, prefeminist society where they join together to seek greater empowerment. Julia has been paralyzed by a gunshot that killed a deer, and through a supernatural intervention presumably dies after Fefu shoots and kills a rabbit. In *Sarita*, Sarita

FIGURE 6. Maria Irene Fornes and Caridad Svich in New York City in 2003. Photo by Michelle Memran.

struggles over her ongoing affair with Julio after she has married Mark. At one point, she engages in a Santería veneration with her mother. In the end, Sarita succumbs to violence when she stabs and kills Julio. She is then sent to live in a mental institution. In *Prodigal Kiss*, Marcela is accosted by Rafael, shot by Coral, and hit by Rafael, yet she survives with some assistance from a supernatural woman who gives her a red sash. In *Tropic of X*, Maura and Mori fight against the rising totalitarian regime in their unnamed Latin American country. Mori is tortured by Fabian, and as Maura searches for him, they connect in a liminal, spirit world. After Maura finds him, she and Mori mysteriously die together. Fornes's and Svich's characters maintain a rigorous determination to survive. However, in Svich's two plays here, only her characters in the United States actually survive, highlighting how many Latin Americans have perished under brutal regimes.

Fornes and Svich create theatrical landscapes where time, space, and location transform from one scene to the next, suggesting that temporal flexibility and shifting realities are integral to Latina theatre. *Fefu and Her Friends*, written in six scenes, includes five locations, with simultaneous scenes in part 2 when the audience migrates from Fefu's living room to the four scenes occurring in and around Fefu's house: kitchen, study, bedroom, lawn. In *Sarita*, Fornes creates five locations: Fela's living room, Sarita's kitchen, the Empire State Building, a beach, and the waiting room in a mental hospital, as time moves linearly from 1939 to 1947 during the play's twenty scenes. Similarly, in Svich's theatrical worlds her characters traverse multiple locations. In *Prodigal Kiss*, Marcela begins in the water between Cuba and Florida, and once on land, travels west by train to San Diego and then by a northeastern train to New Jersey during the play's twelve scenes. The twenty-three scenes in *Tropic of X* occur in diverse spaces: a radio station, an arcade that used to be a bullring, a street, a field, a bone heap, and a sea wall. In both of her works, Svich does not indicate year or time. Thus her plays reflect universality and grant latitude for her characters' journeys to temporally expand or contract in the audience's perception.

Like Fornes, Svich generates plays that experiment with combining text and music. Svich interjects songs in *Prodigal Kiss* that allow Marcela a liminal musical space to reflect on her immigrant experience. The songs provide interludes for Marcela to sing in English and Spanish, deepening the audience's knowledge of her plight. Fornes employs a variety of musical styles in *Sarita* for songs that are more interwoven with the narrative. Each character in *Sarita* sings a solo or duet, whereas in *Prodigal Kiss* only Marcela sings. Svich writes the music and lyrics to her songs, whereas Fornes's lyrics are set to music by Leon Odenz. In both plays, the songs function as interjections of heightened theatricality that reveal and complicate character transformation.

Lastly, Svich has been instrumental in documenting Fornes's legacy. She was Fornes's assistant for the Hispanic Playwrights-in-Residence Laboratory, which she explains entailed "not only setting up the room for work every session but also writing down all the exercises every day for years. This act of transcription was to be the foundation for a book on playwriting Fornes was one day going to write entitled *The Anatomy of Inspiration*."[79] Though Fornes decided not to write that book, Svich chronicled Fornes's work as a teacher, playwright, and director in the volume *Conducting a Life: Reflections on the Theater of Maria Irene Fornes*, coedited with Maria Delgado. This book includes an invaluable consideration of the influence of Fornes's teaching through reflections on and examples of favorite Fornes writing exercises from her students, including Migdalia Cruz, Cherríe Moraga, Elaine Romero, and many others. The book provides a valuable chronology of Fornes's thirty-three-year teaching career. Thus, Svich's training with Fornes at INTAR, her prolific playwriting career, her teaching experience across the globe, her visionary community organizing with the NoPassport collective, and her publication of many Latin@ playwrights through NoPassport Press valiantly imprint the legacy of Maria Irene Fornes.

3

KAREN ZACARÍAS

Navigating Multiple Borders

ARLY TWENTY-FIRST-CENTURY Latina playwrights craft theatrical worlds that question, complicate, and diversify cultural engagement. These playwrights chart and chronicle the experiences of simultaneously inhabiting multiple cultural realms. Karen Zacarías, a playwright of Mexican-Lebanese-Danish descent, emigrated from Mexico to the United States at the age of ten. In her plays, she engages the artistic and spiritual life in Mexico's recent and distant past by navigating many borders. Zacarías uses Mexico as a primary site for considering cultural multiplicity in Latina theatre.

The Fornes frame, when defined as a border, can reflect on the many cultural borders that Latin@s cross to start a new life in the United States. The Fornes frame can also encompass temporal borders between present and past, spiritual borders between natural and supernatural worlds, linguistic borders between diverse languages, artistic borders between creator and creation, and performative borders between actor and character. In *Mariela in the Desert*, Zacarías highlights a female painter's struggle in 1951 Mexico as she confronts the collision of Mexican and American cultures in her home. In *The Sins of Sor Juana*, Zacarías fictionalizes the life of the iconic seventeenth-century Mexican writer and nun Sor Juana Inés de la Cruz (1648–1695), as she contends with Mexican, Spanish, and Aztec cultures in her quest for freedom of expression. In these plays, Zacarías creates characters and narratives that traverse these diverse borders.

Mariela and Sor Juana contest the patriarchal systems in Mexico, which limit their artistic expression and social mobility. Mariela debates art with a Jewish American art historian who influences her return to painting. Sor Juana reconnects with her Aztec servant and her Spanish patroness as she struggles with her desire to continue writing. Zacarías considers the relationship between Mexico's past and present with these narratives that move fluidly between disparate time periods. Mariela contends with her life in the desert juxtaposed against her earlier, more creatively vibrant years in Mexico City. Sor Juana supernaturally travels to her past in order to survive censorship in her present life. Thus, both plays incorporate temporally flexible structures.

Zacarías also utilizes linguistic translation strategies. While *Mariela in the Desert* and *The Sins of Sor Juana* are written in English, the conceit is that the characters are all actually "speaking" Spanish; thus Zacarías "translates" their words, with the invisibility of the Spanish language hovering over the English text.[1] In *Mariela in the Desert*, she creates linguistic "portraits" of her secondary characters in poetic monologues, which exist in a liminal space, as they prepare to engage with the tensions arising in the desert home. In *The Sins of Sor Juana*, she translates and inserts poems by Sor Juana Ines de la Cruz into her play, creating a relationship between her fictional world and Cruz's literary canon. In both plays, Zacarías stages complex cultural intersections as she expands awareness of Mexican narratives that illuminate the Latin@ experience.

MARIELA IN THE DESERT: MEXICAN ARTIST CONFRONTS JEWISH AMERICAN ART HISTORIAN

In *Mariela in the Desert*, Zacarías delves into the lives of a Mexican female painter, her family, and a Jewish American art historian who influences the transformation of her identity. Set on a remote ranch in northern Mexico in 1951, the play presents Mariela Salvatierra, the matriarch of her family, as she confronts her husband, José, a famous painter who is dying, and contends with the arrival of her estranged daughter, Blanca, with her new lover, Adam Lovitz. Adam is a Jewish American art history professor from New York City, with a PhD from Columbia University. He is writing a book on Mexican Expressionism and now teaches in Mexico City,

FIGURE 7. Karen Zacarías rehearsing *Mariela in the Desert* with director Henry Godinez at the Goodman Theatre in 2005. Photo by Liz Lauren/Goodman Theatre.

where he met Blanca, also a painter and his former student. Adam has a keen interest in the work of José Salvatierra and plans to include a chapter on his painting in his new book. Zacarías states, "In *Mariela in the Desert*, the Latinos are in the majority and a sole 'American' character serves as a comparison/contrast of cultural identity."[2] Zacarías offers an important consideration of how cultural collisions can inform Latina identity when Mariela engages with Adam regarding artistic philosophy and practice.

Present and past collide as Zacarías's characters navigate temporal borders throughout her play. In the recent past, Mariela sent a telegram to her daughter, Blanca, who now lives in faraway Mexico City. In an effort to unite her fractured family, Mariela has lied to Blanca by asking her to come home because José has died. As the play opens in the present, Mariela is nursing José, who is still very much alive and cantankerous, though ailing from diabetes. Mariela deceived Blanca about José's death because she felt it was the only way to convince her estranged daughter to return. Mariela then crosses a temporal border to where, twenty years earlier, a young José gropes her in a backroom of their Mexico City home while they are throwing a party for their artistic friends, who include Diego Rivera, Frida Kahlo, David Siqueiros, Rufino Tamayo, Tina Modotti, and Edward Weston. Mariela asks José if he has shown Rivera her own painting. He replies, "He said he hopes you are a better lover than you are a painter."[3] Next, José revels in his plan to move to the desert to create an artistic commune, where their famous friends can visit and work with them.

Zacarías positions José and Mariela as younger contemporaries of Mexico's most acclaimed visual artists of the twentieth century, who traveled the world while pursuing their art. Yet the Salvatierras' careers never reach the same level as their peers. Diego Rivera (1886–1957) painted in Europe for fourteen years before returning to Mexico in 1922 to begin creating murals in Mexico City. In 1929, Frida Kahlo (1907–1954), a young painter, married Diego Rivera, twenty years her senior. Rivera and Kahlo spent time in the United States during the early 1930s, visiting and working in cities such as San Francisco, Detroit, and New York City. The Rivera/Kahlo relationship mirrors the José/Mariela relationship. Mariela echoes Kahlo in that Kahlo was often overshadowed by her famous husband. Yet, Kahlo maintained a vibrant artistic career with international recognition, while Mariela has not emerged from the husband's shadow nor created a major body of work.

Mariela and José's other highly acclaimed friends include muralists and painters David Siqueiros (1896–1974) and Rufino Tamayo (1899–1991), who is considered the "fourth" of the three greats of Mexican Muralism (Rivera, Siqueiros, and Orozco).[4] Lastly, their gathering includes photographer Tina Modotti (1896–1942), originally from Italy, and her lover, American photographer Edward Weston (1886–1958), who moved to Mexico in 1923, after he left his wife in Los Angeles. Art historian Sarah M. Lowe writes: "Weston's trip to Mexico invokes Gauguin's flight from Paris . . . to Tahiti, where he set up a household with a 'native' woman."[5] The Weston/Modotti relationship echoes the Mark/Sarita relationship in Fornes's *Sarita* as well as the José/Mariela relationship. Modotti lived in Weston's shadow, and her photographic works remained less known. However, both Sarita and Modotti seem to have more agency through their urban life than Mariela, who eventually lives isolated in the desert.

Through this collection of Mexico's artistic elite, Zacarías presents a culturally complex milieu where José and Mariela's early artistic life thrives. All of these artists traveled nationally and internationally for their painting, and their work synthesized diverse visual arts aesthetics: Mexican, European, and Aztec. Yet, José and Mariela move to the desert and remain in their rural home for decades. Zacarías juxtaposes a vibrant, cultural, and multivarious past full of possibility with a static present where death echoes through the house: José's failing health as well as the tragic death of their young son, Carlos, many years earlier. While contemporaries of famous artists, José and Mariela remain culturally and artistically isolated.

Blanca and Adam alter the cultural and creative landscape of the Salvatierra home when they arrive late at night. Mariela and Oliva, José's older sister who lives with them, are unaware of Adam's presence in Blanca's life and so are taken aback by his appearance. Before Adam enters, Mariela asks Blanca, "He looks a little old. Are you sleeping with him?" Blanca replies in the affirmative, adding, "There's less of an age difference between us than Papi and you."⁶ An angry Blanca soon runs to see her ailing father when she learns José is still alive.

Zacarías next provides a linguistic "portrait" of Adam. In a liminal space, this Jewish American professor addresses the audience before he crosses the "border" into the Salvatierra home.

> ADAM: It's cold in the desert. I am foreigner in a foreign land, uninvited and unexpected. I like the cold. I like the dry feel of this vast indifferent land. I am here for the funeral of a famous Mexican artist, an artist whose paintings have all but disappeared. I am not here for him, but for Blanca. (Beat) I am an outsider: I am at home where I do not belong.⁷

This poetic moment underscores Adam's minority position and outsider status before he engages with the Salvatierra family. This portrait echoes the musical liminality in Svich's *Prodigal Kiss*, yet unlike Marcela in that play, Adam doesn't long for his home country but exhibits a deep investment in Mexico and the work of José. Zacarías does not make it clear if her character is directly addressing the audience or offering a soliloquy of self-reflection. However, she provides the audience with an opportunity to observe this living portrait of a Jewish American professor. This moment highlights Adam's otherness and sets up an expectation of cultural collision once he enters this Mexican home.

Zacarías immediately introduces the dichotomy between Mariela's Mexican life and Adam's American world through their linguistic differences. Soon after Mariela meets Adam, she compliments him on his ability to speak Spanish. He explains that he taught himself Spanish in middle school after finding a Mexican comic book about Pancho Villa (1878–1923). His claim to have learned Spanish from a comic book may reveal his limited view of the language. However, Zacarías's reference to Villa speaks to the cultural intersections in her play. Historian Alejandro Quintana writes: "[Villa] was an illiterate man who became the most powerful man in Mexico, a defeated soldier who managed to evade over 30,000 U.S. and Mexican troops, and he also served as the governor of Chihuahua, creating laws and policies protecting the poor with the support of the wealthy."[8] Adam claims to have learned the language through reading a comic book written in Spanish about the famous Mexican

FIGURE 8. *Mariela in the Desert*, by Karen Zacarías, produced by the Goodman Theatre, directed by Henry Godinez, in 2005. Mariela Salvatierra (Sandra Marquez) debates with Adam Lovitz (Mark Ulrich). Photo by Liz Lauren/Goodman Theatre.

revolutionary leader who challenged existing political structures and traversed the borders between the United States and Mexico. Adam's interest in Villa is not mentioned again in the play, but the fact that he learned Spanish from this comic book implies he read the narrative numerous times. Zacarías creates layers of cultural complication as this Jewish American art historian, inspired by the story of a Mexican revolutionary, enters the Salvatierra home with some "revolutionary" ideas about art that challenge Mariela and ultimately lead to her liberation.

Cultural and artistic lines are crossed when Adam explains that he is in Mexico City to teach an art history course, "National Identity in Modern Mexican Expressionism."[9] Mariela balks, "An American teaching us about us?" to which Adam replies, "An outside perspective can be helpful sometimes."[10] When Mariela presses him as to why he is not teaching in the United States, he lectures her about American gestural abstraction versus Mexican Expressionism. Mariela then suspects that Adam has been fired from his teaching position in the United States because of his views. Adam responds:

ADAM: Currently, there is an obsession in the United States with gestural abstraction that perplexes me. Critics, academics, collectors are all slobbering over the work of artists like Jackson Pollock. They are so excited about his chaotic process, his splish-splash of color that they do not see he is a man who is communicating nothing. On the other hand, here, Mexican Expressionism gets at the core of why I think art needs to exist.

MARIELA: Ah! And why does art need to exist, Professor?

ADAM: Because at its core . . . art is about communication, a vital human communication, a dangerous dialogue between the artist and the viewer.

MARIELA: So you were fired.

ADAM: Pollock is not abstract, he is random. His work is non-political, impersonal, safe. He throws paint on a canvas. None of his paintings present his point of view. Frida Kahlo slashes open her beating heart and lets it bleed: "This" she paints "is how it feels to love a man more than he loves you." We cannot ignore the brutal truth behind her statement. What do I learn about Pollock when I look at his work? Nothing.

MARIELA: But some would argue that his paintings are beautiful. The vivid colors, the curve of the paint. The energy of the drops.[11]

Adam creates static dichotomies: American abstract expressionism versus Mexican Expressionism, Pollock versus Kahlo, chaos versus order, nihilism versus meaning. Yet, Mariela continually resists his rigid analysis.

Whereas Adam champions Kahlo's work as more valid, Mariela sees value in Pollock's painting. Jackson Pollock (1912–1956), an American abstract expressionist painter, was famous for drip paintings that art historian Evelyn Toynton describes as "like jazz . . . the impression of free-wheeling immediacy and spontaneity—distinctively American quality—exhibiting the same high-wire discipline necessary to avoid spinning out of control."[12] Yet, this description of Pollock as quintessentially American omits the reality of his Mexican cultural influences. Siqueiros, for whom Pollock worked in 1935 through the Federal Arts Project, inspired aspects of Pollock's work. Toynton writes: "Siqueiros's passionate left-wing allegiances led [Pollock] not only to create art for the masses, but also to make art out of non-elite materials, like Duco paint used for automobiles."[13] Conversely, Adam's estimation of Kahlo as unilaterally Mexican negates her bicultural, Mexican-German identity. Kahlo was acclaimed for autobiographical works that novelist Carlos Fuentes declared "are beautiful for the same reason that Rembrandt's are beautiful. They reveal to us the successive identities of a being still in the process of becoming."[14] The juxtaposition of an American artist influenced by a Mexican muralist with a Mexican painter of partial German heritage underlines how Adam's analysis lacks depth of cultural complexity while Mariela's response considers various levels at work in these artists. Adam says he learns nothing from Pollock, whereas Mariela sees energy in his drops of paint on the canvas. This clash between Adam's monolithic interpretation and Mariela's multilayered artistry soon shapes the transformation of Mariela's identity.

The connections between Adam and Mariela are marked by religious difference and potential political affiliations. When Adam discloses to Mariela that he is Jewish, she replies, "I always felt I was Jewish, in a lapsed-Mexican Catholic sort of way."[15] Mariela relates to Adam's religion and admits she is not a practicing Catholic, but Zacarías does not explore this further in the play. In introducing Adam to Oliva, Mariela says, "He's also American, Jewish, possibly a socialist and definitely Blanca's lover."[16] Adam's Judaism is not mentioned again in the play. José and Mariela's political affiliations are not explored either. However, given their close relationship to Rivera and Kahlo, who were active with the Communist party, Adam's possible socialist identity may further connect him to the Salvatierras. Adam's status as Jewish and maybe socialist and an expatriate from late 1940s America highlight his outsider status in his own country as well.

Adam, an American man, places himself between Mariela and Blanca, two Mexican women. Before he leaves the room, Adam assumes Mariela is unhappy with him: "You see an American . . . a gringo standing between you and your daughter."[17] Mariela counters that she sees "a thin, jagged cactus . . . a *palo verde*, green and tugging at the sky, while its tawny roots suck every drop of rain hidden in the crusty dry soil. Yes, a young beautiful cactus. . . . And you professor, are just a little prick, in her side."[18] Mariela paints a poetic image that abstracts this American man into a tiny cactus spine, marginalizing him to a small fragment on the periphery of their lives. Yet her comment traverses both the human and plant worlds and implies Adam is organically connected to the desert landscape. Her analysis also asserts the primacy of her Mexican position over Adam's American reality.

In act 2, Zacarías continues these confrontations along cultural borders as Adam meets José, who first greets him affectionately. When Blanca and Oliva bring in water and flan for José, he asks to share the custard dessert with Adam. As Oliva protests, José replies, "What can a gringo germ do to a man like me?"[19] Zacarías again emphasizes Adam's foreigner status in this Mexican family. First, José uses a slang, potentially derogatory term for foreigner (i.e., "gringo") to describe Adam. Next José refers to Adam as having a germ, which implies that Adam might infect the family. Yet, José asserts his immunity to gringo germs (i.e., American infectious culture).

Frida Kahlo's work next becomes a contentious artistic boundary between Adam and José. Adam offers that he knows Kahlo and is "helping Frida, providing text for her exhibit in Paris. She's the first living woman to have a painting in the Louvre."[20] Adam asserts his cultural and artistic currency through his association with Kahlo. José then declares his superior artistic position by mentioning his close connection with Kahlo and Rivera. He downplays Kahlo's exhibit when he retorts, "The Louvre! Little Frida is a great artist,"[21] and then proclaims his own importance: "I

mean, seriously, I should be showing my work in Paris."[22] José's description of Kahlo as "little" could refer to her diminutive height yet suggests
his jealousy of her success. José adds that Rivera, Kahlo, and many other
Mexican artists visited their desert home in the past. José seems pleased
to learn that Adam knows his friends. Meanwhile, Zacarías highlights
José's lack of mobility. Kahlo travels from Mexico to France for her work,
while José is resentful that he has not left his desert home.

However, Zacarías soon reveals the true level of José's cultural animos-
ity. As Oliva, Blanca, and Adam exit, José proclaims how happy he is that
Blanca has returned; but regarding Adam, he snarls, "I hate him. . . . Bad
for Blanca. Bad for us."[23] When Mariela counters that Adam knows about
art, José retorts, "I know art. He knows nothing. Stupid Americans. They
grab Texas, California, now Blanca."[24] José is referring to the U.S. annex-
ation of Texas and California through the Treaty of Guadalupe Hidalgo
in 1848, which ended the U.S. war against the Mexican Republic.[25] This
event took place over a hundred years before the start of the play, yet José
refers to this historical conflict as if it just happened. More problemati-
cally, José compares his daughter to geography, land, and property, which
reinforces his autocratic, patriarchal position in this family. He intimates
that Adam sees Blanca as property, and if so, this American is "grabbing"
more Mexican territory. In either case, Zacarías aligns gender differences
with historical border schisms between the United States and Mexico.

Zacarías also highlights gender dynamics when José views Adam as a
threat to his marriage. After his tirade, José grows more agitated and falls
out of bed. When Adam rushes in to help, José lashes out: "Mariela? Going
to fuck the professor as soon as I fall asleep?"[26] José's rancor degrades Mariela. She later tells Adam: "Don't worry. I have no plans to sleep with you.
. . . My husband likes to make others uncomfortable."[27] Mariela's dismissal
of her husband's offensive remark speaks to her years of living in a household where denial and not confrontation allow for survival.

The artistic and intellectual connections between Adam and Mariela
soon grow. Mariela does not adhere to her husband's views and advances
a more nuanced approach to their cultural differences. Adam apologizes
for his rude behavior earlier, to which Mariela replies, "It's the best conversation I've had in years, professor."[28] Adam presses on that he heard
that Mariela painted in the past. Mariela asks if Blanca told him that.
Adam replies that Diego Rivera told him years ago that Mariela had

created a painting called *The Bent Woman* that Rivera wanted to trade for one of his own works. Mariela quietly absorbs Adam's compliment and José's lie from years ago about Rivera's estimation of her work. When asked why José stopped painting, Mariela replies that his son died and his daughter ran away. The praise of a male American art historian and a famous male Mexican painter deeply influence Mariela's artistic identity. Zacarías does not supply any female praise of her work by Kahlo or Modotti. Unlike Kahlo, Mariela has not been able to forge a career apart from her famous husband. Zacarías thus highlights the patriarchal confines that Mariela later tries to escape.

Mariela's artistic and cultural identities revolve around a painting entitled *The Blue Barn*, long thought to be "the crown jewel of [José] Salvatierra's work,"[29] and which won Mexico's Presidential Prize in Art. In act 1, a shroud over the painting is removed to reveal a long tear, which Mariela informs was done by José only two days earlier. Adam synthesizes the violence with the painting, saying, "The gash is like a wound. It's almost intrinsic to the painting. The swirls of broken paint, the bleeding color. A vital honest cry of pain. *The Blue Barn* is beautiful, even damaged."[30] In act 2, Adam presses Mariela about why José never signed the *The Blue Barn* and why he used all of his prize money to buy it back from the National Museum of Fine Arts. Mariela skirts the issue. Adam affirms that the masterpiece was praised by Tamayo and Rivera, but repeats the rumor that it was painted by a young man, which Mariela denies.

Zacarías later reveals that Mariela painted *The Blue Barn* when José felt artistically blocked. In a flashback, we see that José was unable to complete a commission he received from a gallery in Mexico City to create new work for an exhibit of twelve paintings each by twelve artists, including Rivera and Siqueiros. He has created eleven but cannot finish the twelfth piece due to his anxiety at being compared to his more famous peers, or insecurity about the quality of his work. Mariela pushes him to complete it, for the gallery will not pay him if the commission is incomplete. In anger, José storms out of his barn studio, knocking over his blank canvas and supplies. Mariela picks up the canvas and, in a moment of inspiration, starts to paint. Her motivation may be as much artistic as economic, but she eventually completes the painting and sends off all twelve to the gallery. However, the obscuring of Mariela's identity behind her famous husband eventually causes tragedy.

The Blue Barn not only signifies Mariela's considerable talent but her complicated artistic relationship with her husband. Her artistic achievement and the very title of the painting are forever linked to family tragedy. In a flashback, we see that Carlos, José and Mariela's emotionally troubled young son, feels the painting's green boy signifies him and the orange bird his older sister, Blanca. He comments that it's not like José's other work. Mariela asks Carlos to finish the painting. He paints a small red flame on the canvas, but begins to have a fit when he feels he has ruined the painting. Mariela assures him that he has not and tells him to hide in the barn and bite his lip when he wants to scream and run away. Back in the present, Zacarías reveals that after José received his prize for *The Blue Barn*, he came home enraged that Mariela's painting had won the accolade, and not one of his eleven. In anger, he set fire to his barn studio. Unbeknownst to José, Carlos was hiding in the barn and died in the fire. After Carlos's death, Blanca ran away and José's grief left him a shell of a man. The loss of their son and the flight of their daughter permanently strained José and Mariela's relationship. Subsequently, Mariela stopped painting altogether.

Zacarías implies that Mariela's identity became secondary to her family regardless of her artistic achievements. In the present, José again berates Mariela about *The Blue Barn*'s prize: "You painted *The Blue Barn* and then you sent it! Why did you send them your painting?"[31] José taunts Mariela that she never properly loved her children, ignored her artistic talent, and that her mothering killed their son. In anger, Mariela intentionally drops and breaks the vial of insulin José needs to survive. When she starts to leave for more insulin, José stops her and essentially asks her to let him die. She haltingly agrees, and soon says good-bye to her husband. The only way to break this cycle of artistic and cultural oppression is for Mariela to kill the patriarch. By doing so, she is able to reclaim her artistic identity. As Mariela weeps alone, Zacarías illuminates the border between the natural and supernatural worlds by having the spirit of Carlos enter. Carlos gives Mariela a paintbrush, and she begins to paint again as the play comes to a close.

Mariela's former self recedes and is replaced by a self with a renewed sense of artistic purpose in part because of her connection with Adam. That Mariela's identity as a female Mexican painter is significantly affected by her interactions with a male American art historian has echoes of imperialism and underscores the gender dynamics of conquest that persist. However, unlike Mark in Fornes's *Sarita*, Adam does not exoticize Mariela. The art historian and painter are equals, with Mariela gradually gaining prominence throughout the play. Zacarías emphasizes that the intersections of artistic, cultural, linguistic, and spiritual borders ultimately empower Mariela to revive her artistic identity.

THE SINS OF SOR JUANA: MEXICAN NUN ENGAGES AZTEC AND SPANISH WORLDS

In *The Sins of Sor Juana*, a fictional rumination on the life of Sor Juana Inés de la Cruz (1641–1695), the iconic seventeenth-century Mexican poet, playwright, and nun, Zacarías theatricalizes multiple border crossings in New Spain (i.e., colonial Mexico) of the late 1600s. Zacarías states that her play "deals with cross-cultural identity in theme, character, language, and plot, where Spaniards, Mexicans, and Native Indigenous people converge in a clash of and bridge of class, religion, race, and gender."[32] In her brief life, Sor Juana wrote over four hundred works of literature, including poetry, prose, and plays. Poet and Nobel laureate Octavio Paz considers Sor Juana one of the "major poets of our hemisphere,"[33] and she is revered in Mexico, where she appears on the one thousand peso bill (roughly a U.S. ten dollar bill). Zacarías constructs collisions between past and present that highlight Sor Juana's poetic talent. Her play also investigates what may have led young Juana to a religious vocation and to becoming the iconic Mexican nun.

Juana Ramírez (who later became Sor Juana Inés de la Cruz) was an illegitimate child born in 1641 in San Miguel Nepantla to a mestiza, Isabel Ramírez, and a Spanish Basque nobleman, Pedro Manuel de Asbaje y Vargas Machuca. A beautiful young woman and prodigy, Juana taught herself by reading her grandfather's books. She was admitted into the viceregal court at age fifteen in service of the vicereine, Doña Leonor Carreto, where she became the vicereine's favorite. At one point, during her time at court, the viceroy tested her knowledge with a gathering of forty learned men; Juana successfully answered their barrage of questions. At age twenty she entered a convent of the Discalced Carmelites, where she continued a life of writing and intellectual expansion. However, her secular poetry drew the ire of the Inquisition, and she was censored in 1691. She ceased writing secular works and died in 1695 at the age of forty-six, after contracting an illness from ailing nuns in her convent.[34]

Zacarías's inspiration for the play came from a discussion with her grandfather Miguel Zacarías, acclaimed film director during the Golden Age of Mexican cinema, who challenged her to write her own version of Sor Juana. Zacarías states:

> When I was a teenager, my grandfather . . . wrote a treatise on Sor Juana, and I didn't agree with his portrayal of her. I saw Sor Juana as a strong, beautiful woman and a remarkable writer who was always searching for answers. In his version, she was a pretty damsel in distress who fainted all over the place. I told him what I thought and he said, "Well, you should write your own Sor Juana." And so I did.[35]

Zacarías's fictional version of Sor Juana portrays her as strong and beautiful, and explores how she chafed against being the "pretty damsel at court" and later struggled to continue her literary career while in the convent. Zacarías's Sor Juana is both sacred and secular, living in the present and the past, navigating a variety of cultural borders as she struggles to gain agency in colonial Mexico.

As in *Mariela in the Desert*, Zacarías also challenges Mexico's patriarchal history in this play. In her 1691 *Response*, Sor Juana writes to her critics and explains, "I entered the convent although I knew the situation had certain characteristics (I am speaking of secondary qualities, not formal ones) incompatible with my character, but considering the total antipathy I had toward matrimony, the convent was the least disproportionate and most honorable decision I could make to provide the certainty I desired for my salvation."[36] The lack of historical documentation surrounding Sor Juana's reasons for entering the convent opens a theatrical space to explore Sor Juana's legacy in colonial Mexico, an era that welcomes revision. Paz reflects: "Although we Mexicans are preoccupied, or more accurately, obsessed with our past, we lack a clear idea of who we have been. . . . Our history is a text in which some passages are written in black ink and others are in invisible ink. One of the periods that has been scribbled over and revised with greatest zeal is that of the viceroyalty of New Spain."[37] Zacarías makes visible this period in Mexican history through dramatizing Sor Juana's fight to retain her agency as a writer by confronting the powers of church and state.

Zacarías's play navigates temporal borders as it negotiates Sor Juana's sacred and secular lives. In the present, Sor Juana is being punished for challenging church leadership and for publishing secular and often physically descriptive poetry, which raises the ire of the Inquisition. In the past, Juana is a lady-in-waiting in the court of the Spanish viceroy and battling an arranged marriage proposal. One way that Zacarías navigates between present and past in the play is through the pivotal character of Xochitl, Sor Juana's Aztec servant at court. Xochitl begins the play by dragging a trunk on stage. Perhaps she is pulling historical baggage or the weight of Sor Juana's past. Next she recites a poem written by Sor Juana. She addresses the audience directly and then becomes a spirit guide through decades of Sor Juana's history. For Xochitl, boundaries between present and past are flexible. In the convent, she often hovers in the shadows out of sight. In the palace, she serves as Juana's confidante, encouraging her to write and serving as an intermediary amid the various factions at court. At one point, Xochitl admits to Juana, "My kind . . . can do anything."[38] That Zacarías chooses an Aztec woman for this role highlights the importance of an indigenous, female voice to recount Mexican history.

Xochitl recites Sor Juana's poems, which are Zacarías's translations and adaptations of the original texts. Zacarías's translation often more firmly establishes the female voice in Sor Juana's poetry. In the prologue, Xochitl recites Sor Juana's sonnet 149, which begins, "With all the hazards of the sea in mind / No one would dare embark / If in advance the dangers were foreseen / She would tread not in the dark."[39] This famous sonnet has been interpreted to reflect Sor Juana's decision to enter the order of the Discalced Carmelites. Latin American studies scholar George Anthony Thomas explains that convent life in seventeenth-century Mexico "meant that a nun would spend the remainder of her life within the cloister. . . . The famous sonnet seems to suggest that the rash decision to enter into the unknown . . . is just as heroic as the contemplative decision to knowingly embark on a lifelong spiritual journey."[40] Zacarías translates the Spanish word *riesgos* not as "risks," but as "hazards," implying that entering convent life contains a degree of danger. She also translates the word *embarcara* not as simply "would embark" but as "would dare

embark," which suggests that being a nun requires bravery. More significantly, she translates *nadie* not with its literal neutered pronoun "no one,"
but as the feminine pronoun "she," thus more fully reinterpreting this
poem as a reflection of a woman's journey.

Zacarías's translation emphasizes that if a woman is to live life fully,
she must exhibit courage. The poem ends with, "But if one chose brave
audacity / Despite the perils therein / And steered a blazing chariot /
To reach Apollo's breath / Then she would live life, its all / Not blandly
endure her days 'til death."[41] Zacarías foregrounds the cultural borders in
this play with an Aztec woman who recites Spanish poetry referencing a
Greek deity. The inclusion of the Greek god Apollo, the god of patriarchal law and moral order, moderation, balance, and form,[42] implies that if
a woman is to reach the highest level of moral order, she must experience
the entirety of her life, which stands in direct contrast to the religious
life, which renounces worldly existence. Thus, before the action of the
play starts, Zacarías presents the collisions of Aztec, Mexican, Spanish,
and Greek cultures through a female perspective. She issues an invitation
to challenge patriarchal structures through the supernatural, as Xochitl
becomes a spirit guide on the journey into Sor Juana's life.

In act 1, Sor Juana's writing scandalizes the church and incurs the
wrath of her confessor, Padre Núñez, the head of the Inquisition. Núñez
attempts to silence her life as a writer. As her books, pen, and paper are
removed from her convent room, Juana, bereft, cries out, "God, why instill
curiosity in women, and then punish them for having it?" She then prays
for the ability to accept her circumstances, "to submit to the authority of
the narrow mind," although she admits, "Lord, in all truth, I prefer this
prayer go unanswered."[43] As opposed to reciting an established Catholic
prayer such as the Our Father or Hail Mary, Juana beseeches God with
a petition she herself creates. At the conclusion of her prayer, deceased
people from Juana's past suddenly begin to emerge from various areas in
her room.

Natural and supernatural intersect as Xochitl suddenly enters Juana's
room from the storage chest. Juana pleads, "Pray for me, Xochitl. Because
I can no longer pray for myself." Xochitl replies, "Pray for you? All right.
In the name of the Father, Quetzalcoatl, and the Holy Spirits, Amen."
When Juana tries to correct her, Xochitl replies, "Fine. I know. I just
don't want to seem partial to anybody up there."[44] Xochitl prays to the

FIGURE 9. *The Sins of Sor Juana,* by Karen Zacarías, produced by the Goodman
Theatre, directed by Henry Godinez, in 2010. Xochitl (Laura Crotte) pleads with
Juana (Malaya Rivera Drew). Photo by Liz Lauren/Goodman Theatre.

Catholic male image of God, to the Aztec creator god, and to the spirits that encompass the Catholic Holy Spirit and the sacred gods of the
Aztec world. Xochitl devises her own petition, which includes an invoca-
tion of Quetzalcoatl, the Aztec plumed serpent god of the wind. Anthropologist Frances Berdan explains that this Aztec deity was "the provider
of human sustenance and patron of the fine arts . . . part creator, part
fertility granter, and part Venus."[45] Additionally, the Aztec deity invoked
is a bifurcation of two animals whose name is created from the Nahuatl
words *quetzal* (bird) and *coatl* (serpent). Xochitl's prayer crosses linguistic
borders between Nahuatl, the Aztec language, and Spanish, reflecting the
intercultural dynamic in Sor Juana's reality.

Xochitl's prayer also incorporates indigenous spirituality and Catholicism. Early Franciscan missionaries to Mexico viewed Aztec religion as
evil. However, the Jesuit order of priests in Mexico during the seventeenth

century preferred a syncretic approach whereby indigenous deities could exist alongside Christian ones. Paz writes: "The Franciscans wanted to put an end to the ancient religions, while the Jesuits wanted to utilize them. And in order to utilize these religions, they had to be stripped of the supernatural."[46] The Jesuits acknowledged Aztec deities as leaders but not spiritual entities. However, Xochitl refutes this by praying to Quetzalcoatl and the Christian paternal God. She resists domination by the Catholic Church and its Spanish language. She treats both deities as equally spiritually necessary. Zacarías here shows that Xochitl can seamlessly negotiate between contentious spiritual worlds.

Supernatural entrances continue when Vicereine, wife of the viceroy of New Spain and Juana's former patroness, enters from the closet. Soon, Vicereine and Xochitl remove Juana's veil to reveal long hair, which Juana says she had shorn. Juana is now transported to her youth when she was living in the court of the Spanish viceroy as a lady in waiting to Vicereine, who grew very close to Juana. That Vicereine enters "out of the closet" may suggest that she had romantic feelings for Juana. In a later scene, when Vicereine attempts to teach the young Juana about male affection, Zacarías's stage directions state that there is a sexual undercurrent between them. However, Zacarías's play does not further explore this dimension of their relationship.

Zacarías next illustrates Juana's ability to see the past and the present simultaneously. After Vicereine appears, Xochitl removes Juana's habit to reveal a colorful, beautiful, alluring gown. Juana looks at herself in the mirror and exclaims, "Look at me . . . Dios mío! It's me. And yet, it's not." Vicereine compliments her beauty, and Xochitl adds, "But underneath, there's a wily old spirit." Then Vicereine spins Juana around to celebrate this duality: "Juana is a wily old spirit! Juana is a wily old spirit! A wily old spirit that looks good in a dress."[47] Zacarías highlights Juana traversing the borders of present/past, natural/supernatural, and the intersections of Mexican/Spanish/Aztec worlds to chart her journey from lady at court to censored nun.

Sor Juana travels back to the present with a renewed awareness of the vow she took to continue to write. She is adamant that she will not compromise her freedom of expression. When the novice brings her paper and pen, she and Sor Filothea reveal Padre Núñez's caveat:

NOVICE: Padre Núñez, in his graciousness, gives you these gifts on the condition that—on your promise—you will write poems in honor of the Church.

FILOTHEA: You are always to share your writing with him. You are to write on subjects he deems appropriate for a woman and for a nun.

NOVICE: Your beautiful poems will honor God.[48]

Juana is then told she must destroy an embroidered verse she created: "What wild ambition drives us / To forget ourselves, our past?"[49] This poem angered Padre Núñez and contributed to his forbidding her to write. Juana rereads her verse, then takes a knife from the novice. Instead of destroying the cloth, Sor Juana cuts her own hand, declaring: "Tell Padre Núñez that I will never tear out these lines. Tell him that I will never be constrained by what he deems appropriate for a woman and for a nun to write."[50]

Zacarías stages the contrasts between Sor Juana's past life as a brilliant young woman of illegitimate birth living among nobility and her present life in the convent. The past world is secular, comical, romantic, and vibrant, while the present reality represented on stage is sacred, tragic, serious, and dire. Zacarías shows the Juana of the past as at risk of being ejected from the court in Mexico City due to her lack of noble lineage. When Vicereine offers to marry her to an older man, Fabio, she reluctantly agrees. Meanwhile, Viceroy is jealous of Juana's sway over his wife. He plots to undo the marriage plan by employing a young rogue, Silvio, who will supposedly dishonor Juana, thereby making her marriage to Fabio impossible. Silvio pretends he is a noble man who wants to publish Juana's poems. Juana soon falls in love with Silvio's intellect. Through a series of misadventures, Juana learns Silvio's true identity, that he is also an illegitimate child. The two plan to be together, until Silvio is killed in a duel. Throughout her entire journey, Juana's intelligence and gift as a writer set her apart and bring her opportunities as well as condemnation. Distraught over Silvio's death, Juana begins writing nonstop and soon agrees to enter the convent as long as she can continue studying and writing.

A sizeable portion of Zacarías's play centers on the secular realm of Juana's relationship with Silvio. Silvio intellectually challenges Juana as she articulates her literary and poetic passions. During their first meeting,

Zacarías additionally considers gender roles as Silvio, who has been hiding in her closet, enters to find an astonished Juana. She puts on Silvio's coat to hide herself (i.e., becoming a man), and she insists that he must be in her private room to borrow a dress, which he then puts on (i.e., becoming a woman).⁵¹ Juana states: "I'm impressed. A man that dares dress like a woman to meet a woman must be quite a man"; to which Silvio replies, "I hear you are quite a woman." After some flirtation, Silvio notices a copy of Cervantes's *Don Quixote* in Juana's room.

> SILVIO: Ah, the clever girl reads. Don Quixote . . . Cervantes . . . quite the master . . .
> *(JUANA looks at him dubiously.)*
> SILVIO: I know the book.
> JUANA: "From reading too much and sleeping too little . . ."
> SILVIO & JUANA: *(In unison.)* "His brain dried up and . . ."
> SILVIO: "He lost his wits."⁵²

Juana and Silvio are reciting lines from chapter 1 of *Don Quixote* where Cervantes describes his protagonist's altered state. The text continues (in Edith Grossman's translation): "he became so convinced in his imagination of the truth of all the countless grandiloquent and false inventions he read that for him no history in the world was truer."⁵³ He becomes obsessed with celebrated knights from France, England, and Spain before he decides to become a knight named Don Quixote de la Mancha. Zacarías complicates gender and cultural borders when this Mexican mestiza young woman dressed as a man and a Spanish young man dressed as a woman recite the lines of a Spanish author whose protagonist's picaresque and fantastical journeys are inspired by reading tales of European knights.

Zacarías leaves Juana in a liminal state between past and present, freedom and censorship, life and death, Old World Spain and the Inquisition and colonial Mexico. In her convent room again, Juana is despondent over being censored and vows never to write again. The figures from her past, Silvio, Vicereine, Viceroy, Pedro, and Xochitl, appear in shadows around her as she rails against them: "I will not speak to you anymore. You are all dead. You are all gone."⁵⁴ All but Silvio retreat. They gaze at each other; he kisses her palm and exits. Sor Juana then asks Xochitl to depart, but the Aztec servant replies, "I will never leave you."[55] Juana's ability to experience the past and present simultaneously strengthens her resolve not to compromise her freedom of expression. She ends the play pushing pen and paper off her desk and waiting with her trusted Xochitl. Navigating these temporal and cultural borders protects Sor Juana from succumbing to the demands of the Inquisition with the hope that her writing will continue.

Zacarías chooses to end her play with a defiant poem that celebrates Sor Juana's resilience in the face of censorship. Xochitl recites:

Come Angels!
View this Wonder
A cut Rose
Lives even longer
She does not wither
But quietly revives
Despite a cruel death
Her aroma survives
There is profit
In cutting her down .
Come Gardeners!
Look and see
A cut Rose
Lives an eternity.[56]

This selection is from Sor Juana's poem 316, a *villancico*, or lyric poem, part of a cycle of poems that Sor Juana dedicated to Saint Catherine of Alexandria, Egypt, which were sung in the cathedral of Oaxaca in 1691.[57] Sor Juana wrote this poem in the year that she was censored by the church, four years before her death. Paz writes: "Catherine was one of [Sor Juana's] symbolic doubles. . . . Catherine, noble virgin of Alexandria, combined the liberal arts with the ardor of her faith, and at the age of eighteen, surpassed most learned males. Maximus, who persecuted all things Christian, convoked the greatest philosophers from far and wide to confound her but she . . . conquered and converted them."[58] When she persuaded the Empress to become a Christian, Catherine was tortured on the wheel, and decapitated.[59] The rose (i.e., Saint Catherine and Sor

Juana) has been cut down (i.e., martyred or censored), but it will continue to live (i.e., via the printed word).

Zacarías's translation emphasizes the remarkable and perhaps supernatural qualities of this rose when she translates the Spanish phrase "*venid a mirar*" (literally, "come and see") as "view this wonder." She continues to highlight the perseverance of this rose when she translates "*porque se fecunda con su propio humor*" (literally, "fertilized by her own humor") as "Her aroma survives." She finishes the poem by translating the Spanish phrase "*una Rosa que vive cortada, más!*" (literally, "a cut rose that lives more") as "A cut Rose / Lives an eternity!" emphasizing Sor Juana's eternal legacy for future generations.

Zacarías closes the play by traversing various cultural borders. Xochitl, whose name in Nahuatl means "flower," is also the "spiritual rose" who has guided the audience on this journey. Therefore, the central image in the Spanish poem is reflected through the Aztec name of the poem's orator. As the play concludes, Zacarías continues to communicate a multilayered reality that incorporates Latin American and African cultures as well as indigenous and Catholic spiritualities as an Aztec woman recites a poem by a Mexican nun about a female Egyptian saint.

Finally, Zacarías navigates borders between performer and performance through the doubling of roles. The actors who play characters surrounding Sor Juana in the convent also play the people of her past life at court. Sor Filothea, the Mexican mother superior who tries to silence Sor Juana, morphs into Xochitl, her Aztec servant, who attempts to help Juana to survive. Sor Sara, a fellow Mexican nun jealous of Sor Juana, changes into Spanish Vicereine, Juana's devoted patroness. Padre Núñez, Sor Juana's confessor and ultimately the one who censors her, becomes Viceroy, who plots Juana's expulsion from the court. Thus the actors inhabit Mexican, Aztec, and Spanish worlds.

The doubling of roles can raise awareness about the relationship between past and present characters. Performance studies scholar Marvin Carlson refers to the "ghosting" that takes place when one actor plays multiple roles over time so that the spirit of past roles infuses the present role the audience is experiencing. Carlson calls this the "recycled body and persona of the actor."[60] There is also a condensed version of this ghosting within a production when an actor plays multiple roles during the course of a single performance of one play. The audience sees the same actor yet witnesses a character transformation layered with aspects of the previous roles.

The "ghost" of the past role hovers over the reception of the current role the actor performs. When Xochitl's Aztec prayer comforts Juana, the spirit of the Catholic mother superior scolding Sor Juana remains. When Spanish Vicereine embraces Juana, the echo of Mexican Sor Sara rejecting Sor Juana reverberates. Finally, in the last scene, "Filothea pulls off her habit and become Xochitl on stage."[61] Zacarías states that this double casting of roles is for "connection between behavior in the Church and the Court."[62] The ways in which both institutions helped and hindered Sor Juana become more apparent through this casting method. Through this "ghosting," Zacarías also reinforces the complexity of the Latin@ body, which traverses many spiritual and cultural borders.

NAVIGATING MULTIPLE BORDERS

Zacarías presents Mexico as a site for navigating multiple borders and not solely as a space for migration northward. Some Latin@ playwrights write about Mexico as the start of a journey to the United States in search of improved economic opportunities. Zacarías celebrates the historical and cultural wealth of her birth country. She emphasizes the complex nature of Mexican culture, where Aztec, Spanish, Mexican, and U.S. realities continually intersect. As in Svich's *Tropic of X*, Zacarías explores the plight of Latin Americans who desire to express themselves freely. However, unlike Mori and Maura, who are silenced in a monolithic, dictatorial state, Zacarías's Mariela and Sor Juana gain agency in a heterogeneous Mexico and begin to reclaim their own voices.

Zacarías also considers the woman as creator (painter and writer) in these plays and the boundaries between a creator and her creation. Mariela, the painter, must revive her connection to creating art by coming to terms with the pain associated with the legacy of *The Blue Barn*. In the end, Mariela chooses to paint again but only after her patriarchal husband has died. Sor Juana, the writer, must contend with the threats to her writing from the Inquisition. At the close of the play, Sor Juana vows never to write again in the face of continuing obstruction from the Church. Both women approach and traverse artistic, cultural, and temporal borders as they attempt to restore the integrity of their creativity. While Mariela regains her artistry, Sor Juana does not. Despite the three centuries between these two time periods, Zacarías highlights the ongoing struggle of women to gain artistic agency in the face of fierce opposition.

Zacarías's portrayal of a painter is connected to Fornes's visual arts influence. In *The Blue Barn*, Mariela does not paint in the social realist style of the Mexican muralists, but creates an abstract expressionistic piece echoing the work of Hans Hofmann (1880–1966), Fornes's teacher. Hofmann had a close connection with Jackson Pollock, whose work Mariela praises. Lee Krasner, Pollock's wife, studied with Hofmann and wanted him to see Pollock's early works. Toynton describes their historic meeting:

> Hofmann looked at Pollock's paintings and, with what may have been a trace of condescension, expressed concern that their subject matter seemed to come entirely from within. Sooner or later, he said, that source would be exhausted, and Pollock would have to venture outside himself for inspiration. "Look at nature," Hofmann advised the younger painter. "I *am* nature," Pollock told him.[63]

This conversation emphasizes the importance of nature, whether internal or external, as a source of inspiration. Mariela is inspired by the desert. Fornes is inspired by internal landscapes and external nature. This echo of Fornes's artistic legacy in Zacarías's play speaks to the significant influence of the abstract expressionist movement on both playwrights.

Whereas many of the leading practitioners of abstract expressionism are male, in *Mariela in the Desert* Zacarías presents a painting in this style by a woman. The term "abstract expressionism" was first coined by *New Yorker* art critic Robert Coates when reviewing an exhibit of Hofmann's work in 1946. Coates writes: "[Hofmann] is certainly one of the most uncompromising representatives of what some people call the 'spatter and daub' school of painting and I have more politely christened abstract Expressionism." Coates praises Hofmann as someone who "thoroughly understands the emotional connotations of color."[64] Abstract expressionism has been further defined as "a tendency among New York painters of the late 1940s and '50s, all of whom were committed to an expressive art of profound emotion and universal themes. The movement embraced the gestural abstraction of Willem de Kooning and Jackson Pollock, and the color field painting of Mark Rothko and others. It blended elements of Surrealism and abstract art in an effort to create a new style fitted to the postwar mood of anxiety and trauma."[65] For *The Blue Barn*, Mariela abstracted her son into a green boy and her daughter into an orange bird. As she crosses the border from blank canvas to artistic creation at the end of the play, Mariela sweeps her brush, and "blue paint, like water, streaks the entire stage."[66] Although it is not clear what form Mariela's new painting will take, Zacarías abstracts and augments Mariela's final gesture to underscore the totality of her newfound artistic identity.

Sor Juana traverses cultural worlds as she contends with the boundaries between her creativity and the Catholic Church. She integrates Aztec, Spanish, and Mexican cultures in her poetry while she grapples with freedom of expression. She negotiates present and past as she tries to make sense of her thirst for artistic fulfillment in the harsh light of the Inquisition. Zacarías further complicates Sor Juana's journey with the recitation of her poetry through the character of Xochitl, an Aztec woman. The mediation of the indigenous poetic delivery emphasizes the layers of cultural complexity in Sor Juana's Mexico. Ultimately, Sor Juana does not reconnect with her writing and remains on the precipice between present and future, when subsequent generations of women will be inspired by her writing.

In these plays, Zacarías navigates cultural, spiritual, temporal, linguistic, and artistic borders. She provides multifaceted ways of seeing Mexico's visual arts and literary legacies. Through the life of an unknown fictional female artist and a historically celebrated writer and nun, Zacarías demonstrates the complex journey of empowerment for Latina voices. Finally, her plays may teach audiences to momentarily view their own multiple border crossings, and those they see on stage, as existing in similar albeit distinct spaces, thus offering a more complex vision and understanding of the Latina experience.

4

ELAINE ROMERO

Viewing Latin@ Realism

MANY LATINA PLAYWRIGHTS incorporate supernatural interventions into their plays that encompass multiple cultures, contest received notions of magic realism, and redefine how the spirit world can be dramatized. In their works, these writers create sacred space and stage rituals, which generate *facultad*, a supernatural way of seeing for their characters and audiences. Elaine Romero, a Mexican American playwright of Spanish heritage, constructs theatrical worlds where her characters seamlessly negotiate the intersections of the natural and supernatural realms.

The Fornes frame can be thought of as a pair of glasses, which connects to the notion of altering sight and in this chapter relates to an alternative vision of realism in Latina theatre. The term "magic realism" has often been used to describe certain Latin@ plays. Literature scholar Maggie Anne Bowers explains that the term "magic realism" was first coined to describe a narrative mode that offers "alternative approaches to reality to that of Western philosophy, expressed in many postcolonial and non-Western works of contemporary fiction by, most famously, writers such as Colombian Nobel laureate Gabriel García Márquez."[1] Bowers's remarks apply to Latin@ theatre, where "magic realism" has been used to describe the depiction of reality expanding past the natural to include the supernatural.

Latina playwrights create worlds on stage that provide alternate views of reality. Latin@ theatre studies scholar Jon Rossini posits that this occurs when "everything is happening within the same event horizon; there is no gap between what might be labeled real and what might be labeled magic."[2] Similarly, Romero's plays embrace the notion that everyday reality exists with no gaps between multiple dimensions. Romero asserts: "The reflection of the idea that concomitant realms might exist, such as this life and the next, and the belief that we might move freely between them, can be found deeply in the Mexican psyche, for example. Such a thought is not inherently supernatural; it just *is*. It is the natural order of things. It is an ordinary experience, not an extraordinary one."[3] Romero contends that the border between the natural and the supernatural worlds is porous in ordinary reality. The realism Romero creates in her plays therefore differs from Western theatrical notions of realism.

Some of the earliest references to Western theatrical realism point to the plays of Henrik Ibsen. Theatre critic Richard Gilman explains: "Ibsen's realism is in the first place a matter of having chosen paradigmatic situations from the life of contemporary society. . . . Ibsen made his social plays out of nothing other than what might have occurred in what we call real life."[4] Romero's realism is also drawn from "real life," but one that is based in a distinctly Mexican and Latin@ context. Romero states: "We are not really writing magical realism. People say we do. People who review us say that we do. They think we have been at home poring over García Márquez. But that is not really the case. For us, there is no separation between this realm and the next. For us, it is all just realism. Latin@ realism."[5] Therefore, I will use the term "Latin@ realism," for this distinguishes Romero's plays, and those of other Latin@ playwrights, from Ibsenian realism. While playwrights of many backgrounds employ non-Ibsenian realism in their plays, I utilize the term "Latin@ realism" for this study, which focuses on considering realism in Latin@ theatre. Latin@ realism complicates other forms of realism by presenting a seamless coexistence of the supernatural and natural worlds in a theatrical setting. Latin@ realism generates fluidity of time, creates sacred space, evokes ritual, generates *facultad*, and provides continual intersections between the physical and spiritual planes. Latin@ realism not only transforms characters' daily lives, but also redefines what a Latin@ play can be.

Romero's characters move freely between natural and supernatural realities and navigate numerous spiritual traditions, including *curanderismo*, Aztec spirituality, Judaism, and Catholicism. In Romero's

FIGURE 10. Elaine Romero teaches her class at the University of Arizona's School of Film, Theatre, and Television in 2014. Photo by Beatriz Verdugo, UA News.

¡Curanderas! Serpents of the Clouds, Paloma, a *curandera* (i.e., healer), and Victoria, a Western doctor, perform *curanderismo* rituals and also mystically travel to Mictlan, the Aztec land of the dead. In *Secret Things*, Delia, a journalist, enters Sephardia, a liminal spirit-world reality, where she encounters the truth about her Jewish heritage. Romero generates multi-dimensional theatrical landscapes through creating liminal sacred spaces where her Latina characters engage in rituals that lead to greater levels of *facultad*, awareness, and transformation.

¡CURANDERAS! SERPENTS OF THE CLOUDS: LATINAS PRACTICE *CURANDERISMO*

In *¡Curanderas! Serpents of the Clouds*, Romero charts the journey of two Mexican American women as they travel from the United States to Mexico. Paloma, a *curandera* (a healer, from the Spanish verb *curar*, which means to heal), practices and puts her faith in the power of *curanderismo*. Victoria, a recent graduate of medical school, firmly believes in the tenets of Western medicine. On this trip to Mexico, Paloma tries to escape the pain of abandoning her husband and four-year-old son, resulting from her husband's infidelity, while Victoria tries to evade the pain caused by the death of her fiancé. Romero presents audiences with a Latin@ realism that traverses Mexican, American, Mexican American, and Aztec cultures as both women transform by engagement with the supernatural through *curandera* rituals.

Each woman's connection to her cultural heritage informs her process of healing throughout the play. Romero describes Paloma as Chicana and Victoria as a *pocha*. Anzaldúa explains a *pocha/o* as "an Anglicized Mexican or American of Mexican origin who speaks Spanish with an accent characteristic of a North American and who distorts and reconstructs the language according to the influence of English."[6] She relates the accusations made toward her when Latin@s heard her speaking English. "*Pocho*, cultural traitor, you're speaking the oppressor's language by speaking English, you're ruining the Spanish language."[7] Romero further complicates the term *pocha* through Victoria, a Chicana in her twenties, who does not speak Spanish at all and is disconnected from her cultural heritage. Paloma fully engages with her Mexican and American cultures, is bilingual, and yet begins the play separated from her true identity as a *curandera* due to her personal crisis. Through the women's growing friendship and supernatural interventions facilitated by an Aztec spiritual guide, Romero positions their cultural identities through spirit-world experiences, which are significant factors in the women's transformation.

The spirit world in Romero's play is not a single experience, but one that is based in multiplicity, mobility, and flexibility. Characters move freely between physical and spiritual realms whose borders become flexible and porous. This spirit world includes travel to the Aztec land of the dead, engaging with a spiritual guide, placing a spiritual phone call, and communicating with both the living and the deceased across spiritual lines. Navigation in this spirit world occurs through the establishment of sacred space and ritual.

Romero aims to create *curanderismo* rituals that address maladies of the body, mind, and spirit. When performed on the stage, these rituals not only allow the audience to view a sacred moment, but also provide a

window into *curanderismo,* "a set of folk medical beliefs, rituals, and practices that seem to address the psychological, spiritual, and social needs
of traditional people."[8] In this tradition, desired healing results from the
melding of disparate spiritual practices. *Curandera* and integrative medicine practitioner Elena Avila explains: "*Curanderismo* does not separate
soul and spirit from the body. . . . A modern medical doctor must go
through a procedural manual, but *curanderismo* uses whatever works:
herbs, counseling, soul retrieval, psychodrama, rituals, spiritual cleansings,
and yes, referrals to medical doctors."[9] *Curanderismo* also results from the
intersection of disparate cultural worlds. Medical writer Bobbette Perrone emphasizes that *curanderismo* "engages transculturally with African
medical practices brought to the Americas through slavery from the sixteenth to nineteenth centuries, through Spanish medical practices incorporating Greek, Roman, and Arabic medicine brought to the Americas
in the sixteenth century through the conquest, and Indigenous medical
practices from Aztec and Mayan cultures, among others, as it diagnoses
the body, heart, and soul of a patient."[10] Thus, Paloma's rituals traverse
diverse traditions and cultures as she aims to heal Victoria and herself.

Romero generated these theatrical rituals based on extensive research.
Of writing the play, Romero says: "I actually spent time interviewing
curandero/as. . . . There was a woman in Tucson, a Mexican American
who studied with shamans in Mexico. . . . Our interview had the big-
gest impact on the play, though I also visited a Yaqui shaman. . . . Later,
I read *Woman Who Glows in the Dark* [by Elena Avila] and a book on
a famous *curandera* from Texas."[11] The rituals in her play include *soba*
(healing through massage), *susto* (diagnosing soul loss), *facultad* (experiencing supernatural sight), and *limpia* (spiritual cleansing.) In her stage
directions, Romero calls these rituals "healing moments."[12] She does not
indicate how to stage these healing moments, thus leaving it to a director
to present what reads as "healing." That the playwright herself chooses to
describe these moments as "healing" and not "magical" indicates that she
trusts the reader of her script to see these curative moments as including
natural and supernatural attributes.

Paloma first creates sacred space when she supernaturally tends to
Victoria on the train to Mexico City where they first meet. Victoria
hurts her finger lifting her heavy suitcase. "Paloma quickly grabs Victoria's finger and does a quick little *soba*—massage to heal the finger. It is

a healing moment. Victoria looks at her finger, surprised and relieved." After Paloma heals Victoria's bruised finger, Victoria asks, "What'd you do? (Denying the healing) It must not have been that bad."[13] Paloma is quickly massaging Victoria's finger but also intuitively addressing her spiritual health. Avila explains that "in the hands of a curandero who understands the emotional and intuitive aspects of massage, it can become a tool for further opening into the psyche."[14] Again, Romero uses the term "healing" to address the physical and spiritual parameters of these rituals.

The next ritual addresses the body and the spirit while initiating sacred space as Paloma divines that Victoria has experienced *susto*. Paloma explains: "It's when something so upsetting happens to a person that their soul leaves their body. It can even lead to death."[15] Victoria, however, does not believe this and, further, lies about the fact that her fiancé has died: "The pyramids. He wanted to see them. . . . Oh my boyfriend. I mean, my fiancé. He wanted to come but . . . Yeah, he was working."[16] Avila writes: "*Curanderismo* teaches us that humans are physical, emotional, mental, and spiritual beings. . . . If we experience a frightening or traumatic event, this can result in soul loss (i.e., *susto*), a state in which we do not feel fully present or as if we are fully ourselves."[17] In this moment, Paloma accesses the supernatural realm. She discerns that Victoria has experienced a trauma. Yet Victoria evades the truth of her past. Throughout the play, Paloma practices *curanderismo* while Victoria represents a Western medical viewpoint that dismisses healing via the spirit world.

Another ritual occurs when Paloma helps Victoria by using a type of quick *soba* that connects the physical to the spiritual. Victoria tells Paloma a story of how she met her fiancé. She becomes very sad, though she still does not tell the truth about his death. Paloma consoles Victoria by patting her on the back. Romero describes it as a "healing moment, something transpires between them even against Paloma's will. Victoria senses something." As Victoria questions Paloma, she feels her heart opening: "Ouch, my heart. Why'd you have to do that? It's making me want to cry." Paloma realizes this is preparing Victoria to delve more deeply into the death of her fiancé. She counsels, "Be strong, mija. You must look into the past and not be afraid."[18] This ritual opens up sacred space where temporal borders become porous, much as in Zacarías's Sor Juana world. Victoria is suddenly transported to the past. She relives the moment when her fiancé prepares to leave on a trip to Mexico without her and challenges her, "How can you make people better if you don't feel their pain?"[19] In this sacred space accessed through ritual, Victoria begins to confront the truth about her complicated relationship with her fiancé as she starts to heal.

Romero also demonstrates additional facets of Latin@ realism through an "Aztec Woman," Paloma's spiritual guide, who "appears in full Aztec regalia."[20] Like Zacarías's Xochitl, the Aztec woman traverses spiritual borders to guide Paloma and Victoria on their journey of healing. The Aztec woman generates sacred space when she appears in various guises: as a train announcer, a hotel clerk, a tour guide, and a dream woman. When Paloma and Victoria visit the National Museum of Anthropology in Mexico City, guided by the Aztec woman, they view an engraved image of Coatlicue, the Aztec serpent earth goddess who conceived all celestial beings out of her cavernous womb.[21] They also examine the Codex Boturini, an ancient scroll depicting the journey of the Aztec to

FIGURE 11. *¡Curanderas! Serpents of the Clouds*, by Elaine Romero, produced by Kitchen Dog Theatre, directed by Christopher Carlos, in 2003. Paloma (Christie Vela) confronts Victoria (Stephanie Ybarra) as the Aztec Woman (Rhonda Boutté) observes. Photo © Linda Blasé, 2003. All rights reserved.

the founding of their capital, Tenochtitlan. While Paloma contemplates the ancient image of a broken tree, the Aztec woman/tour guide questions her: "Think about it, Paloma. How did your tree break? There's a reason to mourn the death of a brave and aged tree. (Beat) You know these things. I've taught them to you."[22] The tree becomes a metaphor for both Paloma's life and her broken relationship with her husband. The Codex Boturini additionally serves as a catalyst to enter sacred space. Mexican historian Federico Navarrete explains that this codex deals with Aztec migration: "In this beautiful sixteenth-century pictorial history, the distance between Aztlán and Mexico is marked by two different lines. The first is a row of footprints representing the path followed by the Mexica [Aztec] in their migration; the second is a continuous line that unites the rectangular year signs that represent the time elapsed during the migration."[23] Thus, this ancient document echoes the spiritual migration of these women.

In the supernatural realm, both women must face the truth about their pasts with the men in their lives in order to continue the healing process. Immediately following their engagement with the Codex Boturini, the Aztec woman as "guide" generates sacred space where both women face complicated relationships with their male significant others. Paloma confronts her husband about his infidelity in "a vision where their spirits speak to each other across time."[24] Paloma also reveals that her marriage is shattered. Next, Victoria speaks to her dead fiancé, Jesús, another "vision which spans across worlds, linking the spiritual world and the physical world,"[25] as they argue over the fact that Victoria lived her life in books while he tried to effect social change as a photojournalist in Mexico. Victoria then acknowledges that her fiancé died of lung cancer. Interestingly, Romero names Victoria's fiancé Jesús but does not give Paloma's husband a name. Victoria's Western world is therefore connected to the central figure in Christianity whereas Paloma's *curandera* world is connected to an anonymous universal masculinity. Romero may be underscoring that Paloma's *curanderismo* embraces a wider spiritual reality than Christianity.

Throughout the play, Paloma exhibits her *facultad*. During their trip to the beach in Acapulco, Victoria also begins to access supernatural sight when she peers into the inner life of a young girl on the beach. Romero states, "Victoria wears a pained expression. It is a healing moment," but Victoria does not yet believe in her supernatural sight.

VICTORIA: (to herself) Oh, little girl, your parents don't love each other anymore.

PALOMA: (Beat) You saw inside her.

VICTORIA: I don't believe in all that.

Paloma tries to convince Victoria that she has a gift of *facultad*, but that acceptance does not come easily to this Western doctor.

PALOMA: You looked inside that child and you saw the future of her heart.

VICTORIA: No.

PALOMA: You have the gift.

VICTORIA: The gift?

PALOMA: You know it's true.

VICTORIA: I don't know about that, but a spirit spoke to me. Yesterday. If I'll only let myself believe it.

PALOMA: It's your journey. I feel it.[26]

That Victoria experiences *facultad* in Acapulco, a traditional tourist destination, may speak to the fact that, at this point, she still feels like a foreigner in Mexico and its tradition of *curanderismo*. However, this moment of consciousness is a turning point in Victoria's journey toward accessing her *curanderismo* abilities.

Throughout the rest of the play, Victoria begins to help heal Paloma. After this ritual of *facultad*, Paloma and Victoria start to discuss Paloma's broken relationship with her husband. During the conversation, the Aztec Woman enters, though Victoria does not see her. Soon the Aztec woman empowers Paloma to make a spiritual phone call, about which Romero says, "on some level, Paloma has reached her husband's soul."[27] Paloma attempts to speak to her husband but cannot. Then, the Aztec Woman takes her hand, Paloma takes Victoria's hand, and all are transported to the spirit world as act 1 comes to a close. Romero here commences to explore another facet of Latin@ realism, when Paloma and Victoria leave the natural realm entirely to be submerged in the supernatural.

At the start of act 2, Romero's characters spiritually descend to the depths of death and darkness. Paloma and Victoria travel to the "bellybutton of the moon," or Mictlan, the Aztec "realm of the ancient dead."[28]

Mictlan here represents a sacred space where the women communicate with the dead, literally (a dead fiancé) and figuratively (a lifeless marriage). Religion historian David Carrasco describes Mictlan as "the ninth level of the underworld where people who died ordinary death resided.[29] . . . The nine levels served as way stations for the souls of the dead as they passed slowly toward the bottom rung, named 'The Place Where Smoke Has No Outlet.'"[30] In Mictlan, Victoria learns from her dead fiancé, Jesús, "You're closer to death than you think."[31] Paloma discovers that her husband regrets his infidelity. Although he pleads for her to return home, Paloma does not accept his apologies. Instead, she says, "I'm sorry . . . I have to—I have to go."[32] Both women must engage with the literal and figurative deaths of their respective relationships in order to continue their journey of transformation.

The climax of the play demonstrates the power of the *curanderismo* ritual to heal and resurrect. When Paloma enters their hotel room, she finds Victoria on the floor, appearing to be dead. Romero then describes Paloma and the Aztec Woman's soul retrieval through a *limpia* (i.e., a spiritual cleansing, from the Spanish verb *limpiar*, meaning to clean):

(She hurriedly moves Victoria's limp arms until they make a cross in an outstretched position and begins her healing work. She fluffs the sheet into the air and lays it down on Victoria's body, covering her completely. Paloma burns copal and herbs. Paloma sweeps Victoria, in the sign of a cross, using a large navel orange. As she sweeps, she recites her version of the Apostles' Creed.)

PALOMA: Creo en Dios, Padre Todopoderoso. I believe in God, the Father Almighty, Creator of heaven and earth.

WOMAN: We believe in the gods, the fathers and the mothers, the creators of the heavens and of the earth, of the rivers that run until they spill into the sea.

PALOMA: And the trees that live for hundreds of years and reach their arms up through the clouds, of the oceans that flow from the sun on to the beach to touch our feet, of all these things that have no end. We ask that you see our daughter, Victoria. We ask that you return her soul to her body, so she may stay here on earth.

WOMAN: (Simultaneously) That you return her soul to her body, so she may stay here on earth.

PALOMA: Amén.
WOMAN: Amén.
(Woman lays her hand on Paloma. A transfer of power. Woman exits. A beat.)[33]

The *limpia* administered by Paloma and the Aztec Woman involves elements of nature: copal (incense), herbs, and an orange; a religious gesture of the Christian sign of the cross, which signifies a blessing of the Holy Trinity: Father, Son, and Holy Spirit; and a prayer containing both Catholic and indigenous spirituality, much like the ritual prayers created by Xochitl in Zacarias's *The Sins of Sor Juana*. Paloma deploys her powers of *curanderismo* to then perform a soul retrieval that resurrects Victoria's body. Avila describes that soul retrieval as "literally a re-membering of ourselves."[34] Victoria dramatically revives and immediately connects to her heritage, as she suddenly becomes bilingual, speaking Spanish and then translating herself: "*Aqui vengo. Mi alma ha regresado a la tierra.* (beat; excited) I spoke Spanish. (Short beat) I'm here. My soul came back to earth." Paloma replies: "You are going to become a serpent. And you will slither through the clouds."[35] Paloma refers to the title of the play, *Serpents of the Clouds*, which Romero explains is the Aztec Nahuatl term for healers.[36] In staging this ritual, Romero complicates many dualities: natural/supernatural, Latin@/Aztec, Catholic/*curanderismo*, English/Nahuatl, serpents (i.e., earth)/clouds (i.e., sky). Romero emphasizes how all these cultural and spiritual elements must coexist for Latin@s to transform.

Paloma and Victoria ultimately utilize their *facultad* to fully inhabit their identities as *curanderas*. When they first meet on the train, Paloma "looks Victoria straight in the eye as if she is peering into her,"[37] as she begins to diagnose Victoria. Paloma tries to encourage Victoria to access her own *facultad*, intuiting that this can lead to ritual and the power of healing; however, Victoria is unwilling to accept this part of herself. Paloma's *facultad* also includes communicating with the spirit world, such as by conferring with the Aztec woman, whom Victoria does not see. By the end of the play, Victoria fully embraces her supernatural sight, which involves relinquishing her past ways of seeing. Romero writes: "Victoria can clearly see into the spiritual realm."[38] Both women are thus able to reconcile their pasts and presents and remain connected to each other. Their mutual connection is curative, as Romero explains: "I thought about these two women meeting on their journeys. I imagined they were both healers of a different order and that they would somehow help heal each other."[39] As Paloma and Victoria traverse borders between the United States and Mexico, between *curanderismo* and Western medicine, their engagement with disparate traditions mirrors their negotiation of the natural and supernatural worlds, which leads to their transformation.

As in Zacarias's *The Sins of Sor Juana*, Romero employs another level of *facultad* through the doubling of roles played by one actor. Through this "ghosting," Romero provides a supernatural view of the multiplicity of roles Latin@s might negotiate as they try to navigate the relationships in their lives. First, the Aztec Woman appears in various guises throughout the play. When she helps these women as the hotel clerk, the audience can see the reverberation of her role as spiritual guide. This ghosting may relate to the notion that healers from the spirit world can also inhabit the ordinary world. When in the guise of the museum tour guide, the Aztec Woman presents the Codex Boturini. The audience views her spirit world identity before she transforms back into the Aztec Woman, who leads Paloma and Victoria to Mictlan. In the Aztec Woman, Romero affirms that these spiritual and cultural realms intersect and coexist.

"Ghosting" additionally occurs when Romero creates the role of Man, who is both Paloma's living husband and Jesús, Victoria's deceased fiancé. The male actor who embodies this part traverses life and death in the supernatural realm. The name of the role suggests an iconic masculinity in Latin@ culture. Here the male portrayal toggles between an unfaithful husband and a social activist fiancé. This movement only occurs in the spirit world where the women connect with them. For example, in Mictlan, first the Man enters as Jesús and informs Victoria that her soul is in peril. Victoria reacts with, "What kind of nightmare is this? My soul's not with the ancient dead," and the Man replies, "It left your body in grief. You cried it through your tears, and then it found its way to me."[40] Jesús tries to tell Victoria to release him, but she cannot. He warns her that holding onto her grief could be fatal. Next the Man transforms into Paloma's husband. Paloma confronts him about his infidelity. He tries to explain how unhappy he had been in their marriage because of Paloma's tending to everyone but her own family. He confesses, "And here I am, broken inside, and you won't heal me." She responds, "Is that my job? To be your nurse? To take care of you?" To which he replies, "You're right. It's not your job. It's my job."[41] Here the Man is trying to coax Paloma into letting go of her anger, yet she will not.

Romero's construction of the character of the Man challenges stereotypical views of Latino masculinity. The audience sees the same actor playing both male significant others in these women's lives. So Jesús's death hovers around Paloma's husband, while his infidelities reverberate in Jesús. The men here exist only in the spirit world, where they attempt to heal their loved ones and confess to their wrongdoings. By staging them in the supernatural realm, Romero also implies that this behavior from these men—this attempted healing and confessing—would be more challenging or impossible in the natural world.

Romero suggests that ultimately while Latin@s must negotiate spiritual and cultural borders, Mexican culture may provide a more ample gateway to the spirit world. While the play is set entirely in Mexico, both women are U.S. citizens. However, they interact with their American culture only in the sacred space when they communicate with the men in their American lives. Although both men are of Mexican descent, they too exist between cultural worlds as Mexican Americans. How these women will negotiate their *curandera* identities when they return to the United States is perhaps another play. Romero creates the expectation that through renewed *facultad* these women will be able to more easily traverse the physical or spiritual borders in their own lives.

Romero also addresses cultural and spiritual intersections on another level, that of writing the play itself. The root of the play comes from found material: the Codex Boturini, which has its own image of a tree. Romero was originally commissioned by the Guadalupe Cultural Arts Center in San Antonio, Texas, where she collaborated with Latin@ and Mexican theatre artists in the creation of the play. Working with a Mexican choreographer, Mexican director, and a Latina composer, Romero began to brainstorm ideas. The choreographer brought a copy of the Codex Boturini to their meeting, and Romero, who had an interest in exploring *curanderas*, found her play. Romero recounts:

> I looked down at the scroll again. I saw a tree that had been cut through the middle. It had living hands and feet. I remember thinking that the tree looked dead, but it was really alive. I asked myself what might seem dead but really still be alive, and I thought of a long marriage. Suddenly, I knew

who had been in the marriage, Paloma and Husband. Then, I saw a little figure perched on top of a rock, crying from a deep place within. It was like the person's soul was pouring out of his or her eyes. I asked myself what could happen to a person to make them mourn from so deep a place, and I thought of Victoria. I imagined she was someone who had never suffered before, who was so used to success she didn't know how to deal with her loss.[42]

Romero's play emerged from considering an ancient Aztec text through her work with a diverse group of Latin@ and Mexican theatre artists. This international collaboration contributes to a theatrical encounter with *curanderismo* where Romero's audiences can view Latin@ reality through a multifaceted engagement with the supernatural.

SECRET THINGS: LATINA JOURNALIST UNCOVERS CRYPTO-JUDAISM

In *Secret Things*, Romero presents Delia, a Latina journalist who discovers and questions her Sephardic Jewish heritage while investigating a news story on crypto-Jews in New Mexico. "Crypto-Jews" is a term that describes Jews who fled the Spanish and Mexican Inquisitions starting in the fifteenth century and who secretly practiced their religion after officially converting to Christianity.[43] In Romero's play, the crypto-Jews are those who fled the arrival of the Inquisition in Mexico in the sixteenth century and moved to northern Mexico, which is now Arizona, Colorado, New Mexico, and Texas.[44] Crypto-Judaism is the result of the same Mexican Inquisition that censored Zacarías's Sor Juana. To engage with this historical global migration, Romero devises supernatural interventions in a sacred space called Sephardia as Delia connects to Judaism.

Romero describes Sephardia as "that mystical location where New Mexico, Texas and California meet,"[45] "an alternate reality."[46] Notably, here Romero uses the word "alternate" to describe this reality, and not the word "magical." "Alternate" connotes a coexistence between both realms, where one can exist in the "primary" or "alternate" reality. This definition fully embraces the heterogeneity and complexity of this spirit world space, which "encompasses dream, the subconscious, the Realm of

Almost Right, a black hole, the Tree of Life and the astral plane."[47] Like Mictlan in *Curanderas*, this sacred space is a place where Delia connects with significant people in her life.

The name Sephardia correlates to Sephardic Judaism. In 1492, the Catholic Monarchs, Ferdinand and Isabella, expelled the Jews from Spain for a variety of motives, including a desire to create a unified Catholic Spain. As Sephardic studies scholar Paloma Díaz-Más writes, "The exact number of Jews who left is unknown. . . . Recent estimates put the number at some one hundred thousand exiles. . . . The exiles called themselves Sephardim, meaning people from *Sepharad*, the Hebrew word for Spain."[48] Hence the name of this sacred space evokes the global community of Sephardic Jews.

Delia gains *facultad* in Sephardia, her ever-shifting spiritual and cultural landscape. As the play opens, Delia appears in a dream in Sephardia and walks into a cabin/house where she meets Aunt, who tells her the house has been in their family for five hundred years. Thus, the house symbolizes the family's Jewish legacy. The house becomes a mansion as Aunt leads Delia to a room sealed off by glass that contains books written by her family. Aunt explains that the books are "many words in many languages" and shows her a pile of books her father wrote. Delia whispers to Aunt: "You tell me our secret things. You pass our secrets on to me in a dream." Delia then asks if any books have been written about love. Aunt replies that there is "one special book—about you and your other half. It's kept hidden away safely in the Tree of Life. Inside the Garden of Pomegranates. Inside Sephardia. Inside you." Aunt tells Delia she can find her book if she lives in her heart. Delia replies, "If I could find my heart,"[49] for she is seeking her true love, her "other half." As Delia continues to question Aunt, the dream fades.

Sephardia offers entrance into a Jewish reality that draws from the Kabbalah, a form of Jewish mysticism that has its origins in medieval Spain. Through this Sephardic Jewish context, Romero echoes Spain's history as Svich and Zacarías have done in their work. Romero describes her creation of Sephardia as "a place where [Delia's] family celebrates an uninterrupted Jewish past";[50] it includes Kabbalistic elements such as the Tree of Life and the Garden of Pomegranates. The Tree of Life is a central Kabbalistic symbol represented by a diagram containing ten attributes (called *sefirots*) that constitute the divine elements of creation. Kabbalah

scholar Perle Epstein asserts that the Tree of Life "epitomizes the emana-
tion of God's 'qualities' into the visible world of men. . . . And since imitat-
ing God eventually led a man to direct knowledge of God, the Kabbalist
exerted himself to perfect each quality on the tree: Humility, Understanding, Wisdom, Judgment, Loving-kindness, Beauty, Majesty, Endurance,
Foundation, and Sovereignty."[51] Through her spiritual quest, Delia seeks
these qualities as well. She also visits the Garden of Pomegranates (Pardes
Rimonim), which refers to a central Kabbalah text written in 1548 by
Moses Cordovero, a Sephardic Jewish rabbi from Safed, Galilee, in which
"he sets forth a comprehensive Kabbalistic account of God, man, and
creation."[52] Additionally, the Jewish tradition states that a pomegranate
has 613 seeds, which represent the 613 *mitzvot* (i.e., the commandments).
During Rosh Hashanah, the Jewish New Year celebration, pomegranates
are then eaten as a symbolic gesture with the hope that one's merits will
multiply like pomegranate seeds. The word for pomegranate in Spanish
is *granada*, which is also the name of the city in southern Spain that was
a seat of power in medieval Muslim Spain (711–1492) where Muslims,
Christians, and Jews coexisted. Thus, the pomegranate echoes Sephardic
Judaism as well. Romero's inclusion of these important Kabbalistic elements suggest the cultural and spiritual complexities that empower Delia
to understand and accept her Sephardic Jewish identity.

Delia negotiates the lines between the supernatural and natural
worlds when she leaves Sephardia and returns to New York City where
she is a reporter at *Time* magazine and receives an assignment to write
about crypto-Jews. She soon travels to her home state of New Mexico
to research her story. In Albuquerque, Delia meets with Abel, a source
lead she received anonymously at work. She confesses to Abel that all she
knows is that "the New Mexican Crypto-Jews claim they have hidden
Jewish roots from the Sephardic Diaspora."[53] Abel is reluctant to speak
further, but she begs him to make the history real for her. Their attraction
is palpable, and they begin to complicate cultural and spiritual intersections as Mexican, American, Spanish, Jewish, Catholic, and indigenous
realities collide:

ABEL: You know how everybody around here insists they're not really
Mexican but Spanish. It's double speak. They mean, "We're not Mexican,
we're Jewish." We are mestizos but there's another dimension within that.

DELIA: Can Catholics, Indians, and Jews co-exist peacefully in one person at the same time? A new Holy Trinity.[54]

Abel's statement describes the duality of Mexican and Spanish cultures in the crypto-Jewish community. Like Fornes's complicated stone (discussed in chap. 1), which has a smooth, dry, clean exterior, but another life underneath, the crypto-Jews rotate between public and private worlds by using the code word "Spanish" to communicate that they are of Jewish heritage from Spain. Abel claims that crypto-Jews are mestizos. Performance studies scholar Diana Taylor writes: "The negotiated subjectivity of the mestizo/a bespeaks alliances far exceeding racial ties, and the intellectual, aesthetic, and political ramifications of the concept of *mestizaje* shape Latin/o American cultural histories."[55] However, with crypto-Judaism, the term "mestizo" also expands to include the spiritual and religious ramifications of the concept.

Delia's question recalls the notion of coexistence (La Convivencia), the era in medieval Muslim Spain when Muslims, Christians, and Jews lived together peacefully. Medieval Spain scholar María Rosa Menocal explains: "In principle, all Islamic polities were (and are) required by Quranic injunction . . . to tolerate the Christians and Jews living in their midst. But beyond that fundamental prescribed posture, *al-Andalus* [i.e., Muslim Spain] was, from these beginnings, the site of memorable and distinctive interfaith relations."[56] Delia asks whether coexistence and religious tolerance are possible in the crypto-Jews' new home, with indigenous spirituality replacing the Muslim faith in this triumvirate of *convivencia*. Delia soon searches for her own *convivencia*, where her worlds (Catholic/Jewish, Mexican/Spanish/indigenous, Sephardia/New Mexico) can coexist in her community and within herself.

Delia next begins to uncover traditions that crypto-Jews practice. Abel tells her that often crypto-Jews are hyper-Catholic, with the women belonging to the Legion of Mary, "a lay association of Catholics who, with the sanction of the Church and devotion to the Virgin Mary, serve the Church and their neighbors on a voluntary basis."[57] Delia then reveals that her mother is a member of the Blue Army, an organization focused on devotion to the apparition of the Virgin Mary at Fatima.[58] Abel encourages her to examine religious gestures for evidence of hidden connections between Jewish and Catholic rituals. Delia continues to receive spiritual insight about these connections in Sephardia, where she awakens to the echoes of Jewish tradition in her mother's Catholic religiosity. As she reenters the spiritual realm, Aunt shows her a prayer shawl decorated with the Star of David (Magen David), a symbol of intertwined equilateral triangles, which represents the shield of King David and is an international sign of Judaism.[59] Delia responds: "My mom has a necklace just like that. The family flower."[60] Through the identification of her mother's traditional Star of David necklace, Delia begins to uncover the reality of her Jewish heritage.

Later, Romero reveals crypto-Jewish rituals in Delia's family. As she speaks with her father, Delia learns of her paternal relatives' mezuzah ritual.

FATHER: Tradición. Men in this family always kiss the doorbell when they come home. But, at some point, it just stopped making sense.

DELIA: *(Realizing.)* My God, Dad, you were kissing words. Sacred words tucked inside an imagined Mezuzah. Words that used to be ours before these other words came and took them away. Have they stolen our words?

FATHER: What words?

DELIA: Our Hebrew words.[61]

Delia and Father discuss the tradition of the mezuzah, "an amulet which is placed on the doorpost of one's house in fulfillment of the commandment in Deuteronomy 6:4–9 and 11:13–21.[62] Part of that commandment reads, "Hear, O Israel: the Lord our God is one Lord, and you shall love the Lord God with all your heart, and with all your soul, and with all your might. . . . And you shall write them on the doorposts of your house and on your gates."[63] Therefore, a Jewish person often touches the mezuzah upon entering the home. However, the crypto-Jews could not risk such an outward public display of their faith. Sephardic studies scholar David Gitlitz explains that for the early crypto-Jews "after Expulsion, nailing a Mezuzah to one's door would have been an unmistakable invitation to martyrdom."[64] Gitlitz goes on to describe ways of maintaining this mezuzah ritual by crypto-Jews, which have included using the "right hand to tap the doorway's stone arch two or three times . . . tapping a certain place on the door frame when entering or leaving their house."[65] Through the discovery of this ritual, Delia starts to fully accept her Jewish heritage.

FIGURE 12. *Secret Things*, by Elaine Romero, produced by
Camino Real Productions, directed by Valli Rivera, in 2013. Delia
(Lila Martinez) discovers a Star of David pendant worn by Aunt
(Salome Martinez Lutz). Photo by Alan Mitchell Photography.

Romero complicates Delia's spiritual quest by interjecting a scientific theory. Delia learns that her father published a book on unified
field theory, which was rejected by the scientific community, and that
he has spent the rest of his life trying to prove his theories. Throughout
Delia's exploration of Sephardia, Romero utilizes this scientific theory
as another means for Delia to navigate the spiritual realm. Romero contrasts the empirical scientific lens of physics with the intuitive spiritual
lens of Sephardia. When Delia speaks with her father, he explains his
unified field theory:

FATHER: The curvature of space and time isn't always smooth, but jagged
and kinky in places. Full of discontinuities. Just when you think it's one

way, you fall into another. And you trick yourself, you say, "When a flag flaps in the wind, is the flag moving or the wind?" You get caught up in the decision between two very obvious choices, and forget the third. It is neither the flag, nor the wind, that moves, but the mind.[66]

Unified field theory "in particle physics [is] an attempt to describe all fundamental forces and the relationships between elementary particles in terms of a single theoretical framework," but such a framework has not yet been found.[67] Sephardia becomes a possible manifestation of the unified field theory, as this sacred space contains all the fundamental forces and key relationships in Delia's life and is a single framework where time jags and space curves to include a house, a cliff, a black hole, the Realm of the Almost Right, the Realm of the Right, and the Garden of Pomegranates. Romero's inclusion of this elusive physics theory not only echoes the supernatural interventions in Delia's life but also reflects the complex dualities she tries to negotiate, including Christian/Jewish religions, Spanish/New Mexican heritage, and intuitive spirituality/empirical inquiry.

Romero expands Delia's spiritual journey through her relationship with Abel. As she interviews him, a romantic attraction grows that mirrors Delia's awakening Jewish faith. Romero explores this attraction by creating glimpses of the Sephardia alternate reality during their meetings. In one section, Delia discovers Abel was the anonymous source who sent her materials on crypto-Jews. She challenges him and says she will continue her story only if she can focus it on him. Then "Lights indicate a shift to an alternate reality" where Delia admits to Abel, "It's just when I met you—I felt understood. Like we were lost in each other's beings. Am I mistaken?" Abel replies, "People used to be one person with four legs and four arms. Until they got split in half. That's what Plato says."[68] Here Romero includes a reference from Plato's *Symposium* where Aristophanes describes this myth and then concludes, "After the division the two parts of man, each desiring his other half, came together, and throwing their arms about one another, entwined in mutual embraces, longing to grow into one"[69] Like Zacarías including Sor Juana's reference to Apollo, Romero includes the classical Greek reference to illuminate the growing connection between Delia and Abel. Interestingly, Abel does not reference the Jewish creation myth that states, "And the Lord God caused a deep sleep to fall upon the man, and he slept; and He took one of his ribs, and closed up the place with flesh instead thereof. And the rib, which the Lord God had taken from the man, made He a woman, and brought her unto the man. And the man said: 'This is now bone of my bones, and flesh of my flesh; she shall be called Woman, because she was taken out of Man.'"[70] Plato's myth presents male and female as equal halves, whereas the Jewish creation myth presents female as secondary, and created out of a man's rib. Perhaps this use of Plato speaks to Abel's desire to expand past received notions of gender or to the fact the he was not raised in the Jewish tradition and is more familiar with secular than sacred texts. However, the truth of their relationship is illuminated only in these interventions of an alternate reality, which then ultimately leads them both into Sephardia.

Delia's far-flung journey back and forth across geographic, cultural, and spiritual borders exemplifies the intersections inherent in her Latina identity, a confluence of Mexican American, Jewish, Catholic, New Mexican, Mexican, and U.S. cultures. When Delia's mother finally admits that her family is Jewish, her father exhorts her to be Catholic, or Jewish, and to love. Time bends again and Delia is catapulted back to Sephardia, to the Garden of Pomegranates. Aunt greets her with the knowledge that Abel is her soul mate, yet Delia cannot fully grasp this revelation. Next, she descends the Tree of Life and begins to finally feel her heart, which had been hardened over the years from failed relationships. Next, she is catapulted back to her hotel room, sitting with Abel, who reveals he actually was with her in Sephardia. As they embrace and kiss, Delia questions whether her Jewish past will be the same for her as it was for him, to which Abel replies, "It will be a lifetime of asking questions. Are you game?"[71] She agrees as she kisses him again, while her voice echoes a passage from the Song of Solomon, the biblical book of love poetry,[72] which is a sacred text for both Jews and Christians.

As she did with the "ghosting" in *¡Curanderas! Serpents of the Clouds*, Romero presents many performative dualities in Sephardia: Delia gains a new name (Delilah), Father is transformed into Rabbi, and Mother becomes Aunt. While Romero gives Delia a new spiritual name, Delilah, this new identity departs from the name's Biblical origin. In the Bible, Delilah sexually tempted Samson in exchange for money, leading the Philistines to cut off Samson's hair and blind and imprison him, which ultimately caused his death (Judges 16:1–22).[73] Here, while Delia/

Delilah's relationship with Abel enters the realm of romance, the result is one of freedom and *facultad*. When the audience sees Delia's Jewish aunt, the memory of her devoutly Catholic mother persists. When Delia meets the Rabbi in Sephardia, the echo of her atheist scientist father remains. By consistently repositioning characters in this sacred space, Romero continually provides a more complex supernatural view of Delia's journey. Romero therefore suggests that navigation of sacred space can provide diverse and transformative spiritual and cultural engagement, leading audiences to see a deeper, more multilayered Latin@ identity.

VIEWING LATIN@ REALISM

Romero's plays allow her audiences to experience various Latin@ realities that are not "magical" but necessitate a shift to an alternate view of reality. As discussed in the introduction, the term Latin@ encompasses a twenty-first-century view of the complexity of the Latin@ community. By applying this term to the notion of Latin@ realism, the @ symbol again provides a sign of the multiple layers of reality. The @ symbol translates to the word *arroba* in Spanish, which additionally means a quantity of solid or liquid measure and is part of the colloquial term *por arrobas*, which means a large quantity. This Spanish meaning suggests the need to remeasure preconceived notions of Latin@ realism in theatre by considering the vast quantity of cultural and spiritual intersections therein. Also, the Spanish meaning relates to the fact that past definitions of Latina theatre such as "magic realism" do not add up and that the meaning needs to be recalibrated. The @ symbol appears above the number 2 on the English keyboard and to the right of the number 2 on the Spanish keyboard; this placement speaks to the collision of two worlds: supernatural/natural, spiritual/earthly, sacred/secular. In order to type the @ symbol, one must "Shift" or "right-Alt," then hit the key, implying that comprehension of Latin@ realism in theatre necessitates shifting or altering one's perception. Latin@ realism complicates other forms of theatrical realism by presenting a seamless coexistence of the spiritual and natural worlds through rituals that evoke sacred space and creation of *facultad*.

Fornes's and Romero's plays affirm that spiritual traditions in the Latin@ community are heterogeneous. In *Sarita*, Fornes juxtaposes

Santería and Christian religions. Sarita and her mother, Fela, venerate Oshun, the Santería deity, in contrast to the traditions of friend Fernando's Catholicism and husband Mark's Protestantism. In *¡Curanderas! Serpents of the Clouds*, Romero presents the intersection of Catholic and Aztec spiritualties within the *curanderismo* tradition. Paloma and Victoria perform *curandera* rituals that navigate the borders between the natural and supernatural realms. In *Secret Things*, Romero's Delia uncovers her Jewish heritage, often hidden within Catholic spirituality. Romero creates Sephardia, in which her characters inhabit a Jewish, mystical, and sacred space. Romero also provides an alternate view of Latin@ spirituality that expands past Catholicism and indigenous traditions to include Judaism.

Romero's characters gain *facultad*, leading to new ways of seeing their spiritual and cultural identities. Through staging Latin@ realism, Romero's plays provide her audiences with *facultad* in seeing and experiencing a Latin@ world in which earthly and spiritual realms coincide. Her characters include journalists who effortlessly inhabit an astral plane, a Western doctor who gains supernatural sight, an Aztec spirit guide who serves as a museum guide, and an atheist physicist who transforms into a Sephardic Jewish rabbi. Romero creates theatrical worlds where various spiritual realities continually intersect with earthly quotidian life. Romero's plays may also help to transform the perceptions of audiences who feel they need to exoticize certain Latin@ plays as "magical." Romero provides the opportunity to view and better understand the multiple ways in which the natural and supernatural worlds can seamlessly coexist in Latin@ realism on stage.

5

CUSI CRAM

Performing Latina Identity

A S LATINA PLAYWRIGHTS navigate cultural borders and provide new understandings of theatrical realism, they also write plays that reconsider Latina identity. Their characters embody multilayered cultural realities that mirror the complexity of twenty-first-century Latin@ society. In her plays, Cusi Cram, a playwright of Bolivian-Scottish descent, complicates cultural representation and upends media forms. She presents bodies on stage that question what it means to be Latin@. Cram reflects, "I write about cultural identity, and identity in general, how you shape it and make it your own."[1] Her characters remind audiences that Latin@s negotiate performativity to embody their cultural complexity.

The Fornes frame can be the shape of a human body, which highlights the importance of the Latina body as a site for performing identity. In *Lucy and the Conquest*, Lucy Santiago enacts the role of a multicultural television detective to fully embrace her Bolivian-Irish-American identity. While in Bolivia, Lucy also encounters a mythical Inca Man who helps her contend with a confluence of U.S., Bolivian, Incan, Spanish, Mexican, and Native American cultures. In *Fuente*, Adela, a Latin American immigrant, supernaturally invokes a 1980s American soap opera, which influences the identities of the residents in her southern desert town. Cram mines the U.S. primetime soap opera *Dynasty*, when Adela causes Soledad, her rival, to channel Alexis Carrington, the TV serial's British female antagonist. Through staging diverse cultural characters

FIGURE 13. Cusi Cram presents her playwriting students'
work at Primary Stages Einhorn School of Performing
Arts in New York City in 2008. Photo by James Leynse.

and manipulating television genres, Cram's plays traverse temporal and
geographic borders, excavate history, and engage performativity to continually shape twenty-first-century Latin@ identity.

LUCY AND THE CONQUEST: LATINA
ACTOR EMBRACES HER INNER INCA

In Cram's *Lucy and the Conquest*, Lucy Santiago, a Bolivian-Irish-
American actor, performs cross-cultural identity. Lucy seeks solace in
a trip from California to Bolivia after being fired from her job playing

Hunter Nevins, a Mexican-Cherokee-American detective, in a television series called *Beach Detectives*. Once she arrives in La Paz, she grapples with her heritage and the legacy of conquest. Lucy encounters her Bolivian relatives and the spirit of her late father. She also meets a mythical Inca Man, the collective soul of all Incas, who forces her to confront Pizarro's conquest of the Incas. By traveling to South America, Lucy gains a deeper sense of her own Latina identity. She must negotiate each disparate cultural world in order to survive.

In the prologue, Cram first presents Lucy's cultural complexities. Calling her Irish American mother on a cell phone from the Miami airport, Lucy reveals she is embarking on a Bolivian adventure. Two other spotlights rise. Tommy, her American boyfriend, pleads to accompany her on her trip. The spirit of her late father, Juan Ricardo Santiago, who was an influential Bolivian ambassador to the United Nations, establishes the dilemma of her cultural navigation:

> JUAN RICARDO: We are looking for a name. South America is a place with no name. South. America. We are Indians and Spaniards, so mixed and melded we can't remember where we begin and where we end. *Somos de aqui y de ninguna parte.* We are from here and nowhere. You want to understand this place, Lucy? First you must understand the power of forgetting."[2]

Her father encourages her to remember the complicated convergence of indigenous and Spanish cultures in South America. Her American boyfriend begs to fly to Bolivia: "I've always wanted, always wanted to see the Andes. Breathe that thin air. Does it really make you dizzy?"[3] By pitting Lucy's diplomatic South American father against her touristic North American boyfriend, Cram establishes the cultural worlds Lucy must confront as she tries to come to terms with her Bolivian American identity.

Throughout the play, Lucy traverses the borders between present and past. After Lucy arrives at the Santiago residence, a "place that once was grand but now shows signs of water damage and neglect,"[4] she reminisces about her travels to this house as a teenager. Time then shifts to six years in the past, when Lucy visits Juan Ricardo and Pacha, her grandmother. A younger Lucy waits to take a trip with her father to Cuzco, the historical Peruvian capital of the Inca Empire,[5] Machu Picchu, the ancient Peruvian city created by the Incas,[6] and Tiwanaku, "the city which is the

Andes sacred center . . . now in ruins, it is to South America what . . .
Stonehenge is to England: the seat of legend, a talisman, a touchstone."[7]
Cram underscores the intricacies of U.S./Latin American/Incan relations by including Machu Picchu in Lucy's desired journey. Anthropologist Johan Reinhard explains: "Machu Picchu's existence was not even
revealed to the outside world until after Hiram Bingham's visit in 1911.
After receiving backing from Yale University . . . Bingham surveyed the
site and has been rightly credited with being the 'scientific discoverer'
of Machu Picchu."[8] That this remarkable Incan ruin was revealed to the
twentieth-century world through the work of a U.S. archaeologist speaks
to the troubled legacy of conquest and the divide between North and
South America.

Lucy admits to a cultural fragmentation between her U.S. and Latin
American worlds. She attempts to shed light on the mysteries of her own
multicultural heritage when she first expresses her cultural knowledge:
"Did you know that Cuzco means bellybutton in Quechua? We're going
to the navel of the Inca Empire. That's so cool."[9] Lucy knows a term in
Quechua, the language of the Incas that is still spoken in several dialects in the Andean regions of Peru and Bolivia,[10] and demonstrates her
attempt to integrate the Bolivian, American, and Incan cultures in her
life. While she waits for her father to prepare for their journey, she exhibits cultural longing: "Sometimes, I feel like it'll never [e.g., the Latin
American continent] be a part of me. I'll always be looking in. It's like I
have this longing for something I've never known."[11] Cram reflects that
Lucy is "forced to confront her own past and her historical past (specifically the history of the Conquest) . . . issues of remembering and forgetting on a personal and historical level."[12] This collision between multilayered past and present and the tension between memory and forgetfulness
highlight the elements Lucy must engage to fully inhabit her Bolivian
American self.

Back in present-day Bolivia, Lucy's Latin American family now
appears. The Santiago aristocratic family history includes three Bolivian
presidents. However, her extended family contains those from divergent
backgrounds, who exhibit varying levels of cultural and class mobility.
Lucy meets Lila, the daughter of the family housekeeper, dressed in jodh-
purs and an army jacket, who "has the personality of a conquistador."[13]
Lila boasts, "I studied abroad. I worked for the airlines. I lived in Miami

AND Denver."[14] Lucy also meets her first cousin, Juan Alberto (aka "the Gringo"), another world traveler, who worked at the Bolivian Mission in New York City. He explains that he is called the Gringo because nobody in his family thinks he is like a Santiago, and that he seems like a foreigner. Lastly, Lucy interacts with Pacha, her one-hundred-plus-year-old grandmother, who loves the wonders of Vicks VapoRub (an American product used to cure a cold through its vaporous ointment) and often narcoleptically freezes, only to be awoken by her grandchildren. Each Bolivian family member references the United States, and Pacha literally spreads a U.S. product on her body. Lucy's engagement with her family furthers a journey into cross-cultural acceptance for them and her. However, the individual who most helps her on this quest is the Inca Man.

Cram introduces an indigenous body that unexpectedly intervenes in Lucy's Bolivian journey. When Lucy begs to sleep on an ancestral bed, Lila warns: "That bed was Simón Bolívar's campaign bed. You sleep on that bed, bad BAD things will happen."[15] Cram's inclusion of Bolívar (1783–1830) interjects a central hero from the Latin American independence movement. This Venezuelan military leader succeeded in driving the Spanish from Venezuela, Colombia, Peru, and Ecuador. Upper Peru was named Bolivia in Bolívar's honor;[16] thus he is literally the namesake of Lucy's cultural heritage, and his cross-cultural legacy informs Lucy's journey. Bolívar's military bed becomes a central site where Lucy must battle her own cultural disruption. After Lucy lies down, the bed "begins to rise toward the ceiling and a man dressed from head to toe in traditional gold Inca clothes emerges from under the bed."[17] Like the Aztec Woman in Romero's ¡Curanderas! Serpents of the Clouds, the Inca Man challenges Lucy to confront history through a liminal sacred space.

Cram chooses the Inca Man to challenge Lucy's cultural fragmentation, which speaks to the relationship between the legacy of Spain's conquest of the Incas and Lucy's journey toward greater self-awareness. The Inca Man recounts the Incan mythological tale about the children of the sun god Inti, who founded an Incan kingdom. When Lucy questions why she is being told this story, Inca Man erupts in anger over the tragedy of the conquest: "I'm pissed at history. . . . From the beginning of the Conquest, we messed up. We did everything wrong. We never had a chance."[18] To substantiate his perspective of the Conquest, he provides the example of the battle at Cajamarca between Pizarro, the Spanish conquistador, and Atahualpa, the Incan king. Geographer Jared Diamond describes:

> Atahualpa was in the middle of his own empire of millions of subjects and immediately surrounded by his army of 80,000 soldiers. . . . Nevertheless Pizarro [leading a ragtag group of 168 Spanish soldiers] captured Atahualpa within a few minutes after the two leaders first set eyes on each other. Pizarro proceeded to hold his prisoner for eight months, while extracting history's largest ransom in return for a promise to free him. After the ransom—enough gold to fill a room 22 feet long and 17 feet wide to a height of over 8 feet—was delivered, Pizarro reneged on his promise and executed Atahualpa.[19]

The Inca Man highlights that while Atahualpa acted honorably, Pizarro broke their agreement, which resulted in the Incan leader's murder. When the Inca Man asks Lucy whether she is angry about this history, Lucy reveals her disconnectedness to Latin America: "I . . . um lived in L.A. for two years. I was on TV. I don't think about history."[20] Lucy's mention of Los Angeles alludes to the perception that certain Southern Californians are not concerned with history. Yet, the history of conquest affects the entire state, since California once was part of Mexico, something Zacarías's José Salvatierra refers to in *Mariela in the Desert*. Lucy confesses that she has been avoiding coming to Bolivia for a long time because she has "these thoughts . . . these memories . . . like an echo in your heart,"[21] and the Inca Man affirms that he is that echo.

Lucy must come to terms with her indigenous, European, and Latin American heritages, which contain the histories of both the conquerors and the conquered. The Inca Man warns that Lucy running away from her family now is "History repeating itself. Turn your back and run. It's in your blood."[22] He exhorts her to remember the myth of Inkarrí and explains: "Inkarrí means the inversion of the world. We believe that a buried Inca's body is slowly becoming whole again. And when it does, the world will return to its former state."[23] Historian Franklin Pease writes:

> The first god is Inkarrí, offspring of the Sun and a savage woman. He is the maker of everything that exists on the earth . . . decided to found the city of Cuzco . . . was captured by the Spanish king; he was later decapitated.

The head of the god was taken to Cuzco and his body is slowly growing under the earth. . . . When the body of Inkarrí is complete he will return and that day will be the Day of Judgment.[24]

Just as the god Inkarrí is fragmented, Lucy too has been culturally torn apart by her lack of connection to her Bolivian heritage. Anthropologist Gary Urton states that the name of Inkarrí is "based on the terms Inca and the Spanish term 'rey' ('king')";[25] thus the name of the mythic king reflects the violent confluence of Spanish and Incan cultures. Perhaps the Inca Man suggests that the myth of Inkarrí may also be a metaphor for Lucy's reparation.

The Inca Man continues to confront Lucy with her reality. He next opens Lucy's bottle of Valium, a drug she takes to deal with her stress, empties the pills, and crushes them. Lucy, distraught, angrily responds, "Are you like . . . like . . . my inner Inca . . . and is this like an Inner Inca Intervention?" The Inca Man admits, "Pretty much."[26] Under the Inca Man's spell, Lucy recalls a trip she took to Cuzco by herself. She describes visiting an Inca temple and seeing an indigenous woman wearing five sweaters and standing next to a llama. Lucy learned that the woman allowed tourists to photograph themselves standing next to her, but the woman did not know her ancestors built the temple because she had been "taught to forget." Lucy subsequently desired to talk to the woman, but the woman spoke only Quechua. In that moment, Lucy confides that she understood about the forgetting and that it was the "first time . . . first time I felt part of this large and ravished place."[27] Cram implies that the disconnections in Lucy's linguistic terrain (English, Spanish, and Quechua) influence her cultural complexity (American, Bolivian, Incan). Cram also highlights how conquest can obliterate memory and how Lucy must recover her own cultural memory in order to survive.

The Inca Man grants Lucy the historical power of the Incan king as well as the geographical fortification of the Altiplano, the Bolivian plateau that was the site of the Incan Empire.[28] As an exultant Lucy raises her arms, the Inca Man recites an incantation over her: "I give you the force of Atahualpa's vengeance blessed with the cold, fierce strength of the Altiplano, so you may forget what you must in order to remember that which will save you and all of us."[29] He also exhorts her to find a balance between forgetfulness and memory. Infused with royalty, spatial

FIGURE 14. *Lucy and the Conquest*, by Cusi Cram, produced by the
Williamstown Theatre Festival, directed by Suzanne Agins, in 2006.
Lucy (Jeanine Serralles) receives an intervention from the Inca
Man (Bernard White). Photo by Williamstown Theatre Festival.

expansion, and cultural recall, Lucy suddenly opens her eyes wide and
collapses into the Inca Man's arms as the first act comes to a close, suggesting how Lucy's world falls apart as she descends more deeply into the
arms of Bolivia's history.

Cram begins to complicate simplistic notions of Latina identity when
Lucy, a Bolivian-Irish-American, performs her TV alter ego, Hunter
Nevins. After act 2 begins, Lucy awakens as Hunter. Before she arrived in
Bolivia, Lucy was fired from her acting job because she refused to wear
a bikini. She argued with her producers that her character, a Mexican-
Cherokee-American with a PhD in forensic psychology, would never
wear a bikini. When ordered to wear the skimpy attire, Lucy snapped
and screamed and was eventually escorted off the TV studio lot. Lucy/
Hunter attempts to help Pacha and explains that "I head up the Special

Beach Force. . . . I speak Spanish. . . . My father was Mexican. . . . My mother is part Cherokee. I also speak Cherokee."[30] Just as Lucy deals with the Spanish conquest of the Inca, her TV alter ego represents the legacy of conquest between the Spanish and indigenous in Mexico and the American and indigenous in the United States. Additionally, Hunter's degree is in forensic psychology, which is the "application of psychology to legal issues, often for the purpose of offering expert testimony in a courtroom."[31] So, her character's training additionally exemplifies hybridity, between the fields of psychology and criminal justice.

Lucy/Hunter provides a performance of the multicultural Latina body. Lucy/Hunter has arrived to head up "investigation Inca," and seeks the woman with the llama while Pacha searches for Lucy. Lucy/Hunter affirms she will help Pacha find her granddaughter but needs to "watch out for someone code name: Pizarro."[32] Lucy/Hunter also looks for a mysterious room, which houses an Inca who is reconstituting himself, as in the myth of Inkarrí. By giving her an alter ego named Hunter, Cram emphasizes that Lucy hunts for her past to make sense of her present. Here, however, Lucy hunts for a person (the indigenous woman) and a location (the mysterious room with the Inca) that will help her unite her fragmented self. Additionally, Lucy/Hunter echoes the "ghosting" in Zacarías's and Romero's plays. Similarly, this ghosting occurs in one actor's body with two characters and multiple cultures coexisting.

Cram demonstrates how Latin@s negotiate increasing levels of cultural intersections. Drew, Lucy's American agent, arrives to take her back to the United States, but he cannot shake Lucy out of her alter-ego state. Meanwhile, Lila and Juan Alberto feel Lucy wants to cheat them out of Pacha's supposed hidden fortune; so they plot revenge. However, Juan Alberto tires of Lila's domination and challenges her about their family history. With rising tension and Lucy still submerged in the role of Hunter, the Santiago family secrets emerge and further complicate these characters. Juan Alberto thought his parents were Alberto and Albertina, Pacha's other two children, who committed suicide because they both loved Juan, the gardener. Pacha reveals that Juan Alberto's father was Juan, the gardener, and his mother was Albertina. When he learns he is not the product of incest, Juan Alberto is elated and wants to celebrate with Lucy, who is still Hunter. Here Cram also touches on received notions of Latin America, as Drew exclaims, "This is like some South American soap opera that I can't get out of."[33] Cram alludes to the cultural tensions between North and South America through Drew's pejorative comment. These revelations cause Lucy to descend into confusion, and she ends up calling out to her boyfriend, Tommy, and her father, Juan Ricardo.

Cram continues to investigate the U.S./Latin American divide as she collapses time and space when the adult Lucy interacts with the spirit of Juan Ricardo. After she confesses that she may be in love with Tommy, Juan Ricardo tries to counsel her. But he ultimately rejects her, saying, "You know NOTHING. You understand NOTHING. You will never learn this world, this country, this house from a book. It is in you, racing in your veins like a disease. . . . GO! GO! GO HOME TO AMER-ICA! Back to Tom Sawyer where you belong."[34] Lucy does not accept her father's demand to leave Bolivia and return to her boyfriend, Tom, whom Juan Ricardo derides as being Tom Sawyer, the main character in the *Adventures of Tom Sawyer*, the 1876 novel by Mark Twain (1835–1910). However, Juan Ricardo's supposedly derisive example of Americana is not the simplistic cultural model that he thinks it is. In Twain's book, Tom, a young American boy, connects with his friend Huckleberry Finn, who, in a later book, travels with Jim, an African American man Huck helped to escape from slavery. Also part of the boys' world is a bicultural Native American, Injun Joe, a criminal.[35] Thus, Twain creates a culturally complex narrative with problematic portrayals of race and class. By having Juan Ricardo refer to Tom Sawyer, Cram indicates that his view of Lucy's American world lacks cultural awareness.

Lucy soon asserts that the two countries compose equal halves in her divided world. The interaction with the spirit of Juan Ricardo awakens Lucy from her Hunter delirium, which she does not seem to remember. Lucy must even forget what happened moments earlier in order to survive. Lila confronts Lucy, and they fight. To stop the physical altercation, Pacha reveals that Lila's father is also Juan Ricardo, so Lucy and Lila are half sisters and her fortune is to be left to her three grandchildren. Lila reconciles with Lucy and says, "You're pretty tough for a gringa." Lucy replies, "I'm NOT a gringa. I'm a half gringa. It's different."[36] By boasting she is half gringa, Lucy rejects her half sister's denial of her Bolivian heritage and finally proclaims herself a bicultural Latina.

In the epilogue, Cram confirms Lucy's hard-won identity. Lucy calls her Irish American mother to let her know that she will be staying in

Bolivia. As the central Simon Bolívar bed rises once again to reveal Juan Ricardo, Lucy confesses that she had never returned to Bolivia previously because she could not learn to forget. Juan Ricardo finally encourages her to end the forgetting by inverting the world, "so one day north will be south and south will be north. Turn the earth upside down, so it makes sense again. . . . You know everything you need to, m'hija."[37] Lucy invokes the myth of Inkarrí and decides to embrace the centuries of memory she has received through her time in Bolivia as she continues to integrate her North and South American worlds. Through this performative journey, Cram emphasizes that Lucy can now consciously remember the cultural complexity of her Latina identity.

FUENTE: SOUTHERN LATINAS LEVITATE SOAP OPERA

In *Fuente*, Cram shapes Latina identity by upending the soap opera model, which serves as a cultural memory that fuels her characters' journeys. Soap opera (or *telenovela* in Spanish) has at times been used as an essentialist, pejorative term to describe Latin@ plays. Here Cram utilizes the soap opera model to examine the complexities of her Latin@ characters, which creates a more nuanced and multifaceted view of Latina identity. Cram's play centers on the residents of Fuente, "a southern, desert place—not as far south as you can go but south nonetheless,"[38] as they struggle with love, loss, and isolation. The Spanish word *fuente* can be translated as "fountain." Thus, the play's title refers to the small, dry, desert town (population fifty) and its residents, who are trying to quench their thirst for a different life.

The action in part 1, titled "Love and Hairspray," focuses on the violent disruption of two couples' lives: Soledad and Chaparro, who are lovers, and Adela and Esteban, who are married. Chaparro loves Soledad, yet Soledad wants more than her life in Fuente; she declares, "I want a life that's all mixed and different than this one."[39] Soon, she runs away from Fuente with Esteban. Adela, now six months pregnant, and Chaparro both try to deal with the aftermath of their respective partners fleeing together. In a homicidal rage, Chaparro attacks and blinds Omar, a convenience store owner, who later reveals he is the father of Adela's child.

Part 1 ends with Esteban and Soledad stranded in the desert as thunder and falling rain surround them.

In part 2, a linear narrative titled "Jesus and the Pacific," Cram considers the legacy of supernatural powers in Blair-Maria, Adela and Omar's teenage daughter, who struggles to live in Fuente. Cram jumps seventeen years forward at the start of part 2 as she introduces Blair-Maria, who is sitting in a chair that is suspended in the air and grasping for a huge white prom dress, also floating in the air and just out of reach. Cram examines generational love as Blair-Maria meets Denver, who is passing through town on his way out west. After the two escape together, Cram reveals that Denver is the son of Soledad and Esteban. Thus the cycle of flight from Fuente continues.

Throughout her play, Cram juxtaposes *Dynasty*, the 1980s U.S. prime-time soap opera, against the lives of the residents of Fuente. *Dynasty* "focused primarily on the lives and loves of Blake Carrington (played by John Forsythe), a wealthy Denver oil tycoon, his wife Krystle (played by Linda Evans), and ex-wife, Alexis (played by Joan Collins), a British ex-patriate."[40] Cram chooses this American soap opera, as opposed to a Latin American *telenovela*, to parallel the lives in Fuente. Thus, a cultural disconnect is created when Latina characters desire to be Anglo and British characters. As a teenager, Adela viewed her rival, Soledad, as Alexis, with both of them fighting over one man, Esteban (i.e., Blake). Young Adela warns a teenage Soledad:

ADELA: This town ain't big enough for two Alexisesssss . . . Know what I mean?
SOLEDAD: I'm afraid I don't.
ADELA: Don't Crystal me, Alexis.
SOLEDAD: I don't know what you're talking about.[41]

Soledad becomes obsessed with Alexis Carrington and begins speaking spontaneously as the conniving British antagonist: "*(as Alexis Carrington)* I'm the sort of woman who says damn you, not thank you."[42] As with the character of Lucy/Hunter in *Lucy and the Conquest*, Cram presents layers of performativity as Soledad performs the character Alexis as portrayed by Joan Collins, which helps her to escape her life in Fuente.

Cram deftly employs and skewers the soap opera model to critique and shape Latin@ identity. Media studies scholar Robert C. Allen identifies four characteristics, "the combination of which made any given text legible to its readers as soap opera":[43]

1. Absolute resistance to [narrative] closure
2. Contemporary setting and emphasis on what we might call "domestic concerns"
3. Didacticism
4. Produced for and consumed by women . . . most of whom spent their weekdays at home, managing households and taking care of children.

Media studies scholar Jostein Gripsrud refutes the third characteristic of didacticism, stating: "the openly didactic character of the early soaps is gone. This is, however, not to say that their didactic function for the audience is gone."[44] Gripsrud highlights the use of the term "opera," stating that soap opera and "opera proper" both share an "emphasis on emotions and 'matters of the heart,' and a leaning towards hyperbole and the excessive."[45] The soap opera model implies perpetual iterations, transformations of human relationships, and a strong connection between popular culture and gender roles.

The choice of *Dynasty* reflects the social differences in Fuente. The American soap opera model implies cultural influence, or even colonization, as American soap operas are broadcast all over the world and often exist as the markers of American culture. Gripsrud's study focuses primarily on the impact of the American television prime-time soap opera *Dynasty* on his native Norway, which raised "questions of cultural identity in an increasingly internationalized media culture."[46] Gripsrud examines how the cultural lives portrayed in the soap opera influenced the cultural ideals and lives of the Norwegian viewers of the program. In *Fuente*, *Dynasty's* wealthy Anglo and European characters are juxtaposed against a working-class Latin@ community. Therefore, the soap opera model also highlights cultural and class intersections; in *Fuente* this is reflected in the diverse characters constantly vying for position and power.

The cultural identities of the women of Fuente exist in counterpoint to Alexis Carrington, a ruthless, power-hungry, British-born expatriate who has spent years living in Mexico. The character of Alexis was introduced at the end of *Dynasty*'s first season when she reappeared in Denver after having spent "sixteen years out of the country, mainly in Acapulco," Mexico's largest resort city. She returns in order to testify to her former husband Blake's violent streak[47] during a trial where Blake is accused of murdering his son Steven's male lover.[48] The development of Alexis's storylines aimed to give her "a power-base from which she could challenge Blake Carrington,"[49] the show's patriarch. Gripsrud ascribes Alexis's appeal to her "uninhibited use of her (and men's) sexuality in her struggle for power . . . which turns her into a partially positive figure whose ruthlessness comes across more or less as an ironic, humorously acceptable feature of the ultimate competitive 'career woman' of the 1980s, the decade of male and female yuppies."[50] Alexis's actions are a parallel to Adela's and Soledad's desire to challenge patriarchal notions of gender roles as well as social status in their community.

In part 2, Cram continues to mine the influence of television on the next generation in Fuente. Blair-Maria reveals, "I'm named after some fat TV actress my Dad thought was pretty and of course the Virgin Mary."[51] She is referring to the television show *Facts of Life* and the lead character, Blair, a wealthy, conceited girl who attends "an exclusive girls school, Eastland."[52] By naming this character after a wealthy Anglo girl and the Spanish name for the Virgin Mary, Cram emphasizes the cultural and spiritual intersections that influence Blair-Maria's identity as a bicultural child of a South American mother and an Arab-American father. Denver reveals he is named after a city because, "My mother liked some old TV show that took place there."[53] Denver, a Latino child, is named after the setting of *Dynasty*, the soap opera about Anglo wealth and power. In both cases, the media-inspired names of these children highlight their complicated cultural identities.

Cram also employs the soap opera paradigm to delve into the linguistic collisions in this southern desert town. In the play's foreword, Cram provides information on the accents of the characters: "For Chaparro, Soledad, and Esteban, English is their first language but the rhythm of their speech is infused with Spanish. Spanish is Adela's first language. Omar was born in an Arabic-speaking country."[54] Cram does not mention Adela and Omar's country of origin, and this omission prevents further knowledge about the specificity of their linguistic background, as Arabic and Spanish are spoken with different dialects in different nations. However, with this note Cram interpolates the musicality of Spanish with English, the syntax of Spanish in English, and the syntax and musicality of Arabic and English. Gloria Anzaldúa recounts: "At Pan-American University, I and all Chicano students were required to take two speech classes. The purpose: to get rid of our accents. Attacks on one's form of expression with intent to censor are a violation of the First Amendment. *Los Anglo con cara de inocente nos arrancó la lengua.*[55] Wild tongues can't be tamed, they can only be cut out."[56] Anzaldúa implies that the use of accented English is not only a form of protected free speech; it is an essential mode of self-expression. The accented language represents the intersection of cultures. Cram is embracing accent as a way to theatricalize the multiplicity of cultural collisions in American society. Cram is not cutting out tongues and she is not taming them. She encourages accents to enrich the play by letting them exist in all their range of expression.

Throughout her play, Cram utilizes accents to theatricalize the influence of Anglo television on the lives of these Latinas. The linguistic collisions are most evident when Soledad begins channeling the voice of Alexis Carrington.

> SOLEDAD: *(in a slightly strange British accent)* Stop your infernal chattering, you're giving me a migraine.
> *(SOLEDAD catches herself, she has never talked like this before.)*
> CHAPARRO: Infernal? Migraine? What . . . what kinda words is those?
> SOLEDAD: My words, my words, that's what they is.[57]

Here the arch, aristocratic language of Alexis is set against the casual, earthy quality of Soledad's language. Cram uses the foreign colonialist accent to irrevocably alter the life of all the characters in Fuente. However, Cram chooses the British accent of the character of Alexis instead of the American accent of her archrival on *Dynasty*, Krystle, creating additional layers of linguistic code-switching through the performance of racial, cultural, and class difference.

Cram also dramatizes supernatural aspects of Latina identity through the soap opera medium. In part 1, Adela is "from a long line of south-of-the-equator witches."[58] She cast a spell on the Aquanet hairspray sold in Omar's store to try to secure Esteban's love: "I put a spell on Omar's Aquanet. . . . But my magic couldn't make a man love me who loved

FIGURE 15. *Fuente*, by Cusi Cram, produced by Barrington Stage Company, directed by Sturgis Warner, in 2005. Chaparro (Michael Ray Escamilla) and Soledad (Lucia Brawley) almost kiss. Photo by Kevin Sprague.

someone else."[59] Cram here utilizes the word "magic" to describe the supernatural. Perhaps this reflects the character's need to reduce the mystery of her powers for the non-South American Chaparro. Adela's spell transforms all the Aquanet in stock; so when Soledad buys the hairspray, this beauty product then becomes a conduit for alternate realities. Whenever Soledad sprays her hair, she begins speaking like Alexis Carrington, which ends up undoing her relationship with Chaparro:

SOLEDAD: I ain't a lady, Chaparro. And I don't never drink beer. *(as Alexis Carrington)*. Champagne cocktail's my particular poison.
(SOLEDAD stops herself. She is not quite sure where these words, this accent, are coming from.)
CHAPARRO: This some game? Something you read 'bout in a lady's magazine? I can play games. I can be Blake. Look at me I'm Blake. What he talk like? Like this? *(in a real Gringo accent)* Well, hello Soledad, fine weather we're having here at the estate.[60]

Soledad, as Alexis, later seduces Esteban: "*(as Alexis Carrington)* You can either love me or hate me. I enjoy it either way."[61] She tells Esteban to call her Alexis and asks him to leave town with her, just as Alexis left Mexico to go back to Denver. Ironically, the action Adela hoped would help her win back Esteban backfires and leads her husband to flee Fuente with Soledad. Cram transforms a product used to immobilize hair into a mobile conduit for complicating Latina identity. Cram therefore upends the cultural landscape of Fuente when Adela, a Latin American woman, creates supernatural hairspray, which turns Soledad, a Latina working-class woman, into a wealthy British expatriate.

Cram presents South American spiritualism versus North American Christianity and thus considers the role of the supernatural in Latina identity. Blair-Maria, Adela and Omar's daughter, tries to come to terms with her supernatural powers. She describes to Omar how she levitates: "Yesterday at cheerleading, I jumped up and didn't come down for a long, long time and finally when I did come down my pom poms stayed in the air."[62] Meanwhile, Adela tries to renounce her former life as a "witch" after her newly found fervor as a Christian. When she sees her daughter levitating, she invites her priest, Padre Gustavo, to their home to attempt an exorcism of Blair-Maria. Blair-Maria pleads with her mother: "All this levitation stuff is crazy and totally scary but it's not evil. Help me understand this magic, Mama, cuz I know you got it in you too."[63] Adela later tells her daughter, "You come from a long line of south-of-the-equator witches, the kind of woman no good, normal, God fearing man will marry, 'cause the power you got is too scary."[64] Nevertheless, Adela and Padre Gustavo continue to attempt an exorcism until Omar returns home, stops the proceedings, and expels Padre Gustavo: "Don't ever come here again. I know our daughter flies and that her prom dress flies and that she's magical in every way."[65] Cram again employs the word "magic" to describe Blair-Maria's supernatural qualities. In fact, words like "mystical" or "spiritual" may better describe Blair-Maria. Cram contrasts Muslim Omar's acceptance of his daughter with Christian Adela's attempt to exorcise her. Here Cram echoes acts of conquest when Latin American indigenous were "exorcised" of their beliefs by Catholic missionaries. Interestingly, Omar, a non-Christian, defends his supernatural daughter against Christian oppression. Blair-Maria hovers in the sky while her conflicted parents argue on the ground. The supernatural intervention highlights that these cultures cannot coalesce and coexist. Blair Maria's levitation signifies her desire to rise above her existence in Fuente and float away to a new life.

Fuente's Latina women mirror *Dynasty*'s strong female characters, like Alexis, who challenge the patriarchy. Television studies scholar Christine Geraghty describes Alexis as "the first woman to assert herself so clearly and capably in this way as a business rival to Blake Carrington. She takes on the masculine attributes of the hero and returns them in spades."[66] Soledad, Adela, and Blair-Maria emerge as resilient and empowered women regardless of the negative actions of the men in Fuente. Yet while they may reflect certain power dynamics in U.S. soap opera icons of the past, these characters' lives catapult them into a varied, diverse present that cannot be contained by the rigid binaries of a wealthy Anglo oil family and their machinations for love and power.

In the end, Cram completely upends the dynamics in the American prime-time soap opera framework to reflect a more culturally complicated world. Cram's *Fuente* embraces, and then ultimately rejects, the world of *Dynasty*. In a contemporary U.S. setting, *Dynasty* portrays domestic concerns by highlighting the lives of the wealthy Anglo and British expatriates living in Denver, Colorado, who often treat each other violently. Cram's contemporary world reflects a working-class, multicultural, southern town, where American, Latin@, and Arab cultures work, mingle, intermarry, and create a hybrid society, with violent ruptures in families. Departing from the didacticism of the soap opera model, Cram's language is nuanced, multilingual, multidialect, and at times whimsical. Unlike soap opera's resistance to narrative closure, Cram's play ends with finite departures. As the two teenagers now face the Pacific Ocean, "Blair-Maria slowly floats upward. Denver looks up at her, just as their hands are about to part, Denver floats up and joins her."[67] Their levitations signify a desire to physically disconnect from the cultural, racial, and class struggles of their lives and find greater happiness in the liminal space between earth and sky. The final image also places lasting value on a supernatural South American reality, which can and does coexist with the characters' North American lives to further expand the complexity of the Latin@ identity.

PERFORMING LATINA IDENTITY

Cram's plays emphasize the performance of identity, as she creates characters within characters. In *Lucy and the Conquest*, Lucy Santiago, a Bolivian-Irish-American actor also performs as Hunter Nevins, a Mexican-Cherokee-American character from a fictional television series. In *Fuente*, Soledad, a southern Latina, channels Alexis Carrington, a British socialite, as performed by Joan Collins in the U.S. television series *Dynasty*. In both plays, the mobility of performance through these female bodies highlights the complex construction of Latina identity. Latina bodies inhabit Latin American, Anglo, European, and indigenous worlds, where cultural differences are continually negotiated. One-dimensional cultural identity is replaced by a variety of cultures that manifest in language, gesture, and action. By rehearsing and performing these roles, these characters generate more complicated constructions of Latin@ identity.

Yet, Cram considers how performance can function in Latina cultural positioning. Lucy performs the role of Hunter, who searches for a room that contains "the pillars of identity, a unique indigenous social order, and the necessary clues to unraveling longing and great personal and historical loss."[68] After channeling Alexis, Soledad tells Chaparro, "I want an Alexis Carrington life with stapled hair and shoulder pad sex."[69] Performance studies scholar Diana Taylor writes: "Performance not only functions as an indicator of global processes, it also opens a space for thinking about them, and about our habits of response. . . . Performances can challenge our assumptions about our role as spectators and our own cultural positioning."[70] However, here performance challenges the character's role as spectator in her own life. Performing Hunter helps Lucy confront the obstacles in her Bolivian family's home. Performing Alexis gives Soledad another view of her small town, leading her to flee Fuente. Both women's performances cause them to question their cultural position. Lucy comes to terms with her Latin American heritage. Soledad rejects the culture of her southern desert town and ultimately has a son she names Denver, a non-Latino name inspired by the world of *Dynasty*. Cram's characters therefore utilize performance as a tool to reshape their lives.

Fornes also highlights the importance of rehearsal and performance in her plays. In *Fefu and Her Friends*, the women gather to rehearse a theatrical fund-raiser for education. Several women perform roles in this rehearsal, led by the dramatic Emma, who explains, "Life is theatre. Theatre is life. If we're showing what life is, can be, we must do theatre." Sue questions, "Will I have to act?" to which Emma replies, "It's not acting. It's being. It's springing forth with the powers of the spirit. It's breathing."[71] Fornes here highlights the close connection between identity and performance. As these women rehearse, they more fully embrace their roles as advocates for female education. Emma performs the prologue from "The Science of Educational Dramatics" by Emma Sheridan Fry, which celebrates the need for intellectual enlightenment. Her rousing monologue ends with "Let us awaken life dormant! Let us, boldly, seizing the star of our intent, lift it as the lantern of our necessity, and let it shine over the darkness of our compliance. Come! The light shines. Come! It brightens our way. Come! Don't let its glorious light pass you by! Come! The day has come!"[72] Likewise, through performance, Cram's characters are awakening to their new lives, shedding light on the truth of their complex cultural identities.

Cram's career as a television soap opera actor reverberates in both plays, which feature powerful female television characters. Cram originated the role of Cassie Callison on the U.S. soap opera *One Life to Live* in 1981 and played the role until 1983. Cassie is the daughter of Dr. Dorian Lord Cramer, a physician and the show's primary female antagonist, and her boyfriend, David Reynolds (nee Renaldi), a pianist. Cassie's backstory reveals that she was born during her mother's med school years and raised by her father, after he stole Cassie and whisked her away to California. Cassie first appears in the fictional Llanview as a teenager to seek out her mother, and is soon adopted by her mother's husband, Herb Callison, Llanview's district attorney.[73] Her character stridently confronts violence. A synopsis for one episode states, "Suddenly a gun shot rings out! Cassie is terrified because she thinks that Kyle murdered the man. But later, Kyle denies it. It was only to frighten him. Cassie doesn't believe him. 'You'd kill anyone—you've proved that!' she says angrily.[74] Cassie's disrupted family echoes Lucy's separated parents—her mother in New York City and her late father in Bolivia. Blair-Maria recalls Cassie, as both were born to unmarried parents and are nonetheless brave, proactive teenage girls.

Cram's professional experience negotiating between actor, soap opera character, and audience response also echoes in these plays. In a 1982 interview, a teenage Cram states, "Cassie is very much like me. She's kind of shy, but she's also very strong. She's a bit more innocent, more naïve, not that I'm a woman of the world or anything. . . . But I do get a lot of mail from teenagers who say that the storyline reminds them of their mothers, all the fighting and stuff. And I always answer the mail. A lot of times, people tell me about their problems and I feel if I can help, I want to."[75] Cram separates herself as actor from her character while her performance as Cassie causes young audiences to reflect on their domestic lives. Likewise, Lucy separates herself from her character Hunter, but that does not stop the audience of her Bolivian family from entertaining preconceived notions of her identity, such as when Lila exclaims, "You want that TV bimbo to take everything we've worked for away?"[76] However, in *Fuente*, as Soledad performs Alexis, she begins to meld with her character and seduces her audience of one: Esteban. Therefore, these Latinas perform television characters that echo Cram's professional soap opera acting career, with her intimate knowledge of the relationship between identity and transformation through performance.

Additionally, Cram's collegiate acting experience may influence her emphasis on the performative. Cram acted in a production of *Fefu and Her Friends* during her first year at Brown University, playing the role of Paula. Cram reflects that the experience taught her what a play could be and began her interest in feminist theory.[77] Paula asks Fefu about her lecture on the radical feminist Voltairine de Cleyre, reflects on the nature of love relationships, and raises the issue of the disconnectedness of wealth and education. Traces of Paula exist in Lucy, Soledad, and Adela, who all seek greater empowerment, self-education, love, and class mobility.

Cram delves into the reception of television performance in the construction of Latina identity. Television roles are broadcast to millions of viewers and can become embedded in popular culture. Cultural studies scholar Jane Feuer asserts, "For a moment in the mid-1980s the television serial *Dynasty* ceased being merely a program and took on the proportions of a major mass-cultural cult."[78] In examining the impact of the soap opera on American culture, she claims, "*Dynasty*'s interpretive communities never merely interpret—they enact, they are counted as demographics, they consume not just a fictional text but a whole range of products as well."[79] Cram chooses prime-time soap operas to influence her characters. It is not clear that the fictional soap opera *Beach Detectives* in *Lucy and the Conquest* is a prime-time soap opera like *Dynasty*; however, both shows contain hyperbolic plotlines and operatic character attributes. The residents of Fuente in *Fuente* and the members of the Santiago family in *Lucy and the Conquest* have a relationship to characters in soap operas. They do not consume products related to the show, but they consume the shows as "cultural products" from other regions and continents. The Latin American-born Adela and the Latina Soledad absorb the world of American *Dynasty*. The Bolivian-born Santiago family obsesses over the American world of *Beach Detectives*. The international reach of these television programs correlates to how the performance of Latina identity can also have national and potentially global influence.

Lastly, Cram's characters may help audiences rehearse and revise their received notions of Latin@ culture. Cram writes: "I feel very drawn to writing Latina/o characters, mostly because I don't see them enough on stage and also there are so many Latina/o actors that I adore and I want to write them interesting parts."[80] Cram speaks of the need for greater Latin@ representation on U.S. stages while acknowledging the existing vibrant community of professional Latin@ actors and the ongoing need for compelling Latin@ theatrical roles. Cram creates opportunities to portray complicated Latin@s characters that inhabit multilayered worlds, with linguistic dexterity, heightened theatricality, and inventive performativity. In presenting these Latin@ bodies performing on stage, Cram's plays provide audiences with an ever-widening view of multidimensional Latin@ identity.

6

QUIARA ALEGRÍA HUDES

Conducting Theatrical Experimentation

L ATINA PLAYWRIGHTS EXPERIMENT with narrative structures, linguistic landscapes, and supernatural interventions to generate works that provide a complex view of contemporary Latin@ worlds. The Fornes frame can be a foundational structure in the sense of a play's structure, the foundations on which a play is built. Latina playwrights upend established theatrical frames and generate innovative play constructions. Quiara Alegría Hudes, a playwright of Puerto Rican and Jewish heritage and winner of the 2012 Pulitzer Prize for Drama, conducts theatrical experimentation in her plays by staging rituals and deconstructing musical forms.

Conducting can refer to a director of a musical performance as well as a material that transmits energy, and derives from the Latin *conducere*, meaning "bring together."[1] In *Yemaya's Belly*, Hudes chronicles the plight of a young boy's attempt to leave his island through staging rituals that transmit the energy of Santería, a "symbolically complex and philosophically subtle religious tradition . . . [that] follows generalized notions of African religious structure, but [whose] practices were altered to fit the social circumstances of enslaved and free Creole Cubans."[2] In *Elliot, A Soldier's Fugue*, Hudes, a Yale-trained composer, deconstructs a fugue to illuminate the life of a Puerto Rican Iraq War veteran and his family, who all served in the U.S. military. Hudes infuses these works with the spirit of Santería. As she explains: "One of my goals has been to write a cycle of plays that explores a different major *orisha* [i.e., saint] in each.

Yemaya's Belly explores Yemaya. *Elliot* subtextually invokes Osanyin. . . . Most people don't know about these things, so I just let it be subtextual. You don't have to know about *orishas* to appreciate a play of mine."[3] In these works, Hudes experiments with both spiritual tradition and musical foundations, which demonstrates to American theatre audiences how theatrical experimentation can shape Latina theatre.

YEMAYA'S BELLY: ISLAND BOY ENCOUNTERS RITUAL

In *Yemaya's Belly*, Hudes charts the journey of Jesus, a twelve-year-old boy who lives on an unnamed island ruled by a dictator. Jesus travels from the countryside to the city, eventually attempting to escape to the United States on a raft. The island in her play has parallels to Cuba through specific Santería references. However, Hudes does not geographically define her setting. Perhaps, in this way, she underscores the universality of this emigration narrative. Hudes does identify aspects of the spirit world as she experiments with the integration of the natural and supernatural worlds through Santería. In order to avoid oppression and/or gain legitimacy, in Santería the *orishas* (i.e., saints) merge with Catholic saints, a tradition in which practitioners "borrowed from Catholic discourse and reinterpreted it in terms of African religions under the guise of an alternative form of folk Catholicism."[4] Yemaya, the great universal mother and deity of the sea,[5] is correlated with La Virgen de Regla, a black saint and patron of the Bay of Havana,[6] whose name symbolizes the merging between Catholicism and African religions. La Virgen (the Virgin) signifies the various manifestations of the Catholic Virgin Mary. *Regla*, which means "rule" in Spanish, is "a word used in Cuba to describe the African-based religions, sects, and practices."[7] Approaching the *orishas'* world can be achieved through divination, sacrifice, possession, trance, and initiation. Hudes's expression of Santería, like Romero's dramatization of *curanderismo*, illuminates her characters' journeys as they negotiate natural and supernatural realms.

Hudes stages four rituals in her play that address female sensuality, modernity, burial, male sexuality, and survival. Hudes explains in her introductory notes: "A ritual involves a body and an object, together in a moment of possession. Rituals are crude, physically exaggerated.

They make the body raw."[8] The ritual objects in her play include a duck feather, a Coke bottle, a coconut husk, and grains of rice. Santería rituals involve the use of food and animal sacrifices. Hudes mirrors this by using rice (food) and a feather (animal). Hudes creates rituals that are not necessarily Santería rituals but incorporate elements of Santería and the connection to the *orishas*. Regarding rituals, American folklorist Michael Atwood Mason writes that "Santería elders do not want to make too much information available to the public";[9] hence the rituals are dedicated to those who are initiated into the Santería practice. Romero's *curanderismo* rituals reflect a tradition that is more accessible to the general public. Hudes must create her own rituals that echo but do not replicate the Santería rituals, which are private and seemingly much less accessible to the general public. Romero's and Hudes's rituals both involve interventions between natural objects and the body. However, whereas the rituals in Romero's plays often focus on healing the body, those in Hudes's plays mark rites of passage for her characters through which they transform. By creating public rituals outside of the private Santería tradition, Hudes may be providing greater access to the *orishas*, free from strict adherence to religious practices.

Yemaya first appears as a young carnival performer when Jesus and his uncle, Jelin, visit an old port city on their island. Hudes notes: "She is young, heavy, and breathtakingly beautiful. Her skin is the richest shade of brown. She wears a regal blue dress adorned with cowries, silver lace, and duck feathers. Underneath the full skirt, her large hips sway like waves. She approaches Jesus and Jelin. Jelin is aroused. . . . She plucks a duck feather from her dress and ruffles it in Jesus's hair."[10] Yemaya puts out a tip cup, saying, "For the spirits," and sings:

Remember me like you remember your ancestors . . .
Many of your ancestors were buried in my belly
blue eyes lie blind in my water . . .
Then when death comes
You will see through the eyes of your parents . . .
you will speak through an eternal voice[11]

Yemaya's song refers to the ocean as a watery grave, which may allude to the slave trade in Cuba and the many Africans who died at sea, thus echoing the African genesis of Santería. The watery grave could also refer to the men, women, and children who perished at sea while attempting to reach foreign shores after fleeing the island. She also may be foreshadowing the possibility of Jesus's death in his attempt to reach the United States.

Through this sacred space invoked by song and dance, Yemaya provides a ritual object of a duck feather, which Jesus takes from her. After Jelin initially scolds Jesus for stealing the feather, Jelin engages in the first ritual in the play:

> Jelin holds the feather. He puts it to his nose and, with a large nasal inhale, he smells it. That's how a woman smells. He puts it back to his nose and sniffs four staccato inhales in a row. Fruit. Fish. Saltwater. Blood. He touches the feather to his nipples, tickling and teasing them. He drags the feather down his torso and finally to his crotch, where he brushes the feather.[12]

Through this ritual, Jelin gains access to the power of female sensuality. When Jesus learns the feather smells like fruit and fish, he says, "Ew," to which Jelin replies, "None of your business. If you're anything like your uncle, you'll get it one day."[13] Jelin then gives Jesus the feather, which will travel with him and lead to other rituals throughout the play. Here the sacred space is not some lofty, faraway place, but a location that is sensual and earthy, generated by a ritual with an animal feather that evokes sexuality.

The feather travels from spirituality and sensuality to commerce and modernity. During that same trip to the city, Jesus visits a grocery store while waiting for Jelin. Lila, the storeowner, asks him if he is going to buy anything. Jesus says he doesn't have any money, but he offers her his feather. Lila then accepts the feather as payment for a bottle of Coke. Jesus promises that one day he will buy her store and become wealthy. This exchange highlights Jesus's desire to escape his life of poverty in the countryside. As Jesus receives the bottle of Coke, he drops it, claiming, "It stung my hand when I touched it."[14] Lila learns that Jesus has never experienced a refrigerated beverage, for his town has no electricity or running water. Lila gives Jesus a second bottle of Coke, and he insists he will return to buy the store. Lila then renames him: "It's the country boys like you that turn into stubborn old mules. . . . Little Mulo. The stubborn one. Be very careful. The bottle's cold."[15] The feather has been exchanged for an American object of modernity and symbol of the outside world. Additionally, the owner of the store replaces Jesus's traditional Catholic name with that of an animal, a stubborn mule. The animal object (the feather) begets a foreign object (the Coke), which leads to an animal name (a mule). Once outside the store, the second ritual ensues as "Jesus holds the bottle of Coke in one hand. When the cold starts to burn that hand, he switches to the other and shakes out the burning hand for relief."[16] The ritual continues with Jesus happily drinking his first Coke and more fully entering the modern world.

Jesus officially changes his name to Mulo after his mountain-farming town is destroyed in a fire, in which his parents perish. On his way back to the city, he encounters Tico, a vendor, mourning the death of his wife, who also died in the fire. Tico serves him coconut juice and then rum. Mulo, traumatized by the loss of his parents, pays Tico in rice before departing. Tico then takes a coconut husk full of rice and performs the third ritual in the play, this one to honor Baldomera, his dead wife, whose remains were consumed by the fire. Tico "holds the coconut husk over his head and turns it upside down. Rice pours down on his head, shoulders, and falls to the ground."[17] The rice metaphorically becomes Baldomera's ashes. This ritual enables Tico to bury the "ashes" of his deceased wife and move on in his life.

The ritual feather gains another very real function when it opens up a path for Mulo's emigration. After Mulo arrives in the city again, he returns to Lila's store where he gets a job doing inventory. Maya, a young girl, enters and sees Mulo's feather on the counter:

MAYA: What's this for?
MULO: It's from the queen of the ocean.
MAYA: I'm not impressed. *(Maya picks up the feather. She inspects it. She smells it. In a teasing sensual manner, she puts it down her shirt and under her bra.*
MULO: That's stealing.
MAYA: Are you going to tell on me?[18]

Yemaya's ritualistic feather here again evokes sensuality. However, when Mulo learns that Maya helps people flee the island, the feather continues to guide his journey, as Mulo and Maya soon escape on a small boat bound for American shores.

Hudes next creates a liminal underwater space. During a storm at sea, Mulo falls overboard and plummets to the bottom of the ocean. On the ocean floor, Mulo is now a famous inventor and dominoes legend. He is treated as a VIP while staying in a hotel's presidential suite. Mulo enters a hotel to find his mother playing dominoes. Tico, who is now the concierge, gives him a coconut husk as a room key. Mulo has invented a new beverage called *coca-nola*, a coconut-flavored Coke, which has become the favorite drink of the president of the United States. Mulo sends the president an invitation to meet at the bar when he learns the commander in chief is also staying at the hotel. This sacred space where Mulo's past and present converge gives him access to communicate with his dead mother (whom he does not recognize but with whom he plays dominoes), the president of the United States, and with Maya, who soon runs in and repeats lines from Yemaya's carnival performer song. Here Hudes contrasts many aspects of Mulo's journey. In the ocean space, Mulo has material wealth, entrepreneurial success, and class agency, whereas on land he has little material, financial, or social status. He again encounters Maya/Yemaya, one of her avatars being Yemaya Olokun, who is found at the bottom of the ocean.[19] Maya's final exhortation, "Come back to me,"[20] portends supernatural power for Mulo that may help him survive. Just as Mulo is navigating this spiritual world, he is simultaneously negotiating and merging a variety of cultures: Caribbean, American, and Yoruban. This experimental sacred space gives Mulo cultural and personal empowerment as an inventor and businessman. However, unlike Romero's characters gaining strength in Mictlan, or Cram's Inca Man empowering Lucy, Mulo's underwater agency soon evaporates once he resurfaces to the raft and his precarious *balsero* existence.

Mulo and Maya gain *facultad* after many days at sea. Mulo moans in his sleep while he has a sexual dream. After Mulo awakens, Maya wonders if she had been the woman in his dream. Mulo then initiates the play's fourth and final ritual.

Mulo reaches his hands out and touches her. His fingers slide up and down her body, making the motion of waves. As he does this, he makes

FIGURE 16. *Yemaya's Belly*, by Quiara Alegría Hudes, produced by People's Light and Theater Company, directed by Shannon O'Donnell, in 2006. Mulo (Mark del Guzzo) and Maya (Joanna Liao) engage in a ritual as Tico (Joe Guzman) and Mami (Mary Elizabeth Scallan) witness. Photo by Mark Garvin.

whooshing sounds through his teeth. Mulo puts his fingers to her breasts and pops his fingertips like sea foam. Maya reaches under her shirt and pulls out the feather. Mulo puts the feather to his nose and smells it. That is how a woman smells.

Mulo describes the odor by using the same words as Jelin did during the first ritual: "Fruit. Fish. Saltwater. Blood."[21] This final ritual marks Mulo's entrance into manhood, as he acknowledges the scent of a woman.

The ritualized feather additionally generates sacred space when a dehydrated Mulo and Maya decide to hold a funeral for their deceased mothers by using the feather as a sort of effigy of the dead women. As they call out their mothers' names, Mulo's mother appears on the water, unbeknownst to them. Mulo and Maya then say prayers for their mothers and both gain a new level of *facultad*. Looking into the distance with eyes that have seen death, sensuality, and underworld spirits, they now begin to see what might be land, or might be the spirit world, as they continue on the next phase of their journey.

In the final scene of the play, as the waves begin to rise and crash into the boat, Maya tells Mulo to look into the distance:

MAYA: Close one eye and squint the other.
MULO: Mosquito?
MAYA: It's land.
MULO: Is that what land looks like?
MAYA: A little bit of green. White dots where the waves are crashing.
MULO: Is that what America looks like?
MAYA: We're still too far away.[22]

It is not completely clear if they have developed the *facultad* that Anzaldúa describes as "a kind of survival tactic that people caught between two worlds . . . unknowingly cultivate."[23] Anzaldúa implies that *facultad* is necessary as a means of survival. She explains how a Chicana must employ this mode of sight in order to withstand the challenges of a world that does not fully accept or value her. However, for Mulo and Maya, *facultad* is more than a tactic. They must use their new vision to literally survive the elements of nature while floating in a liminal water space that contains traces of both countries but is neither nation.

Hudes's exploration of Yemaya provides additional perspective on Jesus/Mulo's and Maya's connection to the ocean. Yemaya is also "the orisha of intelligence and rationality."[24] Hudes underscores her characters' rationale for attempting to leave their island by showing their poverty and lack of options. However, Hudes calls into question the intelligence of their emigration by raft. Perhaps the repetition of Yemaya's appearances throughout the play indicates that her characters continually seek access to greater levels of *facultad* to guide their perilous journey.

As with the "ghosting" in the plays of Zacarías, Romero, and Cram, Hudes doubles the female roles that influence her main character's journey. The actor who performs Mami, Jesus/Mulo's mother from the countryside, also plays Lila, the storeowner in the city. The actor playing Maya, Mulo's friend, performs the goddess Yemaya as well. The liminal space of the ocean provides a location where the dualities of these roles intersect as Mulo encounters his mother and Maya. Mulo does not recognize

Mami, but the audience sees the actor who played Lila; so notions of commerce as well as motherhood hover close to Mulo. Underwater, just as he is about to walk toward his hotel room, Maya grabs him and says, "Remember me like you remember your ancestors."[25] Yemaya echoes through Maya's exhortation as the supernatural and natural worlds collide in the actor playing both roles. Hudes's "ghosting" here provides an expansive view of Latin@ identity, encompassing the rural, the urban, the divine, and the earthly as they coexist in these characters.

The aesthetics of the supernatural can be a challenge in productions of Hudes's play. Although she is staging a version of Santería, many of the interpretations of this play have ignored the intricacy and rawness of this spirit world navigation. Hudes explains:

> *Yemaya's Belly* is a frustrating play for me. . . . The biggest pitfall is that directors make the production poetic, or beautiful, or loosy-goosy. They don't understand that it takes place in very real impoverished circumstances, or that the aesthetic of *Yoruba/Santería/Lukumí*, while ravishingly beautiful and spiritually pure, is also about suffering, loss, violence, and ugliness. I have seen too many productions of *Yemaya* where it looks like a children's book with a palm tree on the set. It's disheartening. . . . It wasn't about storytelling—people think *Yemaya's Belly* is story theater, but it's not. People think it's magic realism, and it's not. It's about psychology and violence and tragic ignorance.[26]

To stage this play as childlike or merely poetic ignores the intersection of the supernatural and natural worlds and its connection to the seriousness of everyday life. Perhaps this informed the production note she includes in the published edition of the play, where she instructs: "Though the text seems poetic, and the rituals give a sense of magic realism, it is imperative that these characters and their situations be as real and specific as possible. Be wary of making this play overly magical. The moments of poetry should be surprises, should stand out against a starker, more impoverished landscape."[27] While she does employ the term "magic realism," she advocates for a realism where the supernatural and natural worlds coexist and inform each other amid a harsh existence.

Through her theatrical experimentation, Hudes juxtaposes ritual and *facultad* against the urgency of human suffering. Whether Maya and

Mulo perish or arrive safely in the United States is not clear. On their ocean journey, Hudes mines the depths of her characters' earthly and spiritual connections as they access the power of ritual. The resulting *facultad* could heal, protect, or purify with the hope of reaching land. Conversely, this supernatural sight could precede their imminent demise, giving them one last vision before they perish at sea. Hudes does not clarify which is the case, leaving the audience to decide whether their liminal sacred space full of mystery and possibility leads to tragedy or survival. Additionally, through experimenting with this staging of Santería, Hudes extends an invitation to her audiences to witness this religious tradition and consider how the spirit world can intervene in the struggle to survive.

ELLIOT, A SOLDIER'S FUGUE: LATIN@ MILITARY VETERANS DECONSTRUCT FUGUE

Hudes composes her play *Elliot, A Soldier's Fugue* by deconstructing a fugue as she delves into the life of a Puerto Rican Marine from Philadelphia confronting a second tour of duty in Iraq. This 2007 Pulitzer Prize finalist is part of a trilogy, which includes *Water by the Spoonful*, her 2012 Pulitzer Prize-winning work, and *The Happiest Song Plays Last*, written in 2013. The entire trilogy is inspired by Hudes's family, most notably the experiences of Elliot Ruiz, her cousin, who served as a U.S. Marine during the Second Iraq War.[28] Hudes explains: "I did not set out to write a trilogy, but a few years after I completed *Elliot* I felt there was still more story to tell, and more structural and stylistic experimentation for me to do in regards to music and playwriting. At that point I planned the trilogy."[29] The trilogy follows Elliot's career as a Marine and then his civilian life as a veteran. The plays consider the reverberations of his military service within the Ortiz family and their Philadelphia community.

In this trilogy, Hudes presents aesthetically complex Latin@ worlds. Each play reflects diverse musical forms: fugue, jazz, and Puerto Rican folk music, also known as *jíbaro* music. Through deconstructing the fugue form, *Elliot, A Soldier's Fugue* dramatizes Elliot in the midst of his military service, which echoes the experiences in this family of U.S. military veterans. In *Water by the Spoonful*, her jazz-influenced play, Hudes gives

FIGURE 17. Quiara Alegría Hudes and her cousin Elliot Ruiz, a former U.S. Marine and Iraq War veteran, attend the Off-Broadway opening of Hudes's *Water by the Spoonful*, produced by Second Stage Theatre in 2014. Photo by Jennifer Broski/BroadwayWorld.com.

equal if not more attention to Elliot's family and their friends. In *The Happiest Song Plays Last*, Hudes considers the lives of Elliot and Yaz, his female cousin, interspersed with *jíbaro* music performed by a live guitarist. The entire trilogy merits a much deeper consideration. However, for the purposes of this chapter, I will be closely examining only *Elliot, A Soldier's Fugue*.

In this play Hudes employs elements from the fugue form to experiment with dramatic structure while delving into the Ortiz family's military service. A fugue consists of a composition for multiple voices or instruments in which "a subject is stated unaccompanied in a single voice (or instrument). Then a second voice enters with the answer. . . . The original voice continues with the counterpoint against the answer. After this, a third voice enters in turn with the subject again while the first two voices continue with counterpoint against it. Finally, a fourth voice enters, now with the answer, while all three of the other voices accompany it with counterpoint."[30] The overall subject of Hudes's play is Elliot Ortiz's military service in Iraq and the question of whether he'll return for a second tour of duty. Hudes here includes four voices: Elliot, Pop, his father, Grandpop, his grandfather, and Ginny, his mother. Each voice repeats and counters the subject by delving into the family members' military service in Iraq, Vietnam, and Korea.

Significantly, Hudes chooses a fugue to structure her play and not a *danzón*, a highly rhythmic form of popular music that is one of the roots of better-known Latin forms such as the mambo and cha-cha,[31] or another Latin American or Caribbean musical genre. In her production notes, Hudes describes the music in the play as, "Flute. Bach, danzónes, jazz, etudes, scales, hip-hop beats. Overlapping lines."[32] Like Svich, Romero, and Cram, Hudes expands the Latin@ experience to include European influences. She also intersects Caribbean and American musical forms in her plays, which again emphasizes Latin@ cultural complexity.

Hudes emphasizes the fugue form closely associated with Johann Sebastian Bach (1685–1750), the acclaimed German composer. Bach composed fugues for instruments (including harpsichord, organ, and violin) and voice. Regarding Bach's *The Art of Fugue* (1742), musicologist Christoph Wolff states: "The governing idea of the work . . . was an exploration in depth of the contrapuntal possibilities inherent in a single musical subject. The carefully constructed subject would generate many movements, each demonstrating one or more contrapuntal principles and each, therefore, resulting in a self-contained fugal form."[33] The structural polyphony in the fugue allows for a multiplicity of voices to echo each other while maintaining their unique identities. In employing the fugue, Hudes creates a multivocal, theatrical landscape that deeply explores one main theme or idea. By extension, this implies a dynamic of constancy versus imitation, or standard versus variation. No matter how far the variation or repetition of the answer strays from the subject, it is always defined in light of the subject as the norm. On one level, Hudes could be stating that the impact of military service is pervasive, and that regardless of generation or military conflict the devastation of war is universal. However, also embedded in this play is the centrality of the Ortiz family's Puerto Rican culture amid their American lives.

Hudes divides her play into fugue and prelude scenes. The four fugue scenes mark major events in the Ortiz men's military lives: first tour of duty, Elliot and Pop killing men during war, Elliot and Pop sustaining leg injuries during combat, and Elliot, Pop, and Grandpop shipping off to war. The ten prelude scenes poetically reverberate with aspects of the Ortiz family's military service: Elliot's press interviews, letters written by Pop to Grandpop during his deployment in Vietnam, and the Ortiz family garden oasis. Time jumps between present and past. Hudes does not address the historical differences between each war but mines the complexities and commonalities of the military lives of Elliot, Pop, Grandpop, and Ginny.

Hudes navigates the relationship between subject and answer by the characters' reflections on one another's histories. In the production notes to her play, Hudes explains that "in the 'Fugue' scenes, people narrate each other's actions and sometimes narrate their own."[34] Through this experimentation, she creates a non-naturalistic, Brechtian-like style in which the audience remains conscious of the play's theatricality while engaging with the characters' journeys. The play's opening scene effectively develops the fugue model as Ginny, Pop, and Grandpop echo the dynamics and reality of Elliot's service. In this scene, Hudes establishes three generations of military service in the Ortiz family. As Elliot prepares to leave for a first tour of duty in the Second Iraq War, Ginny begins the first scene of the play with a description of Elliot's location:

GINNY: A room made of cinderblock.
A mattress lies on a cot containing thirty-six springs.
If you lie on the mattress, you can feel each of the thirty-six springs.
One at a time.
As you close your eyes.
And try to sleep the full four hours.[35]

Next Pop describes the bed sheets, where "the corners are folded and tucked under." Grandpop adds that "the corner of the sheet is checked at 0600 hours, daily." Then Elliot announces his own arrival: "A man enters." In this scene, the fugue functions in several ways: a character's narration of action, a character's narrative answering the main subject, and actual music and song colliding. As the scene continues, time jumps back to 1966, when Pop is serving in Vietnam. Then, time reverts to 1950, when Grandpop is serving in Korea. The scene continues with the main subject

FIGURE 18. *Elliot, A Soldier's Fugue,* by Quiara Alegría Hudes, produced by Page 73 Productions, directed by Davis McCallum, in 2006. Elliot (Armando Riesco), Pop (Triney Sandoval), Grandpop (Mateo Gómez), and Ginny (Zabryna Guevara) present military narratives through fugue. Photo by Monique Carboni.

of Elliot's departure, echoed by the counterpoint of Pop and Grandpop's military service. Timelines intersect as the narrative lines of the Ortiz men harmonize with each other. The scene ends with Grandpop assembling a flute, putting it to his lips, and beginning to play "the melody of a Bach passacaglia." As the flute continues, Pop begins a military chant: "One two three four. / We're gonna jump on the count of four." Lastly, Elliot, his head bobbing while listening to a Walkman, starts to sing the hip-hop tune "Got Yourself a Gun" by Nas: "Uh, uh. And when I see ya I'ma take what I want so / You trying to front, hope ya / Got ur self a gun." In her stage direction, Hudes instructs: "It is three-part counterpoint between the men."[36] The music of three generations of Ortiz men in the military, from the seventeenth-century Bach passacaglia, to twentieth-century military march cadences, to a twenty-first-century hip-hop song, collide in this orchestrated fugue.

Hudes provides a cultural counterpoint in this fugal moment. The passacaglia can be defined as "a through-composed variation form constructed over formal harmonic progressions . . . used widely in the Baroque era but with origins in the Spanish street dance, the *pasacalle*."[37] The term comes from the Spanish verb *pasar* (to pass) and the noun *calle* (street). Hip-hop, also seen in Svich's *Tropic of X*, derives from the African diaspora and draws on North American and Caribbean cultures. The military cadence also has links to Africa. As sociologists David LoConto, Timothy Clark, and Patrice Ware explain: "The music of West African cultures and American military marching cadences appears linked through African American slave songs of the U.S. South that continued through work songs of sharecropping, and has remained part of African American Christian religious practices, and other forms of music (i.e., The Blues, Rap, Hip-Hop)."[38] Therefore, in this first fugue scene, Hudes highlights the multilayered cultural landscape of Latin@ military service where European, Spanish, West African, Caribbean, and North American traditions intersect through the generational musicalities of three Puerto Rican male veterans who served in Iraq, Vietnam, and Korea.

Hudes's subject and answer in the play highlight the history of Latin@s in the U.S. military. Elliot serves as lance corporal in the 3rd Light Armored Recon Battalion First Marine Division, which "conducts reconnaissance, security, and economy of force operations, and within its capabilities, limited offensive or delaying operations that exploit the unit's mobility and firepower."[39] Pop served in the 3rd Cavalry Division during the Vietnam War. Colonel Gilberto N. Villahermosa writes: "Approximately 80,000 Hispanics served in America's armed forces during the country's 10-year involvement in Vietnam, winning 13 of the 239 Medals of Honor awarded during the war."[40] Grandpop served in the 65th Infantry Regiment of Puerto Rico during the Korean War. Villahermosa explains: "With over 4,000 U.S. soldiers, Puerto Rico's 65th Infantry Regiment arrived in Korea in September 1950 well led and well trained. The largest U.S. infantry regiment on the American side, it fought in every major campaign of the war thereafter."[41] Ginny served in the Army Nurse Corps in Vietnam. Colonel Iris West writes: "The officers of the Army Nurse Corps . . . selflessly endured countless hours of their patients' pain, sorrow, screams, blood, mutilation, and at times death. And when it was over, the officers of the Army Nurse Corps quietly came home. All paid an emotional price for that year in Vietnam."[42] Hudes honors her family's military legacy while questioning through these characters the haunting effects of war. While she does not directly address the issues of race in the military, she does foreground the subject of Latin@s in the army and Marines and the challenges veterans face when recovering from war.

Another aspect of the fugue is the countersubject, which occurs when "the material which accompanies the answer is used again against subsequent statements of either subject or answer."[43] Hudes's fugue model designates Ginny, Elliot's mother, as a countersubject through their family garden in Philadelphia. She built the private oasis a few months after her return from Vietnam, transforming an abandoned lot into a lush garden reminiscent of Puerto Rico: "I said, when I'm done with this, it's going to be a spitting image of Puerto Rico. Of Arecibo. It's pretty close. You can see electric wires dangling like right there and there. But I call that 'native Philadelphia vines.'"[44] This garden flourishes and becomes a retreat and refuge for the Ortiz family, and the location in which four of the prelude scenes take place. The garden also juxtaposes U.S., Caribbean, and indigenous influences. Arecibo, the largest city in Puerto Rico and named after an indigenous chieftain, is characterized by the presence of caves and wooded hills bordering the Atlantic Ocean.[45] Philadelphia, the fifth largest city in the United States, is known as the city of brotherly love.[46] Hudes here highlights how the Ortiz family works to integrate their mainland and island lives. The garden becomes a cultural oasis in the midst of an urban environment where the Ortiz family can literally connect to their roots, reminding themselves of who they are and where they come from.

As in *Yemaya's Belly*, Santería plays a role in this theatrical world. Hudes describes her play as subtextually evoking the Santería orisha Osanyin (also known as Osain), who is "the patron of *curanderos* [i.e., healers] and the deity of . . . forests, the bush, and of medicine. Osain is herbalist, healer, and master of the healing secrets of plant life . . . his color is green, reminiscent of vegetation."[47] Thus, this garden seems to evoke the healing Osanyin offers. As Hudes explains in a note on the set: "The 'garden space' . . . is teeming with life. It is a verdant sanctuary, green speckled with magenta and gold . . . holy in [its] own way."[48] Hudes echoes the dynamic in a number of Latin@ plays with roots in the Caribbean, in which the American characters' utopian yearnings for island life often drive the action of the play. Here, the garden becomes a sort of tropical paradise or a Garden of Eden. In the Judeo-Christian creation myth, Adam and Eve are cast out of the garden after eating an apple from the tree of the knowledge of good and evil and Adam is relegated to "till the ground from which he was taken."[49] Being cast out of the Ortiz family garden means one is relegated to accept and experience the harsh realities of war and/or a life in the United States, which does not necessarily embrace the purity and beauty of the Ortiz family's Puerto Rican culture.

In the garden, Grandpop connects the United States, Puerto Rico, and Europe as he describes his love of the fugue. During this prelude scene, Grandpop explains the fugue as untying a knot. The knot is a fixed structure and the fugue untangles the strands, creating an altogether new formation.

> Of everything Bach wrote, it is the fugues. The fugue is like an argument. It starts in one voice. The voice is the melody, the single solitary melodic line. The statement. Another voice creeps up on the first one. Voice two responds to voice one. They tangle together. They argue, they become messy. They create dissonance. Two, three, four lines clashing. You think, good god, they'll never untie themselves. How did this mess get started in the first place? Major keys, minor keys, all at once on top of each other. *(Leans in.)* It's about untying the knot.[50]

Grandpop goes on to describe how he played Bach on the flute for his platoon in Korea. Hudes here links love of Bach to the elder generation's military service. Hence, the knot of the fugue form, which Bach is best known for, connects the subsequent generations of Ortiz men. Hudes deftly describes the dynamics of the fugue while asserting the metaphorical possibilities: the voices could correspond to the Ortiz generations, and the dissonance and messiness could refer to the complexities of military service. The knot could possibly reference the personal entanglements resulting from military service in three different wars: Iraq, Vietnam, and Korea. The knot also echoes a soldier's world, which is systematically organized but can be undone by tragedy. Throughout the play, Hudes's characters attempt to untie themselves from each other to clarify their past and move on.

Hudes's preludes, interspersed among fugue scenes, inhibit the full development of the fugue. In between the four voices of the characters intersecting in fugal synchronicity, Hudes interjects one or two voices in the preludes. Musicologist David Ledbetter discusses the differences between prelude and fugue forms:

> The commonest meaning of the term prelude in the seventeenth-century German tradition is of an improvisation to introduce some more premeditated type of piece. . . . Apart from alerting listeners that the music was about to begin, it had a number of purely practical functions in that it gave singers their pitch, and also allowed instruments, if present, to check their tuning.[51]

All of Hudes's preludes take place in Philadelphia, and not during war, and are either monologues or dialogue with one character on stage speaking to an off-stage voice. The preludes include Elliot's interviews with media, Grandpop's reminiscence of playing his flute, Ginny's ruminations on the genesis of her garden, Pop's letters from Vietnam, and Elliot's elegiac meditation on his life after his war injury. Many of the preludes have an improvisatory quality where the characters' language flows in unexpected poetic patterns. In contrast, the language of the fugue scenes at times follows an almost journalistic reporting style. Similar to their musical counterpart, Hudes's preludes alert her listeners (i.e., audience) to the complexities of the "pre-meditated" subject of her fugue play, Elliot's military service in Iraq. These preludes allow the characters to attune themselves to issues reverberating from this subject. The preludes provide a space for the family to start over and process their war experience. Rather than beginning the play with a prelude and then developing an ensuing fugue, Hudes constructs the play such that individuals constantly interrupt her fugue. These disruptions reveal the fractured nature of Elliot's dilemma, which necessitates an examination of the impact of war on each Ortiz family member. Hudes implies that regardless of the collective destruction of war, the individual cannot be erased or forgotten.

By titling her play *Elliot, A Soldier's Fugue*, Hudes sets up the expectation that the play will contain a simple fugal construction. Yet in the structure of her play, Hudes does not completely adhere to the fugue model. The play goes back and forth in time between scenes titled "Pre-lude" and "Fugue." The four fugues reflect pivotal moments in Elliot and Pop's military service, and the preludes illuminate the influences on Elliot's life before and after his first tour of duty. By moving back and forth between prelude and fugue, the totality of a fugue is never fully developed. By choosing only four fugues and using the preludes to high-light that which influences these moments, Hudes does not continuously delve into the reverberations of Elliot's military service and the physical and psychological impact of war. The spare poetic quality of Hudes's lan-guage infuses the play with a lyrical expression of her characters' strug-gles. However, the back and forth between prelude and fugue scenes pro-vides the audience with only brief glimpses into Elliot and Pop's military experiences. Some of those moments are harrowing, such as the recount-ing of Elliot's war injury in Tikrit, where his leg is severely injured. How-ever, Hudes does not delve into the lasting impact of that wound in sub-sequent scenes, preferring to jump in time. Even as Grandpop states that a fugue creates dissonance and is messy, Hudes's formal elegance at times resists engagement with the ensuing ugliness of war.

In addition, Hudes conducts another degree of theatrical experimen-tation through her fugal deconstruction. Musicologist Hans Eggebrecht reflects on the elements of the fugue, which include

1. connection to the theme—all musical activity proceeds from a single source
2. equality of voices—all voices in a fugue are equal carriers of the theme
3. linear quality—due to the equality of the voices, the polyphonic, inde-pendent character of each voice is imprinted with and characterized by the subject[52]

While the play centers on Elliot's journey, Hudes gives equal weight to each voice (i.e., character). The "solo" or "duet" voices of the preludes con-trast with the polyphonic fugue scenes where all four characters' voices intertwine. Hudes does not create a well-made fugue, but the breakdown of the fugue may indeed be the point. Hudes chooses a fugue, a West-ern European construct, to explore the military complexities of Elliot Ortiz, a Puerto Rican Marine. Hudes does not construct one single flaw-less fugue, for just as Elliot struggles between past and present, military duty and the lure of civilian life, national service and individual desire,

American culture and Puerto Rican culture, the fugue cannot fully express the complexities of Elliot's journey.

Nonetheless, the formalism of the fugue structure also questions the formalism of military structure, where strict regulations must be upheld. With Elliot injured in Iraq and Pop wounded in Vietnam, Hudes demonstrates that these military rules and procedures do not always create a mechanism for survival. The polyphony of fugal voices correlates to the collective of military experiences that cannot exist without each individual's prelude to service and the issues surrounding military duty and veteran life. This interjection of the individual into the collective breaks down the fugue and threatens to break down Elliot's future military career. Therefore, Hudes leaves her audiences to consider the unresolved dangling fugal elements that echo the vast unknown. Yet, as Elliot embarks on his second tour of duty in Iraq, the fugal subject repeats once more.

In the subsequent plays of the trilogy, Hudes continues her stylistic and structural experimentation. In *Water by the Spoonful*, Hudes illuminates Elliot in 2009, five years after his return from war, when he is struggling with haunting memories. The play also follows Yaz, his cousin and a college music professor, and Odessa, Elliot's biological mother and a recovering addict. Hudes utilizes modern jazz form in the play's dissonant, episodic structure as well as in Yaz's profession. Tanya Palmer, director of new play development at the Goodman Theatre, reflects that Yaz's lectures on the jazz of Coltrane "bring the musical underpinnings of the play to the fore. . . . The play exists in both the real and online world and is populated with people from very different backgrounds, each of whom brings a distinct cadence to the play."[53] Elliot and Yaz deal with the death of Ginny, Elliot's adoptive mother, while Odessa and four other recovering addicts connect virtually in her Internet recovery chat room.

Enveloped in Puerto Rican folk music, *The Happiest Song Plays Last* considers Elliot on a film set in Jordan and Yaz in her Philadelphia home in 2010–11 as they attempt to come to terms with their respective pasts in order to move forward. Palmer notes: "The play incorporates stranger-than-fiction details from the real Elliot Ruiz's life: he served as a consultant and then ultimately starred in director Nick Broomfield's feature film about Iraq, *Battle for Haditha*. In the play, the film serves as both a painful reminder of events Elliot would rather forget—and a remarkable second chance for him to seek forgiveness for his actions in war."[54] Elliot reconsiders Middle Eastern culture as he acts on location in Jordan and collaborates with Ali, the film's Iraqi consultant, and his co-star, Shar, a female Arab American actor. Meanwhile, Yaz struggles in her relationships with Agustín and Lefty, two men from her Philadelphia neighborhood. This is the only play in Hudes's trilogy that includes live music, which theatricalizes this family's enduring connection to Puerto Rico.

In the Elliot trilogy, Hudes builds a body of work that reflects a twenty-first-century Latin@ reality. Her trilogy explores diverse cultures, including Latin@, African American, Asian American, Arab American, Anglo, and Middle Eastern. Hudes's plays have a global reach, from the United States (Philadelphia, San Diego, and Puerto Rico) to Vietnam, Korea, Iraq, Japan, and Jordan. Hudes highlights linguistic diversity with intersections of English, Spanish, and Arabic. Her scenes navigate divergent spaces from the realistic to the virtual. Through *Elliot, A Soldier's Fugue* and the entirety of her trilogy, Hudes invites her audiences to witness a theatrical experimentation infused and shaped by musical forms, which echo and complicate the ways that one Puerto Rican family honors and recovers from military service.

CONDUCTING THEATRICAL EXPERIMENTATION

Fornes and Hudes both began their artistic lives outside of the theatre. Fornes worked as a painter before she became a playwright. Hudes trained as a musician and composer before she started writing plays. Fornes's training in the visual arts, such as learning Hans Hofmann's push-pull principle, informed her creative process. Likewise, Hudes's training as a pianist influences her ideas of dramatic structure. Hudes recounts a significant lesson from one of her mentors, Don Rappaport (1929–1995), who taught at the Settlement Music School in Philadelphia for thirty years.[55] "With the simplest of words, he opened my ear to what the world can sound like. He taught me, there are no rules. And that means there can be dissonance. He taught me what dissonance means. He said, 'Play a c-major chord in your left hand.' I did. He said, 'Play an f-sharp major chord in your right hand.' I did. It was dissonant and awful. And I became addicted to dissonance and resolution."[56] Just as abstract expressionism deconstructs and repositions images to generate innovative constructions in visual art, so dissonance in music distorts and reconfigures tonalities to create a new sonic landscape. Both *Yemaya's Belly* and *Elliot, A Soldier's Fugue* explore the dissonance and resolution in their characters' lives. She also applies Rappaport's "no rules" principle to her playwriting, which frees Hudes to conduct her own unique theatrical experimentation in form and content.

Fornes and Hudes both experiment with dramatic structure in their works. In *Fefu and Her Friends*, Fornes stages parts 1 and 3 in the living room of a country house and part 2 in four different locations: the lawn, the study, the bedroom, and the kitchen. The audience must literally migrate from the living room space to the other rooms and areas in and around the house. Hudes experiments with form and space in *Elliot, A Soldier's Fugue* by structuring her play around the fugue and prelude musical forms. However, she also experiments with how space is used by denoting that "the set has two playing areas. The 'empty space' is minimal and transforms into many locations . . . the 'garden space' by contrast, is teeming with life. . . . Both spaces are holy in their own way."[57] As the play shifts from fugue to prelude, the empty stage space becomes a variety of locations: a U.S. military base, a U.S. military transport ship, military barracks in Korea, Philadelphia TV and radio studios, a combat zone in Iraq, and airport tarmacs in Philadelphia and Newark. These locations alternate with the Ortiz's holy garden. Space here is both empty and full, flexible and rigid, secular and sacred. Geography becomes transitory, while the existential emptiness of the space is a constant in which to observe and experience the fraught dichotomies of military and civilian life.

Fornes and Hudes invoke the supernatural world of Santería and weave its spiritual thematic into the fabric of their plays. In *Sarita*, Fornes presents a Santería ritual where Sarita, her mother, and friends worship Oshun, the goddess of love. In *Yemaya's Belly*, Hudes stages a variety of rituals that emanate from a manifestation of Yemaya, the goddess of the sea. In *Elliot, A Soldier's Fugue*, Hudes subtextually invokes Osanyin, the god of healing. In the Santería pantheon, Oshun and Yemaya are sisters and Osanyin "was never born, he simply sprang to earth."[58] While Fornes's ritual to Oshun occurs in one scene only, the goddess's spirit of love permeates the entire play as Sarita must choose between her romantic relationships with Julio and Mark. Hudes takes the representation of Santería further in that Yemaya is a recurring theme throughout the play, as the goddess appears in various guises. Additionally, Yemaya's connection to water figures largely in Jesus/Mulo's survival. While Osanyin is not literally invoked in *Elliot, A Soldier's Fugue*, his spirit of healing permeates the play, as Elliot must try to recover from the wounds of war, both physically, with his injured leg, and spiritually, with the haunting horrors of combat.

Through the transformative stage space and Santería interventions, Hudes presents a Latin@ reality that is not monolithic but comprises numerous countries, locations, cultures, languages, and spiritualties. In her plays, Latin@ is not a fixed term but shifts through continual, expanding redefinition. By conducting theatrical experimentation, Hudes suggests that foundational elements of Latin@ culture can be transformed. Therefore, through questioning established forms and generating new dramatic structures, Hudes leads audiences to reshape their own views of what a Latina play can be.

CONCLUSION

The Legacy of Maria Irene Fornes

MARIA IRENE FORNES'S playwriting and pedagogy will continue to serve as a beacon to generations of theatre artists. Her work emphasizes the importance of the unique voice of the Latina playwright while continually complicating the dualities of Latin@/Anglo, Spanish/English, Cuban/U.S. Latin@, natural/supernatural, realism/experimentalism, and artist/teacher. Fornes's utilization of visual arts techniques such as drawing and visualization continues to impact the development of Latina playwrights. Fornes's work empowers a playwright to discover her individual aesthetic over and above issues of cultural affiliation and to embrace a more intuitive, idiosyncratic approach to writing plays.

The Latina playwrights included in this study have created vibrant works for the theatre that mirror the complexity of early twenty-first-century society. Yet a number of questions still remain. How visible are Latina playwrights in the overall field of American theatre? Where and how often is their work being produced? Are contemporary Latina playwrights being consistently published and anthologized? Are their plays being taught in the academy? Are Latina playwrights teaching playwriting in the academy and, as Fornes did, influencing the next generation of Latina playwrights? Investigating these questions informs how the Fornes frame can continue to shift, advocate for, archive, train, and expand the field of Latina theatre.

THE SHIFTING FRAME

The Fornes frame as a pair of glasses provides more than one lens to view the work of these five Latina playwrights. Fornes's teaching emphasizes the need to envision idiosyncratic theatrical landscapes. However, even though a playwright visualizes a world, does that creation ultimately become visible to theatre audiences? How has the view of Latina playwriting shifted over time? In many respects, Latina playwrights' work has consistently gained greater national visibility. Each playwright examined here has continued to rise to prominence and had an impressively thriving career. Quiara Alegría Hudes and Caridad Svich won prestigious playwriting awards in 2012. Karen Zacarías and Elaine Romero have been playwrights in residence at award-winning regional theatres. Cusi Cram has been a company member of the award-winning LAByrinth Theater Company. All of these playwrights have received world premiere productions in recent theatre seasons.

These Latina playwrights continue to make substantial contributions to the American theatre. Their most recent works are being developed and produced in prominent theatres across the country. What follows is a brief consideration of one or two of their most recent plays and how these works continue to reflect elements of the Fornes frame.

Cusi Cram's *Radiance* premiered in 2013 at the LAByrinth Theater Company in New York City and fictionally explores the true story of Captain Robert Lewis, a pilot in the air force, who is angry, wild, full of life, and a drinker.[1] Lewis was copilot of the *Enola Gay*, which dropped the atomic bomb on Hiroshima in 1945. The play begins with Lewis in a Hollywood bar in 1955, as he tries to avoid appearing on an episode of the *This Is Your Life* television show where he will have to meet Hiroshima survivors. The play then jumps back to 1945 on Tinian Island in the South Pacific, as Lewis prepares to fly in the *Enola Gay*. While none of the characters are Latin@, Cram again considers the complexities of cross-cultural relations (United States and Japan) and the pervasive influence of television. As in *Lucy and the Conquest*, her characters here must deal with the trauma of historical destruction. However, in this play the trauma occurs within the modern context of atomic warfare, and the main character, Lewis, confronts his past actions through the pressure to appear on a popular television program. Cram highlights the complexities of the post–World War II era and the ways in which television can attempt to intervene and mediate ruptures between nations. That Cram chooses to explore these cross-cultural issues in a non-Latin@ context suggests the ways in which military devastation can obliterate borders.

Daphne's Dive, Quiara Alegría Hudes's latest play, premieres in 2016 at the Signature Theatre in New York City, as part of Residency Five, "a unique program that guarantees each playwright three world-premiere productions of new plays over the course of a five-year residency."[2] As in the *Elliot Trilogy*, *Daphne's Dive* explores a North Philadelphia neighborhood. However, here the action involves a group of multicultural characters who find community in a cheap corner bar. Hudes presents Daphne, a Latina bar owner, Inez, her shamanic sister, Acosta, her politician brother-in-law, Ruby, her adopted daughter (any ethnicity), and her patrons, who include Jenn, an Asian American activist, Pablo, a Latino painter, and Ray, a glasscutter (any ethnicity). Spanning eight years, this linear narrative illuminates how this community faces adversity and change as a collective. Before and after the play's five scenes, Hudes also incorporates a pianist performing Caribbean music. Hudes describes the pianist's upright piano as "88 keys of Afro-Caribbean-urban history,"[3] and each of his pieces ushers in a leap forward in time as Ruby announces her age before the next scene starts. Similar to her libretto for *In the Heights*, Hudes stages the lives of an urban community. However, unlike in that Tony Award-winning musical cowritten by Lin Manuel Miranda, Hudes here experiments with how vibrant Caribbean piano music can serve as a counterpoint to the in-depth struggles and tragedies endured by this multicultural group of family and friends.

Elaine Romero is writing a trilogy entitled *U.S. at War*. The first play, *Graveyard of Empires*, winner of the 2013 Blue Ink Playwriting Award, received its world premiere at the 16th Street Theater in Chicago in 2015. The second play, *A Work of Art*, commissioned by the Goodman Theatre and developed in the Goodman Theatre Playwrights Unit, received its world premiere at Chicago Dramatists, in a coproduction with the Goodman Theatre, in 2015. In *Graveyard of Empires*, Romero examines the use of U.S. drones in Afghanistan through a fractured and nonlinear narrative that reflects the trauma of war. The lives of Drew Snider, a military software engineer, his former wife, Shanti, and his son, Nathan, a soldier, tragically intersect with Ramiro Enriquez, a Mexican American air force lieutenant, and his wife, Angela. Snider helped program the UAV (unmanned aircraft, i.e., drones) that Enriquez operates from the Las Vegas desert. Enriquez later stands accused of killing a large portion of a platoon through friendly fire.[4]

In *Work of Art*, Romero explores the aftermath of the Vietnam War, as Sabrina, a young Anglo woman, and her adoptive mother, Carmen, a Mexican American, mourn the death of her biological brother, Kirk, also Anglo, who died in combat. Set in the 1960s to 1970s, the play's multiple locations include "U.S. (Midwest and the West), Vietnam. This world, the next, and all those hard to define places in between."[5] Through reality interwoven with alternate realities, Romero considers another family destroyed by war, as one woman attempts to grieve, heal, and move on in her life. As of this writing, Romero is still composing the trilogy's final play, *Rain of Ruin*. A hallmark of Romero's work is her ability to seamlessly interweave the natural and supernatural worlds on stage as if theatrically attempting to construct a four-dimensional world. Whereas her previous works often contain a measured balance between reality and the spirit world, the first two plays of this trilogy are much more fragmented in their structure, with scenes containing rapid shifts between various realms. Her trilogy, thus far, considers fraught intersections between Mexican American and Anglo characters and provides a haunting experimental representation of how lives fracture through the casualties of war.

Caridad Svich's play *Guapa* received a National New Play Network rolling world premiere in 2013 at Borderlands Theater in Arizona, Phoenix Theatre in Indianapolis, and Milagro Theatre in Oregon. In *Guapa*, Svich considers the life of Guapa, a young Latina *futbolista* (i.e., soccer player) living in a Texas border town with her guardian, Roly, a bicultural Latina, Roly's children, Lebon and Pepi, and her cousin, Hakim, of syncretic ethnicity. Svich situates her play in the "harsh back country of dust and dirt, where along the highway, wayward billboards blare paintchipped ads for stores and sales long gone."[6] She stages the layers of Guapa's desire to escape poverty through her athletic talents. Svich here focuses on a Latin@ family and problematizes Latina identity through a female athlete named Guapa (which means "beautiful" in Spanish). Her play shows how athletic success can be gendered in the Latin@ community. Through Guapa's journey, Svich upends limited expectations for a Latina trapped in poverty. The Latin@ family here is nontraditional.

Guapa, whose parents have abandoned her, lives with a bicultural guardian, her children, and her multicultural cousin. Svich highlights here how contemporary Latina identity continually shifts as Latin@ families struggle against the pressures of economic survival.

The Cincinnati Playhouse commissioned Karen Zacarías's play *Native Gardens*, which premieres there in 2016. Zacarías considers Latin@ and Anglo neighbors who battle over a backyard fence. Tania and Pablo Del Valle, a couple in their thirties, recently purchased a house next door to Virginia Butley, an engineer, and her husband, Frank, a retired government worker. Tania is a Latina PhD student from New Mexico and Pablo is a lawyer, originally from Chile. Zacarías stages the play along the border of the couples' backyards, where "one garden is beautiful English garden with lush grass with a pond filled with fish . . . the other is unkempt, dying peonies . . . straggly rose bushes, grass, a large oak tree, leaves, and acorns."[7] The Del Valles' aim to transform their overgrown yard into a native garden with indigenous plants contrasts with the Butleys' perfectly manicured garden. When the Del Valles discover that their property includes part of the Butleys' garden, a conflict between the couples rapidly escalates. Zacarías considers complications between Anglo and Latin@ worlds through the contestation of physical and cultural borders. Her play *Mariela in the Desert* explored the contrast of Mexican and Anglo characters in 1950s Mexico. Here Zacarías focuses on the intersections between Latina, Latin American, and Anglo cultures within a modern U.S. context. Zacarías presents a young and successful middle-class Latin@ couple as they confront an older and retired middle-class Anglo couple. Zacarías uses the garden metaphor to complicate received notions of border crossing, land appropriation, and indigenousness. Though set in a suburban U.S. neighborhood, the conflict between the Latin@ and Anglo characters over land rights echoes historical conflicts along the U.S.-Mexico border.

Latina playwrights have gained greater visibility through the Arizona Theatre Company's National Latino Playwriting Award, established in 1995, by Artistic Director David Ira Goldstein and Playwright-in-Residence Elaine Romero. Romero has served as an adjudicator for the yearly competition since its inception. Romero reflects: "In my time as a judge for the contest, we have recognized plays that have gone onto long regional lives, published by major publishers, and even awarded a play that was later a finalist for the Pulitzer Prize. We have discovered some of the most significant Latin@ writers working today, supporting writers at all junctures of their careers. Most of our winners have been produced by theatres of all sizes across the country."[8] In its twenty-year history, numerous Latina playwrights have won the award, including Svich and Zacarías.

The visibility of Latina playwrights also continues to shift through the work of the Latina/o Theatre Commons (LTC), which Zacarías cofounded in 2012 while she was a resident playwright at Arena Stage in Washington DC. The LTC is a national movement made up of Latin@ theatre artists, producers, and scholars from across the country. The LTC advances the field of Latin@ theatre by embracing four tenets: art making, advocacy, networking/convening, and scholarship.[9] The LTC held a National Convening in 2013, presented an Encuentro (i.e., encounter), a National Latina/o Theatre Festival, produced by the Los Angeles Theatre Center in 2014,[10] and a Carnaval of New Latina/o Work, produced in association with the Theatre School at DePaul University in Chicago in 2015.[11] One of LTC's latest initiatives is the Sol Project, "a multi-year commitment in New York City for the production of Latina/o plays."[12] The National Convening, the first large-scale formal gathering of the Latin@ theatre community since 1986, brought together seventy-eight theatre artists and scholars from across the country, who met for three days at Emerson College in Boston, Massachusetts. They engaged in conversation about the history of and current challenges, opportunities, and visions for Latin@ theatre-makers in the twenty-first century. The Encuentro hosted nineteen Latin@ theatre companies from across the United States and Puerto Rico. The thirty-day festival presented fifteen works with over one hundred and fifty theatre artists, and provided a powerful national platform for Latin@ theatre ensembles. Los Angeles theatre critic Steven Leigh Morris wrote: "With the range of aesthetics, and the caliber of performance, Encuentro 2014 made its case that Latino theater cannot be ignored in any serious discussion of how the United States is evolving."[13] The Carnaval featured new plays by eight playwrights from across the United States whose work was presented in a series of staged readings featuring award-winning Chicago theatre artists. Zacarías reflects: "The birth of the LTC speaks to the need to give our Latin@ audiences a diverse and authentic repertoire of Latina theater . . . and build a bridge to other audiences and theaters."[14] Zacarías's visionary leadership catalyzed this movement, which promises to significantly transform the field of Latin@ theatre in the years to come.

ADVOCATING THE FRAME

If the Fornes frame is the proscenium arch of a theatre, who is advocating for sustained production of contemporary Latina plays? While the achievements of these five Latina playwrights are impressive, awareness of this work among producers, agents, managers, and artistic directors involved in Broadway, Off-Broadway, regional theatre, and theatre companies of all sizes across the country is continually needed. The diversity of Latin@ theatre needs consistent advocacy. Those who are in the position to produce work do not necessarily appreciate the cultural complexities of the Latin@ community and therefore rely on received notions, such as that all Latinas hail from an urban experience or are all Mexican American, Puerto Rican, or Cuban. Thus, opportunities for greater understanding often falter.

Each playwright in this study has reflected upon the state of Latina theatre and actively advocates for the field. Svich states: "There are amazing Latina playwrights in this country and only two or three are produced in 'visible' venues, which limits the range of what is seen and the diversity that is really out there."[15] Zacarías reflects: "I believe that we are reaching a transformative moment in theatre, when both the population and audiences start to wake up to the idea that we are not a small foreign exotic or domestic entity, but are (and have been, for a very long time) a vibrant, vital part of the American cultural, political, and social landscape. Latina theatre cannot continue to be placed in a niche—it must be recognized and presented, by a wide range of theatres to a wide range of audiences, as part of a universal canon of the American experience."[16] Both Svich and Zacarías advocate for the field through their respective foundational roles in NoPassport and the Latina/o Theatre Commons.

Since winning the Pulitzer Prize for Drama, Hudes has continued to advocate for the field at the national level: "It's worth noting that Second Stage, a major Off-Broadway theatre in New York, programmed a play by me and Tanya Saracho in the same season. It certainly breaks the 'slot' mold we have grown accustomed to—that there is one 'Latino' slot or one 'minority' slot. I had the opportunity to talk to the NEA [National Endowment for the Arts] with Second Stage's artistic director, Carole Rothman, who spoke passionately about audiences of the future. I do think the field is robust right now—ideas catch, and the idea of 'I can do that with my life' is a particularly catchy one."[17] Hudes also supports young writers through being on the board of Philadelphia Young Playwrights, an organization that produced her first play while she was in high school.

Cram addresses the sustainability of a theatre career: "I still feel like there could be more productions of our work, particularly in New York. And then there is the lure of TV—not that writing for TV means that you can't write for theatre, but it is quite consuming. And there is really interesting storytelling happening on TV right now. It's still really hard or next to impossible for most people to make a living as theatre artists, so I think more people, Latina and otherwise, are bypassing that as a real option."[18] While maintaining a thriving playwriting career, Cram has been an Emmy-nominated writer for children's television, a writer on the Showtime television series *The Big C*, and wrote, directed, and produced her first film, *Wild & Precious*, in conjunction with AFI's Directing Workshop for women. Cram also advocates for gender parity in the American theatre through being on the boards of Leah Ryan's Fund for Emerging Women Writers, "which aims to encourage talented but still unrecognized women playwrights,"[19] and the Lilly Awards Foundation, whose mission is "to develop and celebrate women artists by promoting gender parity at all levels of theatrical production."[20]

Romero responds by addressing the emergence of new Latina playwriting voices: "When I serve on panels, I see new people coming from every region of the country. There's a broader range of voices. Playwriting education is up. An MFA used to be rare; now it is the norm. Latina playwrights are writing about everything, and even when the play does not have Latina/o characters, their plays still bring a Latina perspective. There used to be a day when playwrights talked about their own work in terms of 'my Latino and my non-Latino plays.' I don't see playwrights making that distinction anymore. Their plays are Latina plays because they are Latina."[21] Romero continues to advocate for the field especially through her ongoing involvement with the National Latino Playwriting Award. These responses reflect how twenty-first-century Latina theatre is heterogeneous, flexible, transformative, and expansive. All of these Latina playwrights examine this complexity in their plays and work to advocate for and present their unique and diverse experiences to the American theatre community.

Consequently, in the not too distant future, could the theatre community imagine a shift in the programming on U.S. stages? What would happen if there were a regional theatre season in Los Angeles that included new plays by Karen Zacarías, Octavio Solis, Sarah Gubbins, Kia Corthron, and Julia Cho? Could there be a Chicago theatre company season that includes plays by Elaine Romero, Yussef El Guindi, Andrew Hinderaker, Sigrid Gilmer, and Alice Tuan? How would the field change if there were an Off-Broadway season that included works by Cusi Cram, Luis Alfaro, Sarah Ruhl, Naomi Iizuka, and Marcus Gardley? Could there be a season at the Brooklyn Academy of Music that included a site-specific, multimedia, music-filled play by Caridad Svich alongside experimental work by Taylor Mac and the latest opera by Philip Glass? How might the narrative of the American theatre transform if there were a Broadway season that included new plays by Quiara Alegría Hudes, Theresa Rebeck, Stephen Adly Guirgis, Suzan-Lori Parks, and David Henry Hwang? These conjectures are by no means meant to privilege regional, Off-Broadway, and Broadway theatres as the sole markers of success; nor are the pairings meant to suggest that Cram's work can only be done in New York and Zacarías's only in Los Angeles. These hypothetical seasons are meant to emphasize that a shift to cultural and gender parity is essential and that our national stages ought to reflect the cultural diversity within the Latin@ community as well as the cultural diversity in the United States.

THE ARCHIVAL FRAME

The Fornes frame as a grouping of ideas provides a means to document Latina theatre. Once the work is documented in the archive, it also becomes another aspect of the frame. In the introduction to *Chicano Drama: Performance Society and Myth*, Latin@ theatre studies scholar Jorge Huerta writes, "When I wrote my first book in 1980 . . . I could not have written about Chicana (read: female) plays and playwrights because there was only one Chicana playwright in print [i.e., *The Day of the*

Swallows by Estella Portillo Trambley], and, unfortunately, the Chicano Theatre Movement was male-dominated."[22] Is the archive now including more Latina plays? Are Latina playwrights being consistently published and, if so, are they also being anthologized? Of the plays analyzed here, all twelve are published, which is a promising sign. The publishers range from established U.S. theatre publishers such as Samuel French, Dramatists Play Service, Theatre Communications Group, and Smith and Kraus, to newer play publishers such as Playscripts, Inc. and NoPassport Press, to the journal *TheatreForum*, which publishes predominantly experimental work. While the archival frame is expanding, greater access to work by Latina playwrights is still needed. Svich spearheads one such effort by serving as editor of NoPassport Press, an independent press that publishes new plays, translations, and criticism. The NoPassport imprint has published numerous works by diverse writers such as Kia Corthron, Amparo Garcia-Crow, David Greenspan, Karen Hartman, Matthew Maguire, Oliver Mayer, Chiori Miyagawa, and Alejandro Morales.

Four anthologies have provided a significant survey of contemporary Latina theatre. In 1987, Theater Communications Group (TCG) published one of the first anthologies of U.S. Latin@ playwrights. Edited by M. Elizabeth Osborn, *On New Ground: Contemporary Hispanic-American Plays* contains work by Latina playwrights, including Fornes, Lynne Alvarez, and Milcha Sanchez-Scott. The anthology grew out of the TCG's Hispanic Translation Project and includes "new plays written in English by Hispanic Americans."[23] Osborn's editorial work, which incorporates interviews with each playwright, focuses on field formation by publishing Latin@ works not widely known at that time.

In 2000, TCG published another anthology, *Out of the Fringe: Contemporary Latin@ Theatre and Performance*, edited by Svich and Teresa Marrero, containing works by Latina playwrights including Svich, Migdalia Cruz, Cherríe Moraga, Coco Fusco, and Nao Bustamante, Naomi Iizuka, and Monica Palacios. This anthology includes a greater cultural and aesthetic diversity within Latin@ theatre. Marrero reflects: "The heterogeneous space of these texts is marked by a number of characteristics, the most prominent and innovative of which is the foregrounding of sexual identities that defy both Latino and Anglo cultural stereotypes."[24] Through Svich's and Marrero's interventions, this anthology engages critically with the growing complexity of the field of Latin@ theatre.

In that same year, the University of Arizona Press published *Puro Teatro*, an anthology edited by Alberto Sandoval-Sánchez and Nancy Saporta Sternbach dedicated entirely to Latina plays and performance pieces, including work by Romero, Moraga, Dolores Prida, Alicia Mena, Silviana Wood, Janis Astor del Valle, and several others. In publishing only Latina works, Sandoval-Sánchez and Saporta Sternbach explain: "Latinas working in theater have moved from marginal positions backstage to become the central protagonists of an emerging, hybrid, multicultural art form."[25] Sandoval-Sánchez and Saporta Sternbach went on to create *Stages of Life: Transcultural Performance and Identity in U.S. Latina Theater* (2001) to delve deeply into the thematic and theoretical questions raised by these and others works by Latina theatre artists.

In 2011, the University of Illinois Press published *La Voz Latina: Contemporary Plays and Performance Pieces by Latinas*, an anthology of work edited by Elizabeth C. Ramirez and Catherine Casiano. This volume includes plays by Cruz, Moraga, Sanchez-Scott, Evelina Fernández, and Carmen Rivera. Through this anthology, Ramirez and Casiano aim to document "a key period in Latina performance history by a select group of female playwrights from 1980 to the present, working in very distinct forms, styles, themes, and genres."[26] This anthology provides a collection of key works in Latina theatre spanning two decades. While all these editors have introduced influential Latina@ playwrights into the archive, their anthologies tend to focus on Latin@ playwrights from the three major Latin@ cultures: Mexican American, Puerto Rican, and Cuban American, with the largest representation being that of Mexican American playwrights.

Future anthologies need to include a greater cultural multiplicity within Latina theatre if Latina playwrights have reached "new ground," are "out of the fringe," write "*puro teatro*" (i.e., pure theatre), and have "*la voz latina*" (i.e., the Latina voice). New anthologies of Latina playwriting ought to include a range of work that addresses multifaceted Latin@ culture as well as Latina plays that explore topics completely unrelated to Latin@ culture. Titles for new anthologies could include "Multiplicity" or "Intersectionality." The cover art on the existing anthologies vary from a mountain landscape to a painting entitled *Esperanza* (i.e., hope) by Cuban painter Nereida Garcia Ferraz. One features a digital print entitled *Our Lady*, by Chicana artist Alma López, which depicts performance artist Raquel Salinas in a defiant pose as the Virgin of Guadalupe, while another features a photo from the film adaptation of Evelina Fernandez's play *Luminarias*. The cover for a new twenty-first-century Latina play anthology could perhaps include images from contemporary Latina theatre productions: a *curandera* meeting an Aztec woman, a *balsera* singing on a raft in the ocean, Yemaya dancing for a young boy, an Inca man appearing below a levitating bed, a Mexican woman painting her canvas, and a Puerto Rican Marine returning from war.

THE PEDAGOGICAL FRAME

The Fornes frame must be continually constructed and reconstructed. Frame-building knowledge must be shared in order for the frame to be sustainable over time. Since Fornes no longer teaches, those who studied with her are disseminating her methods. However, playwrights need to continue to develop new pedagogical models. The number of Latina playwrights currently being trained in the academy is uncertain. On an anecdotal level, in the past ten years of my university teaching career at various public and private institutions, I have taught playwriting to over two hundred students, and only ten have been Latin@ and only four Latinas. I have also taught playwriting workshops open to the community at large in Los Angeles and Chicago and in those settings encountered several Latina playwrights. If Latin@s make up approximately 16 percent of the U.S. population,[27] they need to be equally represented in academic playwriting programs across the country. The next generation of Latina playwrights will need to gain significant training to hone their craft while negotiating the complexities of culture and learning to discover their unique voices as writers—without the pedagogical mastery of a Fornes.

All the playwrights I have analyzed here teach playwriting in the academy. Cram teaches at New York University as well as the Einhorn School of Performing Arts at Primary Stages and their joint MFA Playwriting Program with Fordham University. Hudes is the Shapiro Distinguished Professor of Writing and Theatre at Wesleyan University. Romero is an assistant professor in the School of Theatre, Film, and Television at the University of Arizona. Svich has most recently taught at Rutgers

University. Zacarías has taught at Georgetown University. Other Latina playwrights teaching in the academy include Marissa Chibas (California Institute of the Arts), Naomi Iizuka (University of California, San Diego), Ashley Lucas (University of Michigan), Cherríe Moraga (Stanford University), Irma Mayorga (Dartmouth College), Monica Palacios (University of California, Santa Barbara), and Edit Villareal (University of California, Los Angeles.) While the array of Latinas teaching theatre is encouraging, it is not yet clear how/if Fornes's pedagogical methods are being utilized and/or transformed in the academy.

Current scholarship needs to continue to bridge the divide between Latina plays being developed and produced in the American theatre and Latina plays being written about and taught in the academy. The number of Latin@ theatre studies scholars continues to increase. Platforms for advocacy in the academy include groups such as the Latina/o Focus Group in the American Theatre in Higher Education (ATHE), whose president-elect, Dr. Patricia Ybarra, is the first Latina to serve in that role in the organization's history. The Latina/o Focus Group, which "supports both the scholarship and practice in Latin@ and Latin American theatre and performance and the collaborative initiatives between members and their respective institutions," has generated a database of Latin@ playwrights[28] and provides mentorship for emerging and established Latin@ scholars.

The Latina/o Theatre Commons (LTC) also provides a space for scholars to build networks of communication. One arena is *Café Onda*, an online journal of the LTC, which "seeks to expand and extend the dialogue and discourse around Latina/o theatre. *Café Onda* reflects current practice and trends in Latina/o theatre around the world."[29] The 2013 LTC National Convening included a series of conversations that involved listening circles and *conocimiento* (i.e., knowledge) groups. Latin@ theatre studies scholar Brian Herrera documented the convening and noted the following about the conversation among those working in academia: "Schools remain slow to integrate courses on Latin@ theater into the curriculum, a fact that contributes to a general lack of exposure to and experience with Latin@ theater among both students and faculty, and continues to produce audiences and theatremakers without even the most rudimentary cultural competence to appreciate the complexity and contribution of Latin@ theater of the last fifty years (let alone the last five hundred.)"[30] The convening concluded by synthesizing action plans in four areas: advocacy, art-making, networking, and scholarship. Among the twelve points in the area of scholarship, one action is particularly relevant to this book: "Establish a task force to develop a plan for the Fornes Institute, which would offer itinerant workshops, permanent retreat/gathering space, and a library."[31] The Fornes Institute will provide a platform to raise greater awareness about Fornes's plays, to advocate for the works of contemporary Latin@ playwrights, and to serve the field of American theatre by continuing Fornes's legacy.

FRAMING THE FRAME

The contingencies of the Fornes frame as a border are that the frame leaves out elements as it includes elements. The frame needs to be a permeable border that many writers can potentially cross. The frame is not about quantifying or exclusivity; it is about reclaiming and reframing the works that have been previously omitted. At some point very soon, there will be no more writers who have had direct contact with Fornes's teaching, and yet they will be entering the frame. I have included an extensive list of Latina playwrights in an appendix. Yet, how will the newest voices in Latina playwriting continue to flourish across the United States?

In my career as a playwright and scholar, I have seen the field of Latina theatre expand artistically, aesthetically, culturally, and spiritually. In 1988, I witnessed a stunning production of Milcha Sanchez-Scott's *Roosters* at the Los Angeles Theatre Center, directed by José Luis Valenzuela and starring Evelina Fernández as Juana, the southwestern mother who desperately wants her husband and children to reunite. From 1990 to 1995, I studied with Fornes in Los Angeles and New Haven. In 1998, I sat beside Fornes in New York City while attending her play *Summer in Gossensass*, about two actresses preparing to perform Ibsen's *Hedda Gabler* in 1891 London. I recall her saying to me, "When you sit in the audience watching your play, it is like you are seeing your play through a mirror on the wall. It's a brand new perspective." Yet, the field of Latina theatre needs to continue to embrace and encourage new perspectives.

Dramaturgical collaborations have also deepened my experience of Latina theatre. In 2000, while I dramaturged Svich's *Prodigal Kiss* at the Playwrights' Center in Minneapolis, I witnessed her teach the cast the haunting melodies she composed for her play. In 2004, as I dramaturged Zacarías's *Mariela in the Desert* at South Coast Repertory in Costa Mesa, I watched her intricately craft Mariela's relationship to Adam's theories on Mexican art. In 2006, I dramaturged Marissa Chibas's *Daughter of a Cuban Revolutionary* for the Center for New Performance at REDCAT, and marveled at her solo work, where she transformed into vibrant, historical members of her Cuban family. Dramaturging my colleagues' plays has inspired and informed my work as a playwright and a scholar.

The next generation of Latina playwrights may emerge from those who are currently studying in the academy, engaging with arts organizations, or staging their works in theatre collectives across the country. However, if the American theatre were to embrace the cultural complexities of all Latina playwrights, now and in the years to come, American theatre audiences would be enriched by experiencing the remarkable diversity in the Latin@ community and our stages would more accurately reflect twenty-first-century Latin@ culture. Received notions that all Latina playwrights hail from one of three main Latin@ cultural groups, or emerge only from an urban milieu, need to be jettisoned and replaced by a deeper appreciation of the cultural and social intricacies of contemporary Latin@ culture. Those who produce, advocate for, and represent superb works by Latina playwrights must continue to allow these plays to reach a broader American audience so that the novice theatregoer, as well as the seasoned professional, can gain greater access to this diverse array of Latin@ theatre, which reflects our contemporary American society. Therefore, I, along with my playwriting colleagues considered herein, will continue to write plays, write about plays, and teach playwriting and theatre studies so that the many voices of Latina playwrights will continue to crescendo, and establish an ever-expanding presence in the life of the American theatre in the twenty-first century.

EPILOGUE

Fornes Is the Frame

FORNES CREATED THE FRAME that informs this study. The theatrical frame of her work continues to be artistically vibrant and timeless. However, her physical frame has become very fragile. Fornes, now in her eighties, no longer writes or teaches, as she suffers from Alzheimer's disease and resides in an assisted living center in New York City. It is particularly heartbreaking that her mother, Carmen, lived to 103 with her mental faculties intact while Fornes now has little, if any, access to her memory of the recent past. For several years, members of her family placed Fornes in a residence in upstate New York, making visiting her very difficult.

Two significant women in Fornes's life valiantly galvanized the theatre community to support an ailing Fornes. In February 2013, Morgan Jenness, her former agent, and Michelle Memran, a filmmaker who has spent the last decade creating *The Rest I Make Up*, a documentary about Fornes that chronicles her career as a playwright and director,[1] successfully advocated for Fornes's transfer to a residence in Manhattan where her friends, students, and colleagues could consistently spend time with her.[2] While I now live in the Midwest, I've been able to visit Fornes a few times in New York City.

On my first visit, I went alone. I felt anxious. I had last seen Fornes over ten years earlier when she was still in relatively good health. We had both attended the 2001 Mark Taper Forum's Latino Theatre Initiative

FIGURE 19.   Maria Irene Fornes and Anne García-Romero at the Mark
Taper Forum Latino Theatre Initiative Retreat, August 2001, Plaza de
la Raza, Los Angeles, California. Photo by Jonathan Ceniceroz.

retreat where she taught a master class and later responded to readings
of new work, including an early draft of my play *Earthquake Chica*. As I
walked up the avenue toward her residence, I did not know how I might
react to being with Fornes in her present state. However, I kept in mind
the advice from friends that Fornes now responds most to music and
Spanish.[3] After I entered her room, I turned on her CD player, filling the
air with the joyful rhythms and forceful voice of Cuban singer Albita.
Then I began to speak to Fornes in Spanish: "Maria Irene eres maravil-
losa, increíble, te quiero mucho. Cuánto me alegro verte." (Maria Irene,
you are marvelous, incredible, I love you very much. I'm so happy to see
you.) While the Caribbean ballads continued, she whispered "Cuba." As
Fornes's childhood memories from Cuba surfaced, she ran her fingers
from her eyes down her cheeks to indicate tears. I gently touched her
arms and began to hold her hand. I recalled that one of my playwriting colleagues who had visited her previously did "hand dancing" with

her, and so I slowly moved her hands in mine while our arms swayed to the music.

A remarkable shift occurred as the third song played. Suddenly, Fornes started talking to me in nonstop Spanish. Sometimes her sentences were linear; other times they ended with a repetition of words like "Mamá" or "Papá." I did my best to engage in conversation. She seemed to tell me a story about what might have been a childhood friend who had something taken out of her hands. She at one point declared, "Soy bonita (I am beautiful), Maria Irene Fornes . . . very beautiful." She later slowly caressed my arms and then my face. She said "Besito" and beckoned me forward so she could kiss my cheek. We continued "hand dancing" while I smiled, relishing the moment. Next, she ordered, "No. Más serio," and I realized she was directing me to be more serious. She then began to make grand gestures with her face and arms, and I started to mirror her. She laughed and looked at me straight in the eyes. She pointed to herself and then to me.

As I said good-bye, a veil descended and a vacant look once again transformed her into an elderly woman with Alzheimer's. However, I left her room incredibly moved and infinitely grateful. We connected deeply even though she did not know who I was. She could not access any recollection of our relationship as teacher/student, yet still we experienced a profound spiritual, cultural, artistic, and emotional exchange. In the classroom, Fornes taught me to explore language, form, character, and structure in innovative ways that empower my theatrical voice. In her residence room, she taught me to use language, gesture, memory, and music to profoundly engage with another. Fornes continues to teach all of us that always the artistic spirit endures.

The frame must continually transform and move on to the future. As the coming generations of playwrights, theatre artists, scholars, students, and audiences continue to consider the work of Fornes and these Latina playwrights, we must journey beyond the frame. In Fornes's *Fefu and Her Friends*, Emma concludes her rehearsal of Emma Sheridan Fry's text with the exhortation, "Let us, boldly, seizing the star of our intent, lift it as a lantern of our necessity, and let it shine over the darkness of our compliance. Come! The light shines."[4] As these Latina playwrights boldly continue to shine light upon Fornes's legacy, I offer the following closing meditation.

If the Fornes frame is a grouping of ideas,
    may we expand upon Fornes's innovative notions of
    what a Latina play can be.
If the Fornes frame is a border,
    may we complicate the cultural, spiritual,
    and aesthetic terrain that Fornes and these Latina playwrights traverse.
If the Fornes frame is a pair of glasses,
    may our theatrical vision be increased by the work of
    Fornes and these Latina playwrights.
If the Fornes frame is the shape of a human body,
    may we continue to nurture a generation of individuals
    whom Fornes's work influences and transforms.
If the Fornes frame is a foundational structure,
    may we build upon the ground-breaking work of
    Fornes and these Latina playwrights.
If the Fornes frame is the proscenium arch of a theatre,
    may we continue to increase the staging of works by Fornes and
    contemporary Latina playwrights.
If the Fornes frame is the frame of a door,
    may we continue to walk through the artistic, theatrical, and
    professional portals that Fornes and these Latina playwrights open
    through their remarkable plays as they raise awareness of the vibrant
    and diverse field of Latina theatre.

APPENDIX A

INTAR HISPANIC PLAYWRIGHTS-IN-RESIDENCE LABORATORY

HISPANIC PLAYWRIGHTS-IN-RESIDENCE LABORATORY (HPRL) AT INTAR HISPANIC AMERICAN ARTS CENTER

The INTAR HPRL Program ran from 1981 to 1992, under the guidance of Maria Irene Fornes. It offered fellowships to Latin@ playwrights from all over the United States. The program consisted of an intensive three-month writing workshop in the fall and a series of staged readings of works in progress at the end of the theatre season in the spring. The HPRL members included:

1981/82:   Eduardo Machado, Manuel Martín, Roberto Monticello, Ana María Simo, Juan Valenzuela, Edit Villareal.

1982/83:   René Alomá, Guillermo Gentile, Manuel Martín, Dolores Prida, Ana María Simo, Cándido Tirado.

1983/84:   Juan Shamsul Alam, René Alomá, Oscar Colón, Federico Fraguada, Eduardo Ivan López, Lorenzo Mans, Peter Mentrie, Milcha Sanchez-Scott, Ana María Simo, Bernardo Solano.

This list was provided by Caridad Svich via INTAR (aka International Arts Relations, Inc.).

1984/85:   Juan Shamsul Alam, Oscar Colón, Migdalia Cruz, Lorenzo
            Mans, Cherríe Moraga, John Pi Román, José Serpa, Ana
            María Simo, Bernardo Solano.
1985/86:   Lourdes E. Blanco, Migdalia Cruz, Leo García, Lisa
            Loomer, José Pelaez, Manuel Pereiras, Ana María Simo,
            Ela Troyano.
1986/87:   Belinda Acosta, Migdalia Cruz, Leo García, Lorraine
            Llamas, Manuel Pereiras, Edwin Sánchez, Al Septién,
            Ana María Simo, Ilion Troya, Ela Troyano.
1987/88:   Alfredo Bejar, Migdalia Cruz, Nilo Cruz, Josefina López,
            Lorenzo Mans, Frank Perez, Ela Troyano.
1988/89:   Roberto Bedoya, Paul Hidalgo-Durán, Lorraine Llamas,
            Lynnette Serrano-Bonaparte, Octavio Solis, Caridad Svich.
1989/90:   Lalo Cervantes, Ezequiel Colon, Nilo Cruz, Chuck Gomez,
            Silvia Gonzalez S., Manuel Pereiras, Caridad Svich.
1990/91:   Oscar Colón, Migdalia Cruz, Nilo Cruz, Leo García,
            Lorraine Llamas, Lorenzo Mans, Caridad Svich.
1991/92:   Nilo Cruz, Lorraine Llamas, Lorenzo Mans, Manuel
            Pereiras, Ana María Simo, Caridad Svich.

CONTEMPORARY LATINA PLAYWRIGHTS

This list includes the names and works of many contemporary Latina playwrights. Each playwright has written more plays than those mentioned here. The titles below are intended to provide an entry point into the body of work of these playwrights and to illustrate the rich diversity in the Latina playwriting community.

Almazán, Raquel. *La Paloma Prisoner*; *The Hopefulness or La Esperanza*

Álvarez, Lynne. *The Guitarron*; *The Snow Queen*

Álvarez, Sofia. *Between Us Chickens*; *Life Drawing*

Anzoategui, Karen. *Catholic School Daze*; *¡Ser!*

Arizmendi, Yareli. *A Day Without a Mexican*

Astor del Valle, Janis. *Trans Plantations*; *Becoming Joaquin*

Avila, Tencha. *Maria y su sidekick*; *The London Impromptu*

Baez, Josefina. *Dominicanish*; *Comrade*; *Bliss ain't playing*

Beech, Maria Alexandria. *Little Monsters*; *What Are You Doing Here?*

I give special thanks to the Latino Focus Group of the Association for Theatre in Higher Education for their initial efforts in compiling this list. https://sites .google.com/site/latinofocusgroup/, accessed June 5, 2014.

Berger Wegsman, Graciela. *Memory Is a Culinary Affair*, *The Dream of Claudia Jade*

Bettis, Hilary. *The Ghosts of Lote Bravo*, *Mexico*

Bofill, Maggie. *Winners*, *Face Cream*

Bofill, Sylvia. *Insideout*, *Windows*

Bustamante, Nao. *America, the Beautiful*, *Inidig/urrito*

Cañel Rossi, Cyn. *Rhythm of the Saints*, *The Undoing of Berta*

Carreño King, Mariana. *Ofelia's Lovers*, *Dance for a Dollar*

Castro Smith, Charise. *Estrella Cruz [The Junkyard Queen]*, *Feathers and Teeth*

Chávez, Denise. *The Flying Tortilla Man*, *The Mask of November*

Chibas, Marissa. *Daughter of a Cuban Revolutionary*, *Brewsie and Willie*

Contreras, Julissa. *Daniel*

Colón, Kristiana. *Octagon*, *Cry Wolf*

Cook, Susana. *The Idiot King*, *The Values Horror Show*

Coppel, Fernanda. *Chimichangas and Zoloft*, *King Liz*

Coronado Castillo, Liz. *Little Girls Don't Do That*, *Aye, No!*

Cram, Cusi. *Lucy and the Conquest*, *Fuente*

Crespín, Patricia. *The Medea Complex*, *We Are Hispanic American Women . . . Ok?*

Cruz, Migdalia. *Fur*, *Miriam's Flowers*

De la Puente, Noemi. *Fountain of Youth*, *The Legend of Suicide Jack*

Del Busto Ramirez, Kimberly. *The Box*, *Hurricane in a Glass*

Díaz Cruz, Evelyn. *Glass Cord*, *Besito Pa' Ti*

Escobar, Georgina. *Sweep*, *Wayfoot*

Farías, Joann. *The Road to Xibalbá*, *The Land of Corn and Power*

Fernández, Evelina. *Solitude*, *Premeditation*

Fornes, Maria Irene. *Fefu and Her Friends*, *Sarita*

Gallegos, Lina. *Wild in Wichita/Locuras en Wichita*, *Carmen's Pearl*

Garcia, Vanessa. *Grace, Sponsored by Monteverde*, *The Cuban Spring*

García-Crow, Amparo. *The South Texas Plays*, *APPEAL—The New American Musical of Mexican Descent*

García-Romero, Anne. *Earthquake Chica*, *Paloma*

Gómez, Magdalena. *The Andalusian Dream*, *Landscapes*

Gomez, Marga. *Memory Tricks*; *A Line Around the Block*

González S., Silvia. *El Vagon/Boxcar*; *Alicia in Wonder Tierra*

Grise, Virgina. *Blu*; *Siempre Norteada*

Hudes, Quiara Alegría. *Yemayá's Belly*; *Elliot, A Soldier's Fugue*

Iizuka, Naomi. *Polaroid Stories*; *36 Views*

Lazú, Jacqueline. *The Block/El Bloque: A Young Lord's Story*

Lewis, Jessica. *Man and Coconut*; *Cashing In*

Loomer, Lisa. *The Waiting Room*; *Distracted*

López, Josefina. *Real Women Have Curves*; *Simply Maria, or the American Dream*

López, Melinda. *Sonia Flew*; *Caroline in Jersey*

Lozano, Florencia. *underneathmybed*; *BUSTED*

Lucas, Ashley. *Doin' Time: Through the Visiting Glass*

Macías, Alana. *Sand and Snow*; *Circle Course*

Martínez, Tere. *Borinquen Lives in El Barrio*; *I Want You by My Side*

Martínez-Cress, Noemi. *From Ali's Internet Café*; *Animus*

Mayorga, Irma. *Cascarones*; *The Panza Monologues*

Mena, Alicia. *Las Nuevas Tamaleras*; *There Comes a Time*

Moraga, Cherríe. *Heroes and Saints*; *Shadow of a Man*

Moreno-Penson, Desi. *Spirit Sex*; *Ghost Light*

Nevárez, Nancy. *Wild Out Sunday*; *Llamada/Rally Cry*

Nieves-Powell, Linda. *Rice and Beans and Other Rican Things*; *Amigos and Dreams*

Ordaz, Evangeline. *Bordering on Love*; *Mass Transit*

Ortiz, Amalia. *Carmen de la Calle*; *Otra Esa on the Public Transit*

Ortiz, Milta. *Más*; *Disengaged*

Palacios, Monica. *Clock*; *Miercoles Loves Luna*

Peláez, Carmen. *City Beneath the Sea*; *Rum & Coke*

Portillo-Trambley, Estela. *Blacklight*; *Morality Play*

Prida, Dolores. *Botánica*; *Screens*

Ramirez, Lisa. *Exit Cuckoo*; *To the Bone*

Rivera Tirado, Carmen. *La Gringa*; *Julia de Burgos: Child of Water*

Rodriguez, Diane. *Living Large in a Mini Kind of Way*; *The Sweetheart Deal*

Romero, Elaine. *Secret Things; ¡Curanderas! Serpents of the Clouds*

Ruiz de Burton, María. *Don Quixote de la Mancha: A Comedy in Five Acts: Taken from Cervantes' Novel of That Name*

Saenz, Diana. *A Dream of Canaries; Lorca at Víznar*

Saldaña, Jenny. *Dancing in the Mirror; PINK: The Chronicles of BC Jenny*

Salinas Schoenberg, Janine. *The Anatomy of Gazellas; Angel of the Desert*

Sanchez-Scott, Milcha. *Roosters; Dog Lady*

Saracho, Tanya. *The Tenth Muse; El Nogalar*

Sevahn Nichols, Adriana. *Night over Erzinga; Taking Flight*

Simo, Ana María. *Exiles; Alma*

Suárez Pico, Tatiana. *Flesh and Blood; Profit*

Sun, Nilaja. *No Child . . .*

Svich, Caridad. *Prodigal Kiss; Tropic of X*

Thome, Andrea. *Pinkolandia; Undone*

Torres, Maria Elena. *Maltinsky; Three Men on a Base*

Treviño Orta, Marisela. *Wolf at the Door; Braided Sorrow*

Troyano, Alina (Carmelita Tropicana). *Post Plastica; Milk of Amnesia*

Valencia, Rita. *A New World War; General Bliss*

Villarreal, Edit. *My Visits with MGM (My Grandmother Marta); The Language of Flowers*

Yanez, Diana. *Viva la Evolución*

Zacarías, Karen. *Mariela in the Desert; The Sins of Sor Juana*

NOTES

INTRODUCTION

1. *Oxford Learner's Dictionaries*, s.v. "frame," accessed May 13, 2014, http://oaadonline.oxfordlearnersdictionaries.com/dictionary/frame.
2. Sandoval-Sánchez and Saporta Sternbach, *Stages of Life*, 35.
3. Mendoza and García Márquez, *The Fragrance of Guava*, 38.
4. Eliade, *The Sacred and the Profane*, 10.
5. Bell, *Ritual*, 11.
6. Ibid., 37.
7. Ibid., 59.
8. Anzaldúa, *Borderlands*, 61.
9. Ibid., 60.
10. Ibid., 61.
11. Ibid., 59.
12. Ibid., 60.
13. Ibid., 99.
14. Ibid., 102.
15. Taylor, *The Archive and the Repertoire*, 94.
16. Anzaldúa, *Borderlands*, 101.
17. Ibid., 101.
18. Ibid., 101.
19. Ibid., 105.
20. López, "Violent Inscriptions," 58.
21. Sandoval-Sánchez and Saporta Sternbach, *Stages*, 53.
22. Ibid., 66.
23. Graham-Jones, "On Attributions, Appropriations," ix.

24. Suárez-Orozco and Páez, *Latinos*, 3.

25. Sandoval-Sánchez and Saporta Sternbach, *Stages*, 42.

26. Graham-Jones, "On Attributions, Appropriations," ix.

27. Ennis, Ríos-Vargas, and Albert, "The Hispanic Population 2010," 3.

28. Ehren, "Octavio Solis Wins."

29. *Maria Irene Fornes*, accessed August 25, 2008, www.mariairenefornes.com.

30. Svich and Delgado, *Conducting a Life*, 285.

31. Migdalia Cruz, along with Caridad Svich, was Fornes's assistant during her time in the INTAR Hispanic Playwrights-in-Residence Lab (HPRL). Cherríe Moraga was also an HPRL student, and Fornes directed her play *Shadow of a Man* at the Eureka Theatre in 1990. Since the aforementioned scholars have already documented the remarkable work of both of these playwrights, I do not consider Cruz or Moraga in this study.

32. Svich, e-mail interview by author, January 15, 2007.

33. *NoPassport*, accessed September 29, 2015, www.nopassport.org.

34. Zacarías, e-mail interview by author, January 2, 2007.

35. *Playwrights' Center*, accessed July 15, 2008, www.pwcenter.org.

36. Romero, e-mail interview by author, January 15, 2007.

37. *Broadway World*, accessed October 1, 2015, http://www.broadwayworld.com/phoenix/article/Matthew-Paul-Olmos-Receives-Arizona-Theatre-Companys-National-Latino-Playwriting-Award-20150629.

38. Cram, e-mail interview by author, January 15, 2007.

39. Hudes, e-mail interview by author, November 28, 2007.

40. *Quiara Hudes*, accessed July 15, 2008, www.quiara.com.

41. "Hispanic Playwrights History," *South Coast Repertory*, accessed June 1, 2014, http://www.scr.org/about/the-scr-story/scr-production-history/scr-play-reading-history/hispanic-playwrights-project-history.

42. *New Dramatists*, accessed July 21, 2008, www.newdramatists.org.

43. *Chicago Dramatists*, accessed June 1, 2014, http://www.chicagodramatists.org/.

CHAPTER 1

1. Scott T. Cummings provides an excellent, comprehensive, and in-depth consideration of Fornes's entire career as a playwright and director in his book *Maria Irene Fornes*.

2. Fornes, *Fefu*, 9–10.

3. Robinson, *The Theatre of Maria Irene Fornes*, 86.

4. Fornes, *Fefu*, 7.

5. Ibid., 15.

6. Svich, e-mail interview by author, January 15, 2007.

7. Fornes directed most of the world premieres of her own work. While this study solely focuses on Fornes's writing and teaching, her award-winning theatrical directing career deserves a more in-depth examination.

8. Svich, e-mail interview by author, January 15, 2007.

9. Romero, e-mail interview by author, January 15, 2007.

10. Cram, e-mail interview by author, January 15, 2007.

11. Paula Vogel began the Brown University MFA in Playwriting program in 1985 and taught there for twenty-four years. A Pulitzer Prize-winning playwright, Vogel is another major force in American playwriting pedagogy. Twenty years younger than Fornes, she continues to teach and write plays. Her students, including Nilo Cruz (also a Fornes student), Quiara Alegría Hudes, and Sarah Ruhl, have had award-winning playwriting careers, gaining Pulitzer Prizes among many other awards.

12. Hudes, e-mail interview by author, November 28, 2007.

13. Zacarías, e-mail interview by author, May 26, 2014.

14. Svich and Delgado, *Conducting a Life*, xix.

15. Ibid., 285–286.

16. Fornes, *Fefu*, 15.

17. Ibid., 11.

18. Ibid., 22.

19. Ibid., 57.

20. Ibid., 44.

21. Ibid., 54.

22. Ibid., 54.

23. Ibid., 57.

24. Robinson, *The Theatre of Maria Irene Fornes*, 87.

25. DeLamotte, "Refashioning the Mind," 154–158.

26. Robinson, *The Theatre of Maria Irene Fornes*, 87.

27. Ibid., 99.

28. "About Isadora Duncan," accessed October 15, 2007, http://www.isadora duncan.org/.

29. Fornes, *Fefu*, 33.

30. Tukesbury, "Emma Sheridan Fry," 341.

31. Osborn, *On New Ground*, 45.

32. Svich and Delgado, *Conducting a Life*, 268.

33. Fornes, *Plays*, 7.

34. Beer, "Beckett's Bilingualism," 215.

35. Robinson, *The Theatre of Maria Irene Fornes*, 223.

36. Another example of Fornes's cross-cultural inspirations can be found in *The Audition*, a short play she wrote for the Mark Taper Forum in the late 1990s as part of the Asian American Theatre Workshop's The Square. When I was working for Fornes briefly as a typist of one of her manuscripts, she told me how she was inspired to write a play about two Mexican actors who loved a famous Mexican film actor who was in actuality a Japanese actor named Toshiro Mifune. "In the slapstick-driven comedy *The Audition*, Fornes explores the idea of cultural stereotypes, with Greg Watanabe and Dennis Dun as struggling Japanese actors preparing for an audition to play Mexicans. The hilarious, zoot-suited Marcus Chong arrives on the scene to give a dazzling 'lesson' in Chicano, Mexicano, and cholo dialects and acting styles." Laura Weinert, "THE SQUARE," *Back Stage West*, July 13, 2000, 19, http://bi.galegroup.com .proxy.library.nd.edu/essentials/article/GALE|A67328262/034587e40 933ac51e9d22bobb381051c?u=nd_ref, accessed May 4, 2014.

37. Fornes, *Fefu*, 17.

38. Ibid., 60.

39. Ibid., 61.

40. Ibid., 4.

41. Years later, Fornes did create a single-set version of her play in which part 2 occurs on the same set as parts 1 and 3. In this main stage version, the four part 2 scenes occur sequentially while characters enter and exit Fefu's living room. This version was directed by Fornes at Muhlenberg College in Pennsylvania in 1996 but has not yet been published. See Cummings, *Maria Irene Fornes*, 75, for a description.

42. Svich and Delgado, *Conducting a Life*, 258–259.

43. Fornes also wrote and directed site-specific productions while in residence at the Padua Hills Playwrights Festival. Sometimes she designed her own sets. Fornes also engaged in cross-gender casting. For her 1989 play, *Oscar and Bertha*, which she staged while I was a student at the Padua Hills Playwrights Festival, she cast Pamela Gordon, an intense actor with a slight build and a smoky vocal quality, in the role of Oscar. Fornes explained she could not find any suitable male actors and felt Gordon best captured the spirit of the character.

44. Fornes, *Fefu*, 32.

45. Ibid., 37.

46. Ibid., 39.

47. Ibid., 29.

48. Ibid., 35.
49. This early lack of multiple productions may be due to the fact that it required an all-Latin@ cast with substantial acting and singing talent, yet it is not a musical. Thus theatre companies may have had difficulty in casting qualified actors for a nonmusical play with songs. Also, the lack of productions is evidence of the long-standing dearth of opportunities for plays with all Latin@ casts with Latina protagonists, a dearth that persists to this day.
50. Fornes, *Plays*, 109.
51. Sweetman, *Paul Gauguin*, 28.
52. Ibid., 16.
53. Ibid., 378.
54. Fornes, *Plays*, 108.
55. Ibid., 126.
56. Fernández Olmos and Paravisini-Gebert, *Creole Religions*, 45.
57. Fornes, *Plays*, 112.
58. Ibid., 113.
59. Sublette, *Cuba and Its Music*, 328.
60. Fornes, *Plays*, 114.
61. Fornes, *Plays*, 116.
62. Ibid.
63. Moroff, *Fornes*, 90.
64. Fornes, *Plays*, 95–97.
65. Cummings, *Maria Irene Fornes*, 108.
66. Fornes, *Plays*, 105.
67. Ibid., 129.
68. Cummings, *Maria Irene Fornes*, 7.
69. Fornes, *Fefu*, 47.
70. Svich and Delgado, *Conducting a Life*, 268.
71. Cummings, *Maria Irene Fornes*, 8.
72. Hofmann and Weeks, *Search for the Real*, 44.
73. Cummings, *Maria Irene Fornes*, 8.
74. "Quotes," accessed June 5, 2014, www.hanshofmann.net.
75. Svich and Delgado, *Conducting a Life*, 190.
76. A complete list of Fornes's students from her INTAR Hispanic Playwrights-in-Residence Laboratory can be found in Appendix A.
77. Svich and Delgado, *Conducting a Life*, xxi.
78. Fornes developed many of her works at the Padua Hills Playwrights Festival, the yearly gathering of playwrights, students, and actors in

Southern California that ran from 1978 to 1995. http://paduaplay
wrights.org/about/the-company/, accessed June 4, 2014.

79. Maria Irene Fornes workshop, Padua Hills Playwrights Festival,
Northridge, California, June 1989.

80. Ibid.

81. Ibid.

82. Maria Irene Fornes workshop, Yale School of Drama, New Haven,
Connecticut, September 1992.

83. *Online Etymology Dictionary*, s.v. "alumnus," by Douglas Harper, accessed
May 26, 2014, http://www.etymonline.com/.

84. Romero, e-mail interview by author, January 15, 2007.

CHAPTER 2

1. Svich, e-mail interview by author, October 20, 2005.

2. Svich, *Prodigal Kiss*, 18.

3. Ibid., 19.

4. Ibid., 20.

5. Ibid., 25.

6. Ibid., 31–32.

7. Ibid., 42.

8. Ibid., 45.

9. Mark 3:17 (RSV).

10. Gitlitz and Davidson, *The Pilgrimage Road to Santiago*, xiii.

11. Acts 12:2 (RSV).

12. Svich, e-mail correspondence with author, July 1, 2015.

13. Svich, *Prodigal Kiss*, 63.

14. *New Catholic Encyclopedia*, s.v. "Louis IX, St. King of France."

15. Ibid., 51.

16. Ibid., 52–53.

17. Albertson, *Bessie*, 195–196.

18. Wald, *The Blues*, 5.

19. Davis, *The History of the Blues*, 9.

20. Stainton, *Lorca*, 220–221.

21. Svich, *Prodigal Kiss*, 55.

22. Ibid., 61.

23. Ibid., 66.

24. Ibid., 68.

25. Ibid.

26. Dever and Dever, *The Poetry and Prose of Rosalía de Castro*, 243.

27. Cooder, video interview, June 25, 2012, accessed April 19, 2014.

28. *New Catholic Encyclopedia*, s.v. "Didacus of Alcalá, St."

29. Svich, *Prodigal Kiss*, 105.

30. Ibid., 116.

31. Ibid., 117.

32. Arie Uittenbogaard, "Sharon Meaning, Sharon Etymology," Abarim Publications, last modified 2014, accessed June 14, 2015, http://www .abarim-publications.com/Meaning/Sharon.html#.VX3BNGZ5dIk.

33. In the staged reading of this play at Midwest PlayLabs, Svich and director Neel Keller cast the roles using non-Latino actors, a casting technique Fornes also employed. This adds a whole other level to Marcela's Anglicization, to say the least. Again, due to the scope of this project, the performativity will not be fully addressed but merits mention here.

34. Svich, *Prodigal Kiss*, 120.

35. Ibid., 125.

36. Bessie Smith with Buck and His Band, *Do Your Duty*, accessed June 30, 2015, https://www.youtube.com/watch?v=9dnlnilzBe8.

37. Patterson, "Cuban Americans," accessed June 14, 2015, http://iipdigital .usembassy.gov/st/english/pamphlet/2012/08/20120822135006.html #ixzz3d4jUdLK8.

38. Svich, *Prodigal Kiss*, 128.

39. Ibid., 129.

40. Ibid., 131.

41. Ibid., 135.

42. Ibid., 136.

43. Ibid., 137.

44. Anzaldúa, *Borderlands*, 104.

45. Svich, *Tropic of X*, 12.

46. Ibid., 65.

47. Svich, e-mail interview by author, October 20, 2005.

48. Rivera, Marshall, and Pacini Hernandez, *Reggaeton*, 6.

49. Cobb, *To the Break of Dawn*, 6.

50. Ibid., 7.

51. Sublette, *Cuba and Its Music*, 525.

52. Ibid.

53. Hebdige, *Subculture*, 25.

54. Ibid., 26.

55. Banks also directed a staged reading of excerpts from *Tropic of X* at the Martin E. Segal Theatre in New York City on December 4, 2006, for an evening titled *Languages at Play in the Theatre—Tropic of X*, a reading + dialogue with Caridad Svich and Marvin Carlson.

56. Banks, *Say Word!*, 4.

57. Svich, *Tropic of X*, 12.

58. Ibid., 15.

59. Ibid., 16.

60. Ibid., 21.

61. Banks, *Say Word!*, 10.

62. Anzaldúa, *Borderlands*, 80.

63. Ibid., 77.

64. Svich, *Tropic of X*, 13.

65. Ibid., 26.

66. Ibid., 42–43.

67. Ibid., 84.

68. Ibid., 47–48.

69. Ibid., 52.

70. Ibid., 67–68.

71. Ibid., 70.

72. Ibid., 96.

73. Ibid., 99–100.

74. Ibid., 102.

75. Ibid., 102–103.

76. Ibid., 105.

77. Ibid., 106.

78. Svich, e-mail interview by author, January 15, 2007.

79. Svich et al., "The Legacy of Maria Irene Fornes," 2.

CHAPTER 3

1. Zacarías has created Spanish-language versions of these two plays. *Los Pecados de Sor Juana* was first produced in 2006 at Gala Hispanic Theatre in Washington DC; *Mariela en el Desierto* was first produced in 2014 at the Aurora Theatre in Georgia. This study concerns the English-language version of her plays. However, a comparative study of the bilinguality of the Zacarías plays does merit consideration.

2. Zacarías, e-mail interview by author, November 20, 2005.

3. Zacarías, *Mariela*, 16.

4. Du Pont, *Tamayo*, 22.

5. Lowe, *Tina Modotti*, 10.

6. Zacarías, *Mariela*, 27.

7. Ibid., 36.

8. Quintana, *Pancho Villa*, x.

9. Zacarías, *Mariela*, 38.

10. Ibid.

11. Ibid., 38–39.

12. Toynton and Pollock, *Jackson Pollock*, 57.

13. Ibid., 3.

14. Kahlo, Dexter, Barson, and Ankori, *Frida Kahlo*, 129.

15. Zacarías, *Mariela*, 43.

16. Ibid., 45.

17. Ibid., 42.

18. Ibid.

19. Ibid., 62.

20. Ibid., 64.

21. Ibid.

22. Ibid., 65.

23. Ibid., 70.

24. Ibid.

25. Luna, "Treaty of Guadalupe Hidalgo."

26. Zacarías, *Mariela*, 74.

27. Ibid., 75.

28. Ibid.

29. Ibid., 77.

30. Ibid., 47.

31. Ibid., 89.

32. Zacarías, e-mail interview by author, November 20, 2005.

33. Paz, *Sor Juana*, 1.

34. Kirk, *Sor Juana*, 15–17.

35. Palmer, "Karen Zacarías," 10.

36. De la Cruz, *Selected Writings*, 163. The original Spanish reads: "Entréme religiosa, porque aunque conocía que tenía el estado cosas (de las accesorias hablo, no de las formales), muchas repugnantes a mi genio, con todo, para la total negación que tenía al matrimonio, era lo menos desproporcionado y lo más decente que podía elegir en materia de la seguridad que deseaba de mi salvación."

37. Paz, *Sor Juana*, 11.

38. Zacarías, *Sor Juana*, 41.

39. Ibid., 3. The original Spanish reads: "Si lós riesgos del mar considerara, ninguno se embarcara; si antes viera bien su peligro, nadie se atreviera ni al bravo toro osado provocara."

40. Thomas, *The Politics and Poetics of Sor Juana*, 12.

41. Zacarías, *Sor Juana*, 4. The original Spanish text reads: "Pero si hubiera alguno tan osado que, no obstante el peligro, al mismo Apolo quisiese gobernar con atrevida mano el rápido carro en luz bañado, todo lo hiciera, y no tomara sólo estado que ha de ser toda la vida."

42. Leeming, *Oxford Companion to World Mythology*, s.v. "Apollo."

43. Zacarías, *Sor Juana*, 14.

44. Ibid., 28.

45. Berdan, *Aztec Archaeology*, 234.

46. Paz, *Sor Juana*, 152.

47. Zacarías, *Sor Juana*, 16.

48. Ibid., 46.

49. Ibid., 47.

50. Ibid., 47.

51. This cross-dressing scene echoes Sor Juana's play *Los Empeños de Una Casa* (*The Trials of a House*) in which one of the male characters cross-dresses as a woman to escape discovery.

52. Zacarías, *Sor Juana*, 28.

53. Cervantes, *Don Quixote*, 21.

54. Zacarías, *Sor Juana*, 47.

55. Ibid.

56. The original Spanish reads: "Venid, Serafines, venid a mirar una Rosa que vive cortada, más; y no se marchita, antes resucita al fiero rigor, porque se fecunda con su proprio humor. Y así, es beneficio llegarla a cortar: venid, Jardineros, ¡venid a mirar una Rosa que vive cortada, más!"

57. Octavio Paz offers an in-depth exploration of these *villancicos* in his book *Sor Juana, or, The Traps of Faith*.

58. Paz, *Sor Juana*, 434–435.

59. *New Catholic Encyclopedia*, s.v. "Catherine of Alexandria, St."

60. Carlson, *The Haunted Stage*, 53.

61. Zacarías, *Sor Juana*, 47.

62. Zacarías, *Sor Juana*. Zacarías made this note in the 2001 Dramatic Publishing version of the play.

63. Toynton and Pollock, *Jackson Pollock*, 20.

64. Coates, "Art Galleries Abroad," 83–84.

65. Wolf, "Abstract Expressionism," accessed June 5, 2014, http://www .theartstory.org/movement-abstract-expressionism.htm.
66. Zacarías, *Mariela*, 98.

CHAPTER 4

1. Bowers's book provides a thorough history of the term "magic realism" as it relates to literature, film, and painting, but does not discuss its use in theatre. Bowers, *Magic(al) Realism*, 1.
2. Rossini, Contemporary Latina/o Theatre, 148.
3. Romero, e-mail interview by author, June 1, 2014.
4. Gilman, *The Making of Modern Drama*, 63.
5. Romero, interview by author, August 5, 2015.
6. Anzaldúa, *Borderlands*, 77.
7. Ibid.
8. Perronne, Stockel, and Krueger, *Medicine Women*, 86.
9. Avila, *Woman Who Glows*, 17.
10. Peronne, Stockel, and Krueger, *Medicine Women*, 37–38.
11. Romero, e-mail interview by author, May 27, 2008.
12. Romero, *¡Curanderas!*, 27.
13. Ibid., 2.
14. Avila, *Woman Who Glows*, 73.
15. Romero, *¡Curanderas!*, 7.
16. Ibid., 10.
17. Avila, *Woman Who Glows*, 64.
18. Romero, *¡Curanderas!*, 27.
19. Ibid., 29.
20. Ibid., 1.
21. Anzaldúa, *Borderlands*, 68.
22. Romero, *¡Curanderas!*, 39.
23. Navarrete, "The Path from Aztlán," 31–48.
24. Romero, *¡Curanderas!*, 40–41.
25. Ibid., 43.
26. Ibid., 51.
27. Ibid., 55.
28. Ibid., 57.
29. Carrasco, *Daily Life of the Aztecs*, 267.
30. Ibid., 45.
31. Romero, *¡Curanderas!*, 59.

32. Ibid., 64.
33. Ibid., 83–84.
34. Avila, *Woman Who Glows*, 192.
35. Romero, *¡Curanderas!*, 85.
36. Ibid., iii.
37. Ibid., 7.
38. Ibid., 85.
39. Romero, e-mail interview by author, January 15, 2007.
40. Romero, *¡Curanderas!*, 58.
41. Ibid., 61–62.
42. Romero, e-mail interview by author, January 15, 2007.
43. Jacobs, "Women, Ritual, and Secrecy," 97.
44. Ibid., 97.
45. Romero, *Secret Things*, 6.
46. Ibid.
47. Ibid.
48. Díaz-Más, *Sephardim*, 7.
49. Romero, *Secret Things*, 10.
50. Romero, e-mail interview by author, November 11, 2005.
51. Epstein, *Kabbalah*, 15–16.
52. Cordovero and Robinson, *Moses Cordovero's Introduction to Kabbalah*, xxiv.
53. Romero, *Secret Things*, 15.
54. Ibid., 19.
55. Taylor, *The Archive and Repertoire*, 94.
56. Menocal, *The Ornament of the World*, 30.
57. "Legion of Mary," accessed June 4, 2015, http://www.legionofmary.ie/.
58. "About the Apostolate," accessed June 4, 2015, http://wafusa.org/the-apostolate/.
59. *Jewish Virtual Library*, s.v. "The Star of David—*Magen David*," accessed June 4, 2015, https://www.jewishvirtuallibrary.org/jsource/Judaism/star.html.
60. Romero, *Secret Things*, 23.
61. Ibid., 39.
62. Gitlitz, *Secrecy and Deceit*, 52.
63. Deuteronomy 6:4, 9 (RSV).
64. Gitlitz, *Secrecy and Deceit*, 528.
65. Ibid.
66. Romero, *Secret Things*, 56.

67. *Encyclopædia Britannica Online*, s.v. "unified field theory," accessed May 31, 2014, http://www.britannica.com/EBchecked/topic/614522/unified-field-theory.

68. Romero, *Secret Things*, 33.

69. Plato, *Symposium*, accessed March 1, 2015, http://classics.mit.edu/Plato/symposium.html.

70. Genesis 2:21–23 (RSV).

71. Romero, *Secret Things*, 68.

72. *The Concise Oxford Dictionary of the Christian Church*, s.v. "Solomon, Song of," http://www.oxfordreference.com/view/10.1093/acref/97801996 59623.001.0001/acref-9780199659623-e-5414.

73. Judges 16:1–22 (RSV).

CHAPTER 5

1. Cram, e-mail interview by author, November 15, 2005.

2. Cram, *Lucy*, 8.

3. Ibid.

4. Ibid., 9.

5. Reinhard, *Machu Picchu*, 5.

6. Ibid.

7. Sullivan, *The Secrets of the Inca*, 24.

8. Reinhard, *Machu Picchu*, 12.

9. Cram, *Lucy*, 10.

10. *The Concise Oxford Dictionary of Archaeology*, s.v. "Quechua," accessed May 15, 2014, http://www.oxfordreference.com/view/10.1093/acref/97 8019953 4043.001.0001/acref-9780199534043-e-3411.

11. Cram, *Lucy*, 11.

12. Cram, e-mail interview by author, November 15, 2005.

13. Cram, *Lucy*, 5.

14. Ibid., 12.

15. Ibid., 15.

16. *A Dictionary of World History*, s.v. "Bolívar, Simón," accessed May 1, 2015, http://www.oxfordreference.com/view/10.1093/acref/9780192807007 .001.0001/acref-9780192807007-e-488.

17. Cram, *Lucy*, 20.

18. Ibid., 20.

19. Diamond, *Guns, Germs, and Steel*, 68.

20. Cram, *Lucy*, 21.

21. Ibid., 22.
22. Ibid., 40.
23. Ibid.
24. Pease, "The Andean Creator God," 173.
25. Urton, *Inca Myths*, 73.
26. Cram, *Lucy*, 41.
27. Ibid., 43.
28. *The Oxford Companion to Archaeology*, s.v. "Tiahuanaco Empire," accessed May 15, 2014, http://www.oxfordreference.com/view/10.1093/acref/978 0195076189.001.0001/acref-9780195076189-e-0446.
29. Cram, *Lucy*, 43.
30. Ibid., 50.
31. *Encyclopædia Britannica Online*, s.v. "forensic psychology," accessed March 10, 2015, http://www.britannica.com/EBchecked/topic/1373311/ forensic-psychology.
32. Cram, *Lucy*, 51.
33. Ibid., 57.
34. Ibid., 62.
35. *The Oxford Companion to American Literature*, s.v. "Tom Sawyer, the Adventures of," accessed April 20, 2015, http://www.oxfordreference .com/view/10.1093/acref/9780195065480.001.0001/acref-978019 5065480-e-4812.
36. Cram, *Lucy*, 65.
37. Ibid., 68.
38. Cram, *Fuente*, 5.
39. Ibid., 9.
40. Sharon Mazzarella, "Dynasty," on Museum of Broadcast Communications website, accessed May 23, 2014, http://www.museum.tv/eotv/ dynasty.htm.
41. Cram, *Fuente*, 24.
42. Ibid., 14.
43. Allen, *Speaking of Soap Operas*, 137–138.
44. Gripsrud, *The Dynasty Years*, 164.
45. Ibid., 163.
46. Ibid.
47. Ibid., 203.
48. Bates, *Dynasty High*, 107.
49. Gripsrud, *The Dynasty Years*, 206.
50. Ibid., 233.
51. Cram, *Fuente*, 68.

52. "The Facts of Life," on *TV.com*, accessed June 1, 2014, http://www.tv .com/shows/the-facts-of-life/.

53. Cram, *Fuente*, 68.

54. Ibid., 5.

55. Translation: "The Anglos, with a look of innocence on their faces, cut out our tongue."

56. Anzaldúa, *Borderlands*, 76.

57. Cram, *Fuente*, 8–9.

58. Ibid., 58.

59. Ibid., 45.

60. Ibid., 10.

61. Ibid., 14.

62. Ibid., 51.

63. Ibid., 56.

64. Ibid., 58.

65. Ibid., 59.

66. Geraghty, *Women and Soap Opera*, 65.

67. Cram, *Fuente*, 73.

68. Cram, *Lucy*, 52.

69. Cram, *Fuente*, 9.

70. Taylor, *Archive and Repertoire*, 234.

71. Fornes, *Fefu*, 22.

72. Ibid., 47–48.

73. "Cassie Callison Carpenter," on *soapcentral.com*, accessed April 8, 2015, http://soapcentral.com/oltl/whoswho/cassie.php.

74. *Soap Opera Digest*, November 23, 1982, 70.

75. Brown, "Cusi Cram," 113.

76. Cram, *Lucy*, 18.

77. Cram, e-mail interview by author, January 15, 2007.

78. Feuer, "Reading Dynasty," 444.

79. Ibid., 458.

80. Cram, e-mail interview by author, November 15, 2005.

CHAPTER 6

1. *Oxford Dictionary of English*, s.v. "conductor," accessed May 5, 2014, http://www.oxfordreference.com/view/10.1093/acref/9780199957111 23.001.0001/m_en_gb0170940.

2. Mason, *Living Santería*, 8.

3. Hudes, e-mail interview by author, December 1, 2005.

4. Fernández Olmos and Paravisini-Gebert, *Creole Religions*, 38.
5. Ibid., 52.
6. Ibid.
7. Ibid., 256.
8. Hudes, *Yemaya's Belly*, 6.
9. Mason, *Living Santería*, 61.
10. Hudes, *Yemaya's Belly*, 14.
11. Ibid., 15.
12. Ibid., 16.
13. Ibid.
14. Ibid., 18
15. Ibid., 19.
16. Ibid., 20.
17. Ibid., 27.
18. Ibid., 31.
19. Fernández Olmos and Paravisini-Gebert, *Creole Religions*, 43.
20. Hudes, *Yemaya's Belly*, 43.
21. Ibid., 46.
22. Ibid., 48.
23. Anzaldúa, *Borderlands*, 61.
24. Fernández Olmos and Paravisini-Gebert, *Creole Religions*, 52.
25. Hudes, *Yemaya's Belly*, 43.
26. Hudes, e-mail interview by author, December 1, 2005.
27. Hudes, *Yemaya's Belly*, 6.
28. Hudes, *Elliot*, vii.
29. Hudes, e-mail interview by author, August 28, 2012.
30. Verrall, *Fugue and Invention*, ix.
31. *Encyclopedia of Popular Music*, s.v. "Mercerón Mariano," accessed May 10, 2015, http://www.oxfordreference.com/view/10.1093/acref/9780195313734.001.0001/acref-9780195313734-e-18782.
32. Hudes, *Elliot*, 6.
33. Wolff, *Johann Sebastian Bach*, 433.
34. Hudes, *Elliot*, 5.
35. Ibid., 7.
36. Ibid., 15.
37. *The Oxford Companion to Music*, s.v. "passacaglia," accessed May 18, 2014, http://www.oxfordreference.com/view/10.1093/acref/9780199579037.001.0001/acref-9780199579037-e-5014.
38. LoConto, Clark, and Ware, "The Diaspora of West Africa," 106.

39. "3D Light Armored Reconnaissance Bn," on the Marine Corps website, accessed June 7, 2015, http://www.1stmardiv.marines.mil/Units/3DLAR BN.aspx.

40. Villahermosa, "America's Hispanics," 62–66.

41. Ibid.

42. West, *The Women of the Army Nurse Corps*, 5.

43. Verrall, *Fugue and Invention*, 19.

44. Hudes, *Elliot*, 20.

45. Magaly Rivera, "Arecibo," on Tour Puerto Rico website, accessed June 1, 2014, http://www.topuertorico.org/city/arecibo.shtml.

46. *Oxford Encyclopedia of the Modern World*, s.v. "Philadelphia," accessed June 20, 2015, http://www.oxfordreference.com/view/10.1093/acref/97 80195176322.001.0001/acref-9780195176322-e-1235.

47. Fernández Olmos and Paravisini-Gebert, *Creole Religions*, 59.

48. Hudes, *Elliot*, 4.

49. Genesis 3:22–23 (RSV).

50. Hudes, "Elliot, a Soldier's Fugue," 37.

51. Ledbetter, *Bach's Well-Tempered Clavier*, 54.

52. Eggebrecht, *The Art of Fugue*, 61–62.

53. Palmer, "The Making of a Trilogy," 12.

54. Ibid., 13.

55. Valerie M. Russ, "Donald Rappaport, 66, Caring Music Teacher," on *Philly.com*, posted December 11, 1995, accessed March 10, 2015, http:// articles.philly.com/1995-12-11/news/25671258_1_music-teacher -settlement-music-school-teen-student.

56. Hudes, e-mail interview by author, November 28, 2007.

57. Hudes, *Elliot*, 4.

58. Fernández Olmos and Paravisini-Gebert, *Creole Religions*, 59.

CONCLUSION

1. Cram, "Radiance," unpublished manuscript, 2014, 3.

2. http://www.signaturetheatre.org/Explore/Residencies/Residency-Five .aspx, accessed March 29, 2015.

3. Hudes, "Daphne's Dive," unpublished manuscript, 2015, 2.

4. Romero, "Graveyard of Empires," unpublished manuscript, 2015, 3.

5. Romero, "A Work of Art," unpublished manuscript, 2015, 3.

6. Svich, "Guapa," unpublished manuscript, 2012, 2.

7. Zacarías, "Native Gardens," unpublished manuscript, 2015, 1.

8. Romero, e-mail interview by author, September 29, 2015.

9. http://howlround.com/latina/o-theatre-commons, accessed June 1, 2014.

10. http://thelatc.org/encuentro2014/, accessed March 12, 2015.

11. http://howlround.com/2015-carnaval-of-new-latinao-work, accessed June 29, 2015.

12. http://howlround.com/latina/o-theatre-commons, accessed October 18, 2015.

13. http://www.laweekly.com/arts/the-fantastic-encuentro-2014-festival-showed-the-power-of-latino-theater-5207079, accessed March 12, 2015.

14. Zacarías, e-mail interview by author, May 26, 2014.

15. Svich, e-mail interview by author, January 29, 2008.

16. Zacarías, e-mail interview by author, May 26, 2014.

17. Hudes, e-mail interview by author, April 7, 2014.

18. Cram, e-mail interview by author, May 21, 2014.

19. www.leahryansfeww.com, accessed October 23, 2015.

20. http://www.thelillyawards.org/, accessed October 23, 2015.

21. Romero, e-mail interview by author, June 4, 2014.

22. Huerta, *Chicano Drama*, 11.

23. Osborn, *On New Ground*, vi.

24. Svich and Marrero, *Out of the Fringe*, xvii.

25. Sandoval-Sánchez and Saporta Sternbach, *Puro Teatro*, xi.

26. Ramirez and Casiano, *La Voz Latina*, 1.

27. Ennis, Ríos-Vargas, and Albert, "The Hispanic Population 2010," 3.

28. https://sites.google.com/site/latinofocusgroup/, accessed April 23, 2015.

29. http://howlround.com/cafe-onda, accessed July 2, 2015.

30. Herrera, Benjulian, and Gahlon, *The Latina/o Theatre Commons*, 79.

31. Ibid., 133.

EPILOGUE

1. http://documentingirene.com/, accessed June 1, 2014.

2. Koznin, "Theater World Friends."

3. A portion of this section was previously published in *Innovation in Five Acts: Strategies for Theatre and Performance*, edited by Caridad Svich, New York: Theatre Communications Group, 2015.

4. Fornes, *Fefu*, 48.

BIBLIOGRAPHY

"About LFG." *Latino Focus Group.* Accessed April 23, 2015. https://sites.google
.com/site/latinofocusgroup/.

Albertson, Chris. *Bessie.* New Haven, CT: Yale University Press, 2003.

Allen, Robert Clyde. *Speaking of Soap Operas.* Chapel Hill: University of
North Carolina Press, 1985.

Anzaldúa, Gloria. *Borderlands/La Frontera: The New Mestiza.* San Francisco:
Aunt Lute Books, 1987.

Aristotle. *Poetics.* Translated by S. H. Butcher. New York: Hill and Wang, 1961.

Arrizón, Alicia. *Latina Performance: Traversing the Stage.* Bloomington: Indiana University Press, 1999.

Arrizón, Alicia, and Lillian Manzor, eds. *Latinas on Stage.* Berkeley, CA:
Third Woman Press, 2000.

Avila, Elena. *Woman Who Glows in the Dark: A Curandera Reveals Traditional
Aztec Secrets of Physical and Spiritual Health.* With Joy Parker. New York:
J. P. Tarcher/Putnam, 1999.

Baker, George Pierce. *Dramatic Technique.* Boston: Houghton Mifflin, 1919.

Banks, Daniel. *Say Word!: Voices from Hip Hop Theater: An Anthology.* Ann
Arbor: University of Michigan Press, 2011.

Bates, Billie Rae. *Dynasty High: A Guide to TV's Dynasty and Dynasty II: The
Colbys.* North Charleston, SC: Booksurge, 2006.

Beauvoir, Simone de. *The Second Sex.* Translated by H. M. Parshley. New
York: Knopf, 1953.

Beer, Ann. "Beckett's Bilingualism." In *The Cambridge Companion to Beckett*, edited by John Pilling, 209–221. Cambridge: Cambridge University
Press, 1994.

Bell, Catherine M. *Ritual: Perspectives and Dimensions*. New York: Oxford University Press, 1997.

Berdan, Frances. *Aztec Archaeology and Ethnohistory*. Cambridge: Cambridge University Press, 2014.

Bessie Smith with Buck and His Band. "Do Your Duty." Recorded 1933. OKEH Records. YouTube video, 3:36, posted by "cdbpdx," March 4, 2009. Accessed June 30, 2015. https://www.youtube.com/watch?v=9dnlnilzBe8.

Bhavnani, Kum-Kum. *Feminism and Race*. New York: Oxford University Press, 2001.

Blau, Herbert. *The Dubious Spectacle: Extremities of Theater, 1976–2000*. Minneapolis: University of Minnesota Press, 2002.

Boal, Augusto. *Theatre of the Oppressed*. Translated by Charles A. McBride. New York: Theatre Communications Group, 1993.

Bowers, Maggie Ann. *Magic(al) Realism*. Oxon, UK: Routledge, 2004.

Browman, David L. "Tiahuanaco Empire." In *The Oxford Companion to Archaeology*. Oxford: Oxford University Press, 1996. http://www.oxfordreference.com/view/10.1093/acref/9780195076189.001.0001/acref-9780195076189-e-0446.

Brown, Meredith. "Cusi Cram Keeps Her Innocence." *Soap Opera Digest*, November 23, 1982, 113.

Broyles-Gonzalez, Yolanda. *El Teatro Campesino: Theater in the Chicano Movement*. Austin: University of Texas Press, 1994.

Butler, Judith. *Bodies That Matter*. New York: Routledge, 1993.

———. *Gender Trouble: Feminism and the Subversion of Identity*. New York: Routledge, 1990.

"Café Onda." *HowlRound*. Accessed July 2, 2015. http://howlround.com/latina/o-theatre-commons.

Carlson, Marvin. *The Haunted Stage: The Theatre as Memory Machine*. Ann Arbor: University of Michigan Press, 2003.

Carrasco, David. *Daily Life of the Aztecs: People of the Sun and Earth*. With Scott Sessions. Westport, CT: Greenwood Press, 1998.

Case, Sue Ellen. *Split Britches*. New York: Routledge, 1996.

"Cassie Callison Carpenter." *Soapcentral.com.* Accessed April 8, 2015. http://soapcentral.com/oltl/whoswho/cassie.php.

Cervantes Saavedra, Miguel de. *Don Quixote*. Translated by Edith Grossman. New York: Ecco, 2003.

Chibas, Marissa. "Daughter of a Cuban Revolutionary." Unpublished manuscript, 2007.

Coates, Robert. "The Art Galleries Abroad and at Home." *New Yorker*, March 30, 1946, 83–84.

Cobb, William Jelani. *To the Break of Dawn: A Freestyle on the Hip Hop Aesthetic.* New York: New York University Press, 2007.

Cooder, Ry. "Ry Cooder about Carlos Núñez." YouTube video, 1:13, posted by "Galicianpipes." Last modified June 25, 2012. Accessed April 19, 2014. https://www.youtube.com/watch?t=32&v=FN1yiWIpP2A.

Cordovero, Moses ben Jacob, and Ira Robinson. *Moses Cordovero's Introduction to Kabbalah: An Annotated Translation of His Or ne'erav.* New York: Michael Scharf Pub. Trust of Yeshiva University Press, 1994.

Cram, Cusi. "Fuente." Unpublished manuscript, 2004.

———. *Fuente.* New York: Samuel French, 2009.

———. "Lucy and the Conquest." Unpublished manuscript, 2006.

———. *Lucy and the Conquest.* New York: Samuel French, 2009.

Cummings, Scott T. *Maria Irene Fornes.* Abingdon, Oxon: Routledge, 2013.

Darvill, Timothy. "Quechua." In *The Concise Oxford Dictionary of Archaeology.* Oxford: Oxford University Press, 2008. http://www.oxfordreference.com/view/10.1093/acref/9780199534043.001.0001/acref-9780199534043-e-3411.

Davis, Francis. *The History of the Blues.* New York: Hyperion, 1995. Accessed June 14, 2015. http://search.alexanderstreet.com/view/work/441835.

De la Cruz, Juana Inés. *Selected Writings.* Translated by Pamela Kirk Rappaport. New York: Paulist, 2005.

DeLamotte, Eugenia C. "Refashioning the Mind: The Revolutionary Rhetoric of Voltairine de Cleyre." *Legacy* 20, no. 1 and 2 (2003): 153–174.

De Lauretis, Teresa. *Technologies of Gender.* Bloomington: Indiana University Press, 1987.

Dever, John P., and Aileen Dever. *The Poetry and Prose of Rosalía de Castro: A Bilingual Facing Page Edition.* Lewiston, NY: Edwin Mellen Press, 2010.

Diamond, Jared M. *Guns, Germs, and Steel: The Fates of Human Societies.* New York: Norton, 1998.

Díaz-Más, Paloma. *Sephardim: The Jews from Spain.* Chicago: University of Chicago Press, 1992.

Dolan, Jill. *The Feminist Spectator as Critic.* Ann Arbor: UMI Research Press, 1988.

———. *Presence and Desire: Essays on Gender, Sexuality, Performance.* Ann Arbor: University of Michigan Press, 1993.

Du Pont, Diana C., ed. *Tamayo: A Modern Icon Reinterpreted.* Santa Barbara, CA: Santa Barbara Museum of Art, 2007.

Eder, Richard. Review of *Fefu and Her Friends*, by Maria Irene Fornes. *New York Times*, January 14, 1978, 10.

Eggebrecht, Hans Heinrich. *J. S. Bach's The Art of Fugue: The Work and Its Interpretation*. Ames: Iowa State University Press, 1993.

Ehren, Christine. "Octavio Solis Wins ATC's 2002 Latino Playwriting Award." *Playbill*. Playbill, Inc., 2002. Web. Accessed June 3, 2014. http://www.playbill.com/news/article/73349-Octavio-Solis-Wins-ATCs-2002-Latino-Playwriting-Award-Entries-for-2003-Sought.

Eliade, Mircea. *The Sacred and the Profane: The Nature of Religion*. Translated by William R. Trask. New York: Harcourt, Brace, 1959.

Ennis, Sharon R., Merarys Ríos-Vargas, and Nora G. Albert. "The Hispanic Population 2010." *2010 Census Briefs*. Washington DC: U.S. Census Bureau, 2011.

Epstein, Perle. *Kabbalah: The Way of the Jewish Mystic*. Boston: Shambhala, 2001.

Farías, Joann. "Road to Xibalba." Unpublished manuscript, 2006.

Fernández, Evelina. "Liz Estrada in the City of Angels." Unpublished manuscript, 2006.

Fernández Olmos, Margarite, and Lizabeth Paravisini-Gebert. *Creole Religions of the Caribbean: An Introduction from Vodou and Santería to Obeah and Espiritismo*. New York: New York University Press, 2003.

Feuer, Jane. "Reading Dynasty: Television and Reception Theory." *South Atlantic Quarterly* 88, no. 2 (1989): 447–448.

Feyder, Linda, ed. *Shattering the Myth: Plays by Hispanic Women*. Houston: Arte Público Press, 1992.

Flynn, Gerard C. *Sor Juana Inés de la Cruz*. New York: Twayne, 1971.

Fornes, Maria Irene. *Fefu and Her Friends*. New York: PAJ Publications, 1992.

———. *Plays*. New York: PAJ Publications, 1986.

———. *Sarita*. Directed by Maria Irene Fornes. INTAR Theatre, 1984. Billy Rose Theater Collection, New York Public Library. DVD.

Fornes, Maria Irene, and Bonnie Marranca. "Interview: Maria Irene Fornes." *Performing Arts Journal* 2, no. 3 (Winter 1978): 106–111.

Freedman, Samuel G. "A Choice of 9 Plays on the Boards." *New York Times*, February 10, 1984.

Friedman, Thomas L. *The World Is Flat: A Brief History of the Twenty-First Century*. New York: Farrar, Straus and Giroux, 2005.

García Canclini, Nestor. *Hybrid Cultures: Strategies for Entering and Leaving Modernity*. Translated by Christopher L. Chiappari and Silvia L. Lopéz. Minneapolis: University of Minnesota Press, 1995.

Garcia Crow, Amparo. "Under a Western Sky." Unpublished manuscript, 1997.

———. "Esmeralda Blue." Unpublished manuscript, 2006.

García Lorca, Federico, and Caridad Svich. *Federico García Lorca: Impossible Theater: Five Plays and Thirteen Poems*. Hanover, NH: Smith and Kraus, 2000.

Geraghty, Christine. *Women and Soap Opera: A Study of Prime Time Soaps*. Cambridge, UK: Polity Press, 1991.

Gilman, Richard. *The Making of Modern Drama: A Study of Büchner, Ibsen, Strindberg, Chekhov, Pirandello, Brecht, Beckett, Handke*. New York: Farrar, Straus and Giroux, 1974.

Gitlitz, David M. *Secrecy and Deceit*. Albuquerque: University of New Mexico, 2002.

Gitlitz, David M., and Linda K. Davidson. *The Pilgrimage Road to Santiago: The Complete Cultural Handbook*. New York: St. Martin's Griffin, 2000.

Gonzalez, Miranda, Diane Herrera, Tanya Saracho, and Marisabel Suarez. "Sólo Latinas." Unpublished manuscript, 2005.

Graham-Jones, Jean. "On Attributions, Appropriations, Misinterpretation, and Latin American Theatre Studies." *Theatre Journal* 56, no. 3 (October 2004): ix.

Gripsrud, Jostein. *The Dynasty Years: Hollywood Television and Critical Media Studies*. London: Routledge, 1995.

Grise, Virginia, and Irma Mayorga. *The Panza Monologues*. Austin: Allgo and Evelyn Street Press, 2004.

Grumbling, Megan. "Them Belly Full: But You Might Be Left a Little Bit Hungry." Review of *Yemaya's Belly*, by Quiara Alegría Hudes. *Portland Phoenix*, March 17, 2005.

Harbison, Lawrence. *New Playwrights: The Best Plays 2013*. Portland, ME: Smith and Kraus, 2013.

Hart, James D., and Phillip W. Leininger. "Tom Sawyer, The Adventures of." In *The Oxford Companion to American Literature*. Oxford: Oxford University Press, 1995. http://www.oxfordreference.com/view/10.1093/acref/9780195065480.001.0001/acref-9780195065480-e-4812.

Hebdige, Dick. *Subculture: The Meaning of Style*. London: Routledge, 2002.

Herrera, Brian Eugenio, Jayne Benjulian, and Jamie Gahlon. *The Latina/o Theatre Commons 2013 National Convening: A Narrative Report*. Boston: HowlRound.com, 2015.

Hoban, Phoebe. "3 Generations of Soldiers' Stories in a Melancholy Key." Review of *Elliot, A Soldier's Fugue*, by Quiara Alegría Hudes. *New York Times*, February 7, 2006. http://www.nytimes.com/2006/02/07/theater/reviews/07fugu.html?_r=0.

Hofmann, Hans, and Sara T. Weeks. *Search for the Real, and Other Essays: A Monograph Based on an Exhibition, Covering a Half Century of the Art of Hans Hofmann, Held at the Addison Gallery January 2–February 22, 1948.* Andover, MA: Addison Gallery of American Art, Phillips Academy, 1948.

The Holy Bible, Containing the Old and New Testaments, Revised Standard Version. New York: Thomas Nelson and Sons, 1972.

Hudes, Quiara Alegría. "Adventures of Barrio Grrrrl!" Unpublished manuscript, 2006.

———. "Elliot, A Soldier's Fugue." Unpublished manuscript, 2006.

———. *Elliot, A Soldier's Fugue.* New York: Theatre Communications Group, 2012.

———. *The Happiest Song Plays Last.* New York: Theatre Communications Group, 2014.

———. "Yemaya's Belly." Unpublished manuscript, 2006.

———. *Yemaya's Belly.* New York: Dramatists Play Service, 2007.

———. *Water by the Spoonful.* New York: Theatre Communications Group, 2012.

Huerta, Jorge. *Chicano Drama: Performance, Society, and Myth.* Cambridge: Cambridge University Press, 2000.

———. *Chicano Theater: Themes and Forms.* Ypsilanti, MI: Bilingual Press/Editorial Bilingüe, 1982.

Irigaray, Luce. *That Sex That Is Not One.* Ithaca, NY: Cornell University Press, 1985.

Jackson, Buzzy. *A Bad Woman Feeling Good: Blues and the Women Who Sing Them.* New York: Norton, 2005.

Jacobs, Janet Liebman. "Women, Ritual, and Secrecy: The Creation of Crypto-Jewish Culture." *Journal for the Scientific Study of Religion* 35, no. 2 (1996): 97–108.

Jerome M. Levi. "Structuralism and Kabbalah: Sciences of Mysticism or Mystifications of Science?" *Anthropological Quarterly* 82, no. 4 (2009): 929–984. http://muse.jhu.edu/login?auth = 0&type = summary&url = /journals/anthropological_quarterly/v082/82.4.1evi01.html.

Kahlo, Frida, Emma Dexter, Tanya Barson, and Gannit Ankori. *Frida Kahlo.* London: Tate Publishing, 2005.

Kanellos, Nicolás. *A History of Hispanic Theatre in the United States: Origins to 1940.* Austin: University of Texas Press, 1990.

Kent, Assunta Bartolomucci. *Maria Irene Fornes and Her Critics.* Westport, CT: Greenwood Press, 1996.

Kerr, Walter. "Two Plays Swamped by Metaphors." *New York Times*, January 22, 1978.

Kirk, Pamela. *Sor Juana Inés De La Cruz: Religion, Art, and Feminism*. New York: Continuum, 1998.

Koznin, Allan. "Theater World Friends Bring Ailing Playwright Closer To Home." *New York Times*, February 6, 2013.

Krøløkke, Charlotte, and Ann Scott Sørensen. *Gender Communication Theories and Analyses: From Silence to Performance*. Thousand Oaks, CA: Sage Publications, 2006.

Ledbetter, David. *Bach's Well-Tempered Clavier: The 48 Preludes and Fugues*. New Haven, CT: Yale University Press, 2002.

Leeming, David. "Apollo." In *The Oxford Companion to World Mythology*. New York: Oxford University Press, 2005. http://www.oxfordreference.com/view/10.1093/acref/9780195156690.001.0001/acref-9780195156690-e-110.

LoConto, David G., Timothy W. Clark, and Patrice N. Ware. "The Diaspora of West Africa: The Influence of West African Cultures on 'Jody Calls' in the United States Military." *Sociological Spectrum* 30, no. 1 (2009): 90–109.

López, Melinda. "Sonia Flew." Unpublished manuscript, 2006.

López, Tiffany Ana. "Violent Inscriptions: Writing the Body and Making Community in Four Plays by Migdalia Cruz." *Theater Journal* 52, no. 1 (2000): 51–66.

Lowe, Sarah M. *Tina Modotti: Photographs*. New York: H. N. Abrams in association with the Philadelphia Museum of Art, 1995.

Luna, Guadalupe T. "Treaty of Guadalupe Hidalgo." In *The Oxford Encyclopedia of Latinos and Latinas in the United States*, edited by Suzanne Oboler and Deena J. González. New York: Oxford University Press, 2005. http://www.oxfordreference.com/view/10.1093/acref/9780195156003.001.0001/acref-9780195156003-e-932.

Macias, Alana. "The Watchers." Unpublished manuscript, 2006.

———. "When the Tigris Runs Black." Unpublished manuscript, 2006.

Mann, Alfred. *The Study of Fugue*. New Brunswick, NJ: Rutgers University Press, 1958.

Marnham, Patrick. *Dreaming with His Eyes Open: A Life of Diego Rivera*. New York: Knopf, 1998.

Marranca, Bonnie. "The State of Grace: Maria Irene Fornes at Sixty-Two." *Performing Arts Journal* 14, no. 2 (1992): 24–31.

Mason, Michael Atwood. *Living Santería: Rituals and Experiences in an Afro-Cuban Religion*. Washington DC: Smithsonian Institution Press, 2002.

Mazzarella, Sharon. "Dynasty." *Museum of Broadcast Communications.* Accessed May 23, 2014. http://www.museum.tv/eotv/dynasty.htm.

McKendrick, Melveena. *Theatre in Spain, 1490–1700.* Cambridge, UK: Cambridge University Press, 1989.

Mendoza, Plinio A., and Gabriel García Márquez. *The Fragrance of Guava: Conversations with Gabriel García Márquez.* London: Faber and Faber, 1988.

Menocal, Maria Rosa. *The Ornament of the World: How Muslims, Jews, and Christians Created a Culture of Tolerance in Medieval Spain.* Boston: Back Bay Books, 2003.

Mitchell, Tony. *Global Noise: Rap and Hip-Hop Outside the USA.* Middletown, CT: Wesleyan University Press, 2001.

Moraga, Cherríe. *Heroes and Saints and Other Plays.* Albuquerque, NM: West End Press, 1994.

Moreno-Penson, Desi. "Devil Land." Unpublished manuscript, 2007.

Morley, Ian. "Philadelphia." In *Oxford Encyclopedia of the Modern World.* Oxford: Oxford University Press, 2008. http://www.oxfordreference.com/view/10.1093/acref/9780195176322.001.0001/acref-9780195176322-e-1235.

Moroff, Diane. *Fornes: Theater in the Present Tense.* Ann Arbor: University of Michigan Press, 1996.

Morris, Steven Leigh. Review of the Encuentro Latino Theatre Festival. *LA Weekly,* November 13, 2014. Accessed March 12, 2015. http://www.laweekly.com/arts/the-fantastic-encuentro-2014-festival-showed-the-power-of-latino-theater-5207079.

Mulvey, Laura. *Visual and Other Pleasures.* Bloomington: Indiana University Press, 1989.

Muñoz, Jose Esteban. "Feeling Brown: Ethnicity and Affect in Ricardo Bracho's *The Sweetest Hangover (and other STDs).*" *Theater Journal* 52, no. 1 (2000): 67–79.

Navarrete, Federico. "The Path from Aztlan to Mexico: On Visual Narration in Mesoamerican Codices." *RES: Anthropology and Aesthetics,* no. 37 (Spring 2000): 31–48.

Neipris, Janet. *To Be a Playwright.* New York: Routledge, 2005.

Ortiz, Fernando, and Enrico Mario Santí. *Contrapunteo cubano del tabaco y el azúcar: advertencia de sus contrastes agrarios, económicos, históricos y sociales, su etnografía y su tranculturación.* Madrid: Cátedra, 2002.

Osborn, M. Elizabeth. *On New Ground: Contemporary Hispanic-American Plays.* New York: Theatre Communications Group, 1987.

Palmer, Tanya. "A Conversation with Karen Zacarías." *Onstage* (Goodman Theatre) 25, no. 5 (June–July 2010): 10.

———. "The Making of a Trilogy." In *The Happiest Song Plays Last*, Goodman Theatre Playbill, April 2013, 12.

Patterson, Mary Jo. "Cuban Americans, Union City, New Jersey." *IIP-Digital*. Last modified August 31, 2012. Accessed June 14, 2015. http://iipdigital.usembassy.gov/st/english/pamphlet/2012/08/20120822135006.html#ixzz3d4jUdLK8.

Paz, Octavio. *Sor Juana, or, The Traps of Faith*. Cambridge, MA: Belknap Press, 1988.

Pease, Franklin. "The Andean Creator God." *Numen* 17, no. 3 (1970): 161–175.

Perkins, Kathy A., and Roberta Uno. *Contemporary Plays by Women of Color: An Anthology*. London: Routledge, 1996.

Perrone, Bobette, H. Henrietta Stockel, and Victoria Krueger. *Medicine Women, Curanderas, and Women Doctors*. Norman: University of Oklahoma Press, 1989.

Phelan, Peggy. *Mourning Sex: Performing Public Memories*. New York: Routledge, 1997.

———. *Unmarked: The Politics of Performance*. New York: Routledge, 1993.

Phillips, Michael. "Goodman's 'Mariela' Wanders in Vain." Review of *Mariela in the Desert*, by Karen Zacarías. *Chicago Tribune*, February 11, 2005.

Plato. *Symposium*. Translated by Benjamin Jowett. New York: Pearson, 1956. http://classics.mit.edu/Plato/symposium.html.

Pressley, Nelson. "Signature's 'Belly': Not Quite Full." Review of *Yemaya's Belly*, by Quiara Alegría Hudes. *Washington Post*, December 16, 2005.

Quintana, Alejandro. *Pancho Villa: A Biography*. Santa Barbara, CA: Greenwood, 2012.

Ramirez, Elizabeth. *Chicanas/Latinas in American Theatre: A History of Performance*. Bloomington: Indiana University Press, 2000.

Ramírez, Elizabeth, and Catherine Casiano. *La Voz Latina: Contemporary Plays and Performance Pieces by Latinas*. Champaign: University of Illinois Press, 2011.

Ramos-García, Luis, ed. *The State of Latino Theater in the United States: Hybridity, Transculturation, and Identity*. New York: Routledge, 2002.

Reel, James. "Magical Mystery Tour: Exploring the Invisible World at Invisible Theatre." Review of *¡Curanderas!* by Elaine Romero. *Tucson Weekly*, December 14, 2000.

Reinhard, Johan. *Machu Picchu: Exploring an Ancient Sacred Center*. Los Angeles: Cottsen Institute of Archeology Press, 2007.

"Residency Five." *SignatureTheatre*. Accessed March 29, 2015. http://www.signaturetheatre.org/Explore/Residencies/Residency-Five.aspx.

Rivera, Carmen. "Julia de Burgos—Child of Water." Unpublished manuscript, 1998.

———. "La Gringa." Unpublished manuscript, 1996.

Rivera, José. *References to Salvador Dalí Make Me Hot and Other Plays*. New York: Theatre Communications Group, 2003.

Rivera, Magaly. "Arecibo." *Tour Puerto Rico*. Accessed June 1, 2014. http:// www.topuertorico.org/city/arecibo.shtml.

Rivera, Raquel Z., Wayne Marshall, and Deborah Pacini Hernandez, eds. *Reggaeton*. Durham, NC: Duke University Press. 2009.

Robinson, Marc, ed. *The Theatre of Maria Irene Fornes*. Baltimore, MD: Johns Hopkins University Press, 1999.

Roman, David. "Comment: *Theatre Journals*." *Theatre Journal* 54, no. 3 (2002): vii–xix.

Romero, Elaine. "Catalina de Erauso." Unpublished manuscript, 2006.

———. "¡Curanderas! Serpents of the Clouds." Unpublished manuscript, 2015.

———. *¡Curanderas! Serpents of the Clouds*. In *Women Playwrights: The Best Plays of 2000*, edited by David L. Lepidus. Grantham: Smith and Kraus, 2002.

———. "Secret Things." Unpublished manuscript, 2005.

———. *Secret Things*. New York: Playscripts, Inc., 2007.

Rossini, Jon D. *Contemporary Latina/o Theater: Wrighting Ethnicity*. Carbondale: Southern Illinois University Press, 2008.

Russ, Valerie M. "Donald Rappaport, 66, Caring Music Teacher." *Philly .com*. Accessed March 10, 2015. http://articles.philly.com/1995–12–11/news/ 25671258_1_music-teacher-settlement-music-school-teen-student.

Saborío, Linda. *Embodying Difference: Scripting Social Images of the Female Body in Latina Theatre*. Lanham, MD: Farleigh-Dickinson Press, 2012.

Sanchez-Scott, Milcha. *Roosters*. New York: Dramatists Play Service, 1988.

Sandoval, Chela. *Methodology of the Oppressed*. Minneapolis: University of Minnesota Press, 2000.

Sandoval-Sánchez, Alberto. *José Can You See? Latinos On and Off Broadway*. Madison: University of Wisconsin Press, 1999.

Sandoval-Sánchez, Alberto, and Nancy Saporta Sternbach. *Stages of Life: Transcultural Performance and Identity in U.S. Latina Theater*. Tucson: University of Arizona Press, 2001.

———, eds. *Puro Teatro: A Latina Anthology*. Tucson: University of Arizona Press, 2000.

Schechner, Richard, and Willa Appel. *By Means of Performance: Intercultural Studies of Theatre and Ritual*. Cambridge: Cambridge University Press, 1990.

Schmitt, Natalie Crohn. *Actors and Onlookers: Theater and Twentieth-Century Scientific Views of Nature*. Evanston, IL: Northwestern University Press, 1990.

Sevan, Adriana. "Taking Flight." Unpublished manuscript, 2006.

Shell, Marc. "Marranos (Pigs), or from Coexistence to Toleration." *Critical Inquiry* 17, no. 2 (Winter 1991): 306–335.

Siegel, Ed. "Play's Southwestern Town, Inhabitants Fall Flat." Review of *Fuente*, by Cusi Cram. *Boston Globe*, July 13, 2005: E3.

Smiley, Sam. *Playwriting: The Structure of Action*. Englewood Cliffs, NJ: Prentice-Hall, 1971.

Sofer, Andrew. *The Stage Life of Props*. Ann Arbor: University of Michigan Press, 2003.

Solomon, Alisa. "Seeing and Nothingness." *Women's Review of Books* 10, no. 9 (1993): 22.

Stainton, Leslie. *Lorca, a Dream of Life*. New York: Farrar, Straus, and Giroux, 1999.

"State and County Quick Facts." *United States Census Bureau*. Accessed July 2, 2015. http://quickfacts.census.gov/qfd/states/00000.html.

Styan, J. L. *Modern Drama in Theory and Practice*. Cambridge: Cambridge University Press, 1981.

Suárez-Orozco, Marcelo M., and Mariela Páez. *Latinos: Remaking America*. Berkeley, CA: University of California Press, 2002.

Sublette, Ned. *Cuba and Its Music: From the First Drums to the Mambo*. Chicago: Chicago Press Review, 2004.

Sullivan, Lawrence Eugene. *Native Religions and Cultures of Central and South America: Anthropology of the Sacred*. New York: Continuum, 2002.

Sullivan, William. *The Secrets of the Inca: Myth, Astronomy, and the War Against Time*. New York: Crown, 1996.

Svich, Caridad. "Prodigal Kiss." Unpublished manuscript, 1999.

———. *Prodigal Kiss*. South Gate, CA: Lizard Run Press, 2009.

———. "Tropic of X." Unpublished manuscript, 2006.

———. *Tropic of X*. New York: NoPassport Press, 2007.

Svich, Caridad, Brooke Berman, Migdalia Cruz, Julie Hébert, Anne García-Romero, Jennifer Maisel, Oliver Mayer, Han Ong, Lisa Schlesinger, Alisa Solomon, and Alina Troyano. "The Legacy of Maria Irene Fornes: A Collection of Impressions and Exercises." *PAJ: A Journal of Performance and Art* 31, no. 3 (September 2009): 1–32. http://www.jstor.org/stable/20627931.

Svich, Caridad, and Maria Delgado, eds. *Conducting a Life: Reflections on the Theater of Maria Irene Fornes*. New York: Smith and Kraus, 1999.

Svich, Caridad, and María Teresa Marrero, eds. *Out of the Fringe: Contemporary Latina/Latino Theatre and Performance*. New York: Theatre Communications Group, 2000.

Sweetman, David. *Paul Gauguin: A Life*. New York: Simon and Schuster, 1995.

Taylor, Diana. *The Archive and the Repertoire: Performing Cultural Memory in the Americas*. Durham, NC: Duke University Press, 2003.

———. "Transculturating Transculturation." *Performing Arts Journal* 13, no. 2 (1991): 90–104.

Thomas, George A. *The Politics and Poetics of Sor Juana Inés De La Cruz*. Farnham, Surrey, England: Ashgate, 2012.

Thornham, Sue. *Feminist Film Theory: A Reader*. New York: New York University Press, 1999.

"3D Light Armored Reconnaissance Bn." *Marines*. Accessed June 7, 2015. http://www.1stmardiv.marines.mil/Units/3DLARBN.aspx.

Toynton, Evelyn, and Jackson Pollock. *Jackson Pollock*. New Haven, CT: Yale University Press, 2012.

Treviño-Orta, Marisela. "Braided Sorrow." Unpublished manuscript, 2006.

Triplett, William. "'Sins of Sor Juana': An Emotional Sacrifice on the Altar of Idealism." Review of *The Sins of Sor Juana*, by Karen Zacarías. *Washington Post*, November 11, 1999.

Tukesbury, Beatrice L. "Emma Sheridan Fry and Educational." *Educational Theatre Journal* 16, no. 4 (1964): 341–348.

Urton, Gary. *Inca Myths*. Austin: University of Texas Press, 1999.

Valdez, Luis. *Zoot Suit and Other Plays*. Houston: Arte Público Press, 1992.

Velasco, Sherry M. *The Lieutenant Nun: Transgenderism, Lesbian Desire, Catalina De Erauso*. Austin: University of Texas Press, 2000.

Verrall, John. *Fugue and Invention in Theory and Practice*. Palo Alto, CA: Pacific Books, 1966.

Villahermosa, Col. Gilberto. "America's Hispanics in American Wars." *Army Magazine* 52, no. 9 (Sept. 2002): 62–66.

Wald, Elijah. *The Blues: A Very Short Introduction*. New York: Oxford University Press, 2010.

Wattenberg, Richard. "Barrio Grrl Fights Demons in Plot Full of Fun and Fantasy." Review of *The Adventures of Barrio Grrl!* by Quiara Alegría Hudes. *The Oregonian*, March 23, 2005.

West, Iris J. "The Women of the Army Nurse Corps During the Vietnam War." http://www.vietnamwomensmemorial.org/pdf/iwest.pdf.

Westhoff, Ulrike. Review of *Tropic of X*, by Caridad Svich. Translated by Erik Abbott. *StadtRevue*, June 2007.

Wilson, Christopher. "Passacaglia." In *The Oxford Companion to Music.* Oxford: Oxford University Press. http://www.oxfordreference.com/view/ 10.1093/acref/9780199579037.001.0001/acref-9780199579037-e-5014.

Wolf, Justin. "Abstract Expressionism." *The Art Story.* Accessed June 5, 2014. http://www.theartstory.org/movement-abstract-expressionism.htm.

Wolff, Christoph. *Johann Sebastian Bach: The Learned Musician.* New York: Norton, 2001.

Yarbro-Bejarano, Yvonne. "The Female Subject in Chicano Theatre: Sexuality, 'Race,' and Class." *Theater Journal* 38, no. 4 (1986): 389–407.

Zacarías, Karen. "Mariela in the Desert." *Theater Forum* 28 (Winter/Spring 2006): 12–35.

———. "Mariela in the Desert." Unpublished manuscript, 2006.

———. "The Sins of Sor Juana." Unpublished manuscript, 2010.

———. *The Sins of Sor Juana: A Play in Two Acts.* Woodstock, IL: Dramatic Publishing, 2001.

Zarrilli, Phillip B., and Gary Jay Williams. *Theatre Histories: An Introduction.* New York: Routledge, 2006.

INDEX

ABOUT THE AUTHOR

Anne García-Romero is a playwright and theatre studies scholar. Her plays include *Paloma, Provenance, Earthquake Chica, Mary Peabody in Cuba, Mary Domingo, Land of Benjamin Franklin, Girlus Equinus, Desert Longing, Juanita's Statue,* and *Santa Concepción.* Her plays have been developed and produced at the NYSF/Public Theater, the Eugene O'Neill National Playwrights Conference, Mark Taper Forum, Hartford Stage, South Coast Repertory, Arielle Tepper Productions' Summer Play Festival (Off Broadway), INTAR, HERE, New Georges, the Orchard Project, National Hispanic Cultural Center, Borderlands Theater, Nevada Repertory Company, Jungle Theater, East LA Repertory, Open Fist Theater Company, Wordbridge Playwrights Laboratory, and the Los Angeles Theater Center. She's been a Jerome fellow at the Playwrights Center of Minneapolis, as well as a MacDowell Colony fellow. Her plays are published by Broadway Play Publishing, Playscripts, Smith and Kraus, and NoPassport Press. Her article on Latina playwrights was published in the Latin American Theatre Review. She is a founding member of the Latina/o Theatre Commons. She holds an MFA in playwriting from the Yale School of Drama and a PhD in theatre studies from the University of California, Santa Barbara. She is the Thomas J. and Robert T. Rolfs assistant professor in the Department of Film, Television, and Theatre at the University of Notre Dame. She is a recent member of the Goodman Theatre Playwrights Unit, an alumna of New Dramatists, and a resident playwright at Chicago Dramatists.